AF615496

AS HE LEADS

Is Joy

Dora M. Taylor

Missionary Nurse
in
Honduras

As Told
to
Marie E. Cutman

through
Dora's journals and the
letters she wrote to her parents.

Copyright ©1999 by Marie E. Cutman

Printed in the United States of America

Front Cover:
Picture of Dora at the Trujillo clinic
discharging a patient leaving by
local ambulance.

Library of Congress Catalog Card Number: 99-74269

ISBN 0-9672285-4-9

Designed and Published by:

MecPublishing
Marie E. Cutman
125 West Main Street
P O Box 22
Morgantown PA 19543

To

My Lord, Jesus Christ

Who in love saved me and gave me joy

Who called me and used me

and Who led to this book

and to

My parents, who prayed

To my gracious, faithful, congenial co-workers

this book is humbly dedicated

for the glory of God alone.

AS HE LEADS
Is Joy

Table of Contents

Photographs and Documents

Preface

I threw myself down by the bed and silently cried to God, "Lord, You know where my journals are; if You want me to have them back, and I think You do, please bring them back to me." Unburdened, I went to bed and slept.

That was in 1972. I had returned to Pennsylvania that night after visiting friends and acquaintances in Honduras where I worked from 1951 to 1963. My sister, Joyce Mast, met me at the airport in Philadelphia, and as we drove home she told me the house where Mother and I lived had been robbed. Mother was staying with my sister, Muriel Mack, while I was gone, and when they went to water her house plants Sunday afternoon, they found total chaos—drawers dumped, cupboards ransacked, the freezer door ajar, etc. Although the family had cleaned much of the house, my room was as the robber had left it.

Mother and I talked for an hour or so and then decided to go to bed. I opened my bedroom door—I had to clear a path to get in! But it was when I looked in the closet that I was hit with utter dismay—my two file cases were gone! One held important business papers, and the other one held four large notebooks, the journals I had kept during the years I worked in Honduras. The loss of the business papers didn't bother me, but the journals! They held so many memories and so many facts that the very thought of losing them drove me to my knees.

The next morning Muriel called. She said a patient in the office of her husband, Dr. Noah Mack, had told them that her son had found some things with my name on them in a dump on Welsh Mountain. I could get them at the patient's home approximately ten miles away. And so I got my journals back—damp and partly rain-soaked, but restorable. *And it shall come to pass, that before they call, I will answer; and while they are yet speaking, I will hear.* (Isaiah 65:24)

In the years since, many people have suggested and encouraged me to write my Honduras story. I did not feel led to do it myself;

however, I believe God led me to ask an author friend, Marie E. Cutman, to take on the challenge. She has done it using my journals and the weekly letters I wrote home. They were not written for the public eye, but I open them up to you now with the prayer that God will be glorified.

Dora M. Taylor

Foreword

Except for the grace of God, I could have lived a life of sin. My heart has all the capabilities of sin that anyone else's has, but that grace was and is sufficient to forgive and cover all shame and regrets. His grace has brought me a life of abounding joy and satisfaction. When I lie down at night, there is a singing in my heart and at times during the day when I have time to reflect, there are such surgings of joy that I can only praise Him.

True, I didn't have a husband or children, but the Lord gave infinitely more than enough to compensate and I could not ask for more than He has given me. Not that I despise those things. I am human and, I believe, a normal woman, but spiritual joys far surpass temporal ones.

As my body grew cold approaching death in 1952 when I had falciparum malaria, I experienced things that one rarely does in the land of the living. I could feel God's presence beside the bed and in my spirit I heard His promise to be with me. I was ready to pass right over to be with Him and then He spoke the words, "Go home and tell." At that moment I knew I would not go to Him just then. He still had work for me to do.

That presence of God was so vivid that the things of this earth have never since had the value they had before. I was a Christian and was serving the Lord, but part of that experience was the joy of knowing His unlimited forgiveness and the knowledge that nothing stood between us—that was peace and joy beyond description.

As He Leads was the motto of our graduating class in 1933 at Eastern Mennonite College, Harrisonburg, Virginia. At many points in my life I spoke the words and I really meant them, but since 1952 I know in a new way that **AS HE LEADS is Joy**.

You too can experience the joy of God's love, forgiveness, acceptance, and leading because of His grace. All that is needed is to accept Him as your Savior and follow Him with all your heart.

Dora

Map of Central America

Dora M. Taylor
1948

1910 - 1951

I hadn't been in Trujillo long before my forty-first birthday rolled around. Thinking no one in Honduras would know, I decided to celebrate without telling anyone. I planned light refreshments and invited the people who usually attended the evening prayer meeting to meet at my house. Someone, however, did know it was my birthday and spread the word. Needless to say, the inner excitement of having my own secret party faded into embarrassment as trays of flowers and gifts started arriving at four o'clock in the afternoon. That was how I learned that Hondurans make a big production of birthdays.

I doubt if there was a party on my birth date, October 28, 1910, in the little old stone house across from Warren Shops near Malvern, Pennsylvania. I was the first child of 20-year-old Verna Martin Taylor, a housewife, and Edgar Taylor, an almost 22-year-old blacksmith and wheelwright for Warren Shops. My parents named me Dora Mary for my two grandmothers, Dora May Wright Martin and Mary Elizabeth Showalter Taylor, but Granny Taylor suggested they call me Dora May because she already had one namesake granddaughter, hence my name became Dora May.

When I was two, my sister Muriel was born, followed by Glenn two years later. Four years after that Lois came, and when I was 16 my youngest sister Joyce made Father and Mother the parents of five. One child, a baby boy, had died shortly after birth in 1922.

We were a close and happy family. An important part of our daily lives was the time spent together for family devotions. My father read the Bible aloud and then we knelt for prayer. I remember one morning especially. We always knelt facing the backs of our chairs with our arms resting on the chair seats. As we turned to rise to our feet that day, we couldn't help giggling. Our pet cat had joined us, quietly sitting on Mother's back.

Unless sickness prevented, we rarely missed Sunday morning services at the Mennonite church at Frazer, and on Sunday afternoons we usually went to services at Bacton Hill Chapel, a mission outpost a few miles away.

I started school at Frazer, Pennsylvania, but a few months later we moved to Lionville, where Father was the village blacksmith. There I attended a one-room school, and I remember my two good teachers—

Miss Bessie, and when she retired, Miss Margaret. Seventh and eighth grades were taught in one side of the Friends' Meeting House by another fine teacher, Miss Edith.

I remember a big snowstorm which piled the drifts so high we couldn't see even the outline of the highway at some places. Father helped shovel the road open, by hand, and told us of drifts that were too high to see over. When Sunday came, the Eby family arrived from their farm in a bobsled and invited us to join them. Soon we were all snuggled in the straw with plenty of blankets and on our way to church. At some places we had to go through the fields.

The snow froze at night and for several days we walked to school on top of high drifts. As the snow melted, we discovered there were places where we had been walking on top of the picket fence in front of our yard.

When I was eight years old, typhoid fever struck two people in Lionville, Mrs. Elmer Ruth and me, and I was in bed for four weeks. At the same time, Muriel had measles and Glenn and baby Lois had both measles and whooping cough. People gawked at the three quarantine tags on the front door. Needless to say, Mother had her hands full, and for awhile a neighbor, Mrs. Bond, came and helped.

As my fever climbed, my mind withdrew into a dreamlike existence. Wind blew through the tree outside the window, and, through barely opened eyelids, I watched the wavy patterns etched by sunlight and shadows. Back and forth the designs moved as the branches swayed. Gradually, to my feverish mind the hypnotic movement took on meaning. No longer did I see shadows of waving leaves; instead, the activity became missionaries hurrying back and forth across the ocean to tell the world about Jesus.

At church I had often heard speakers such as T. K. Hershey, a missionary to Argentina, talk about the people who needed to hear about Jesus. In Sunday School I also heard stories about missionaries, and one of our favorite songs was "Over the Ocean Waves" which says the heathen *are living far, far away waiting for the day when missionaries will hasten to them with glad tidings and the bread of life*. In my delirium, I saw the missionaries hurrying to foreign lands.

I was 11 years old when I made the decision to accept Christ as my Savior. Along with others, I was baptized by Bishop Noah Mack and became a member of Frazer Mennonite Church. As years went by, I grew in understanding and in commitment to the Lord. My parents gave me a Bible for Christmas and from it I memorized many verses. Daily Bible reading and prayer became a part of my life.

When I was 13 Father worked for awhile at the country home of the Clothiers a few miles from Malvern. They were co-owners of the well-known Strawbridge and Clothier Department Store in Philadelphia. Father kept their riding horses shod and did metal work for Mrs. Clothier. One beautiful thing he made was a cut-out iron sign which was put up at the entrance of the estate. Later he made one as a Christmas gift for my sister Lois and her husband. At the end of their lane the sign announced "Wil-Lo-Farm, D. Wilbur Erb." It has trees, the stream, and a horse in profile cut with chisel and hammer. Today, in 1999, this beautiful and greatly-admired piece of work hangs outside their apartment at Virginia Mennonite Retirement Community.

I had my first nursing experience when Joyce was born. Grandma Martin was there, but I took care of Mother and the baby at night. Dr. Kurtz told me I ought to take up nursing, but it was because of Katherine Rohrer, my Sunday School teacher and a loved and respected community nurse, that I first thought I could be a nurse.

By that time my parents had purchased a house on the outskirts of Malvern. There was no high school in Malvern, so when it was time for me to enter ninth grade, my Martin grandparents of New Holland, Pennsylvania, opened their home to me during the school year. I lived with them one year and then with Bishop Noah Mack and his wife while attending tenth and eleventh grades in the New Holland High School.

The fall of 1927 I registered for twelfth grade at Eastern Mennonite School in Harrisonburg, Virginia, and graduated in the spring of 1928 in the tabernacle in Park Woods. By 1933, when my sister Muriel and I graduated from junior college and our brother Glenn from high school, Eastern Mennonite School (EMS) had become Eastern Mennonite College (EMC). Our class motto in 1933 was **As He Leads** and this really became my life motto.

God used many people to train and prepare me for His work. Harry and Myrtle Brackbill, who lived in the tenant house on the Haldeman farm and had a roadside market along Route 30 west of Malvern, were a couple I look back on as fine examples of true Christianity. I worked in their home the summer of 1924 and helped take care of their two little girls. For several years I also worked in the home of Harry's younger brother, Milton, one of the pastors at Frazer Mennonite Church. Milton was married to Myrtle's sister, Ruth. They lived in Paoli during the winter and on the farm in the summer. They had five daughters. In both these homes I experienced wonderful Christian love.

Eastern Mennonite Board of Missions and Charities was looking for workers in 1935 for their Spanish Mission in Ybor City, Tampa, Florida. Approximately 30,000 people, mostly Cubans, but some Spaniards and Italians, lived and worked in Ybor City. The majority of them were employed rolling the famous Havana cigars. Anna Kauffman, who had worked at the mission for many years, was retiring and my sister Muriel and I were asked to take her place.

In January 1936 John Mellinger and Christian Hiestand drove us, in three days, from Pennsylvania, a land of ice and snow, to Tampa, Florida, the land of the burning sun. Our first night on the road we stopped in Harrisonburg, Virginia, with friends of our EMS and EMC years. The second night we found shelter in a two-room cabin in Georgia. A fireplace was in the room the men shared, and I still declare Muriel and I endured the coldest night of our lives in that second room. The bedding was far from adequate, and no heat from the fireplace reached us!

A more enjoyable memory of the trip was seeing miles of bluebirds lined up on the telephone wires like beads on a string.

Anna Kauffman continued at the mission a short time to acquaint us with the work. She introduced us to her kindergarten of seven or eight children, and clued us in on ways she used to keep the little ones busy with stories and pictures in catalogs and treats of one raisin each.

Our home on Fourth Avenue was a row house five rooms deep. We had a front porch, a bedroom, two rooms turned into one large room for church services, a living room, a kitchen, a tiny bathroom, and a back porch.

Besides Muriel, there were Mary Mack, Laura Histand, Mary Graybill, Edith Kennel, and Irene Stauffer who worked with me between the time I started in 1936 until I left in August 1944. Muriel stayed less than a year because she was engaged to be married in September to Dr. Noah K. Mack, and they were under appointment with the Eastern Mennonite Board of Missions and Charities for mission work in Tanganyika, later Tanzania, Africa.

During a short period when I was the only mission worker living at the Fourth Avenue house, Annie Maniscalco, a young girl from around the corner, came to stay with me. Eventually she accepted the Lord at a revival meeting and was baptized on Pearl Harbor Day. Later she graduated from Eastern Mennonite College, married, and spent some time in the Philippines in mission work. She lives with her husband in Oregon and is still serving the Lord.

Annie told me how excited her three little boys were the day they rushed into the house shouting that they had found an *angel mouse*. "Come and see it," they cried. It was a huge bat!

Learning Spanish was a necessity for my work in Ybor City, and I discovered I picked it up quickly, hearing it every hour of the day. By September I conducted a cottage meeting in Spanish, but I wonder how it sounded. Years later I found myself thinking in Spanish, and I still do at times.

The people we worked with were very clean. They took baths every afternoon, and then the mothers washed all the clothes on washboards. Most of the houses had a hole in one corner of each room to serve as a drain for the water used to scrub the bare floors.

Paul and Alice Sauder were the pastor family at Ida Street Mission two miles away. They had twin boys named Joseph and John, another boy named William, and a girl, Anne. We had good working relationships and enjoyed our times together. They were followed by an older couple, George F. and Anna Brunk, who were like parents to us mission girls.

Recently, among some papers I saved over the years, I found something I wrote while working in Ybor City. It follows:

> *The mission worker doesn't need to work for her living, all she has to do is visit the sick and see why Johnnie wasn't in Sunday School and do her washing and write the mission news for publication and answer the telephone and sweep the church and clean the lice from an orphan girl's head and study Spanish and go to the store and study her Sunday School lesson and go to see the new Jones baby and help Julia cut out a dress and give out some fish donated to the mission and visit in fifty homes and make out the financial report and check out books in the children's library and guard the hour set apart for her private devotions and answer the doorbell and can some tomatoes and write a few letters and present the claims of Christ to Dorothy when she drops in and order the Sunday School supplies and make out a Christmas program and pay the rent and do visitation work in the hospital and entertain callers from the neighborhood and get the meals and call Nancy's mother to the phone and settle a dispute between Doris and Anna and see that no bed bugs have been carried in and get the housecleaning done and prepare for Children's Meeting and go to sing for old Jennie and lend her typewriter and*

answer a request for information about the mission and comb a sick neighbor's hair and explain a passage in the Bible to William and see if there is anything in the house to set before unexpected guests and mend the hymn books and get Mary to fold the Spanish Way *and fix a meal for a tramp and balance it with something for his soul and teach Martha to keep her coverings neat and go to Spanish class and darn her stockings and show some tourists through the mission and take care of requests for clothing and distribute the* Way *and go with Mrs. Martínez to try to get work and do some sewing for the new converts and make a note about taking Helen to prayer meeting and try to fix the rocking chair and take Catherine to the doctor and iron and get after the weeds in the back yard and see what Jimmy's mother wanted and take a baby to the clinic and help Alice with her arithmetic.*

The next important step in my life began when I enrolled at the La Junta Mennonite Hospital School of Nursing in September 1945. At the age of 34 years and 11 months I just skimmed under the enrollment guideline limit which stated students were to be between the ages of 18 and 35.

The work was hard, and because it was wartime there was a shortage of nurses. The school had a high rating, however, and good training, and it was an honor to them that after graduation I was awarded the Linda Richards medal for the state of Colorado. I completed the three-year course of study, graduated in 1948, and then spent the next year working at the hospital. It was standard procedure at that time for the La Junta Mennonite Hospital to request their student nurses to return for a time of employment following graduation unless they went into other work for the church.

During the years I spent in La Junta, I attended the Spanish Mennonite Church, and there as well as at the hospital with Mexican patients I continued to use Spanish.

A school nurse was needed at Eastern Mennonite College beginning September 1949, so shortly after completing my year of service in La Junta, I headed back to Harrisonburg, Virginia. Two students on the roster at that time were twins Bill and Bob Detweiler, who later became well-known radio preachers. One of them was a patient in the infirmary for awhile.

During the years at La Junta and at EMC, I continued to grow in my Christian life and in fellowship with the Lord. My desire was to please Him and I offered myself to Him for whatever He should choose. I had no leading to volunteer but trusted the Lord to make each next step known. It was a precious experience living *As He Leads*.

The mission board regularly sent representatives to the college to recruit workers, and I thought that possibly I might be one of the persons contacted by them. However, just at the time they were due to arrive on campus, Mother was hospitalized in Philadelphia, and I was called home to help take care of her. When I returned from my short leave, the representatives had been there and gone. I took it to be *As He Leads*.

During the year I was nurse at EMC, Mennonite Central Committee (MCC) and the Mennonite colleges arranged a work/travel summer in Europe, and God opened the way for me to go. Orientation occurred in Akron, Pennsylvania, and that evening Orie Miller, secretary of Eastern Mennonite Board of Missions and Charities, called me across the street to his home and asked if I would consider going as a nurse to the mission field in either Ethiopia or Honduras. I told him I would.

Orie said, "Maybe you want to think about it awhile. Most people do."

So I told him how I had already felt God's call and had yielded myself for any work He might have for me. I believed this was the call He had been preparing me to answer. I left the decision for placement to the mission board. My sister Muriel and her husband, Noah K. Mack, were medical missionaries in Tanganyika, so Africa held an attraction for me. However, Honduras would be the more practical choice because of my familiarity with the Spanish language. It wasn't until I returned from Europe three months later that I learned I would be going to Honduras.

The morning following my talk with Orie, the group I was with left from New York for Europe. From the beginning of June to the end of August 1950, we spent six weeks traveling in two Dutch buses visiting Mennonite sites in Luxembourg, Belgium, Holland, Germany, Switzerland, and Italy, and then six weeks in work camps.

I was first assigned to Prali Ghigou, a village high in the Italian Alps where Waldensians were building a retreat center. From that location we could look into France. I had two jobs: working on the road first, and later helping in the kitchen. There were people from 13 nations working together on the project. The food was mainly pasta—

ten buckets of water and one bucket of pasta, but one evening raw bacon was served. We Americans took ours outside and fried it over a fire.

In France we spent some time at Valdoi renovating an old chateau to become a Mennonite children's home.

♔

After I was informed that my mission assignment was Honduras, I received a letter from Anna Atwood. She and her husband, Robert, were missionaries working up the coast east of Trujillo. She told me what a beautiful old place Trujillo was and also said that much of the time it was without a doctor. That prompted me to ask the mission board for two things: a course in midwifery and some exposure to or training in tropical diseases. Both requests were granted. Fortunately one of the three places in the U.S.A. where midwifery training was offered was at Preston Maternity Hospital in Philadelphia, 25 miles from Malvern. Only one or two midwives were trained at a time, but due to a cancellation and God's leading, I was accepted.

For six months, over the winter of 1950-51, I studied midwifery at Preston. Miss Stella Mummert had succeeded Katherine Rohrer, the nurse I had known in my childhood, as superintendent. Miss Mummert was a capable and exacting midwife with a wealth of experience. She prepared maternity nurses, many of them Mennonite girls from Lancaster County, Pennsylvania, to care for mothers and babies after home deliveries. In addition, she trained midwives one or two at a time.

In 1960, Preston Maternity Hospital became affiliated with Pennsylvania Hospital and Miss Mummert retired after assisting or supervising 10,000 deliveries in her 40 years of service. Preston was built in 1836 and opened for patients in 1866. They had 25,000 deliveries and had taught 413 students, of which 81 were licensed as midwives by the state of Pennsylvania.

I had 70 deliveries under Miss Mummert's tutelage. Dr. Hirst was responsible for complicated deliveries and gave me instructions in using forceps and in making and suturing episiotomies.

When I left Preston Miss Mummert gave me a box of things I might find useful in Honduras. Many a time I blessed her for that gift. When I needed a glass connector, just a little thing, but what do you do when you desperately need it and there just isn't one in the clinic? Look in the box and sure enough there is one Miss Mummert thought to include.

Another thing she gave me I still use in my retirement apartment.

It is a glass washboard 8½" x 18" with its advantages printed on the back—*Ideal for silks, hosiery, and lingerie or handkerchiefs. Just the right size to fit a bucket, pail or lavatory. Packs easily into suitcase or traveling bag. Columbia Washboard Co*. It's probably valuable as an antique now.

The only tropical medicine course available for nurses was at the Adventist Hospital in Loma Linda, California. Another alternative was to study firsthand with Dr. Thaeler at the Moravian Mission Hospital in Bilwaskarma, Nicaragua. I wrote to him, but by the time I was nearly ready to leave Preston I still had not received an answer. The women I worked with there thought I should be worried, but somehow I knew God was in charge and just before the deadline to decide if I should go to California, a letter came inviting me to Bilwaskarma.

Picture taken in 1950 and used on a prayer card when I left for Honduras.

Dora M. Taylor

1951

Early in the summer of 1951, my commissioning service was held at a Mennonite church in Lancaster, Pennsylvania. On bended knees I was given the charge by Stoner Krady using Romans 10:10-28. *"Dear Sister,"* he said, *"since you have been appointed for the Honduras field to which the Lord has called you and the Holy Ghost has set you apart and consecrated you to teach and witness to the gospel of our Lord Jesus Christ as the power of God unto salvation to everyone that believeth, you are hereby commissioned by the church to go and teach and exemplify the gospel of our Lord Jesus Christ, also the order and practice of the Mennonite church under whose direction you are going. This being your first term of service, many friends and precious souls are awaiting your coming. You will not be responsible for their salvation, but for pointing out the way of salvation through our Lord Jesus Christ. To this end we wish you the grace and blessing of our Lord Jesus Christ who through His death and resurrection has made such a witness possible. The grace of our Lord Jesus Christ be with you to make you strong in every good work. Amen."*

That was a very serious and responsible commitment, and as I went I claimed these words from John 10:4: *and when he putteth forth his own sheep, he goeth before them.* I was not equal to the task, but I already had experienced God's enabling and that is what I trusted. Not that I always followed as I should have; I failed many times and after my days in Central America were past Satan tried to discourage me by bringing those things to my remembrance, but I know they are repented of, confessed, and forgiven—how great His mercy is! Anything that was accomplished for the Lord—all praise goes only to Him.

The *West Coast Champion* carried me by rail to Tampa, Florida, on June 12, 1951. Mission workers and friends I had known from my days in Ybor City met me at the station. As we drove toward the new location on Ninth Street, I felt a flutter of excitement as familiar sights came into view. Even more pleasurable was the opportunity to greet and visit more friends and former acquaintances. The first evening I attended a Spanish meeting led by Timothy Brenneman, a pastor from Sarasota. The Spanish sounded as good to my ears as the *helado de coco* (coconut ice cream) tasted to my mouth.

As I visited in the homes of various friends, I rejoiced to see how faithful some had remained in spite of hardships. Often, however, I was grieved to see the results of willful living. On the faces and in the lives of several girls, where I had once seen radiant joy, the deceiver had done a work of destruction. As Charles Hostetter gave a clear message of salvation at a Wednesday evening meeting, I prayed for several persons I knew who were still wavering on the brink of a decision.

My days in Tampa were few, but I witnessed many ways that the rejection of the Savior affected people's lives. George F. and Anna Brunk visited me, and George warned me they would not be able to come to Honduras to take care of me if I became ill. Anna's jolly laughter lingered in my memory long after I forgot the details of an amusing story she told about learning to catch mackerel.

I left Tampa by bus for Dothan, Alabama, with a happy, satisfied feeling that my visit was a lovely gift from the Lord. During a layover I did my best to comfort a woman suffering the news of her daughter's broken marriage. My medical missionary nursing work would begin in Honduras, but I could witness for the Lord wherever I found myself with a needy person.

Elam Hollinger and his wife, mission workers in Brewton, Alabama, met me at the Brewton bus station and took me to their home. Next morning his wife and I visited friends, and in the evening I spoke at the Bible School program telling of the work waiting for me in Honduras.

Elam's prayer as I waited for the bus to New Orleans returned to my memory many times in the hours to come. "Lord," he prayed, "direct all the details of Dora's trip and give rest to her body during tonight's journey."

I did rest during the long trip, and even slept a little in the New Orleans bus station in the morning before getting breakfast. It was upon my arrival at Piety Street Wharf that I started to wonder about the way the Lord was directing the details of my trip—my ship had sailed without me! The *S. S. Céfalu* was supposed to sail at 10:00 a.m., but had left at 7:00 the evening before because a threatened dock strike was to start at midnight. Fear struck at my heart, then I remembered: *God is in control. He certainly knows every step of my journey, and He permitted this to happen. He will take care of me.* A calmness descended and stayed with me all the way.

I took a taxi to the Standard Fruit and Steamship Company office. There I was told I would be given a plane ticket to Havana, Cuba where I could join up with the *S. S. Céfalu.* After spending the night in a nearby hotel, I boarded the plane, which had a stop in Tampa. My phone call from the airport to Irene Stauffer during the short layover, certainly surprised her. She was even more surprised to learn I was back in Tampa.

Before evening, however, I was surrounded by a babbling of Spanish as I went through customs in Havana. The city reminded me of an old-world city. Houses were big, heavy-looking buildings of stone or stucco. Windows opened directly onto the sidewalks, with only shutters providing protection and privacy at night. As I walked by, I could look right into the houses and could have even reached into some rooms. The streets were crowded with hand carts and lots of bicycles. It seemed as though every second car had the red license tag proclaiming *alquilar* (to rent) or taxi. From lunch until about 3:30 in the afternoon, shops closed and people disappeared from the streets. After that time people were back on the streets and the coffee shops were filled with well-dressed customers.

The *S. S. Céfalu* was in dock the next day when I visited the shipping office and before long I was in the Gulf of Mexico off Havana, with about 50 other passengers. I could see no reason the Lord had kept me from boarding at New Orleans, but I really didn't need to know His reason. He had kept me safe and made my path smooth.

The Standard Fruit & Steamship Company's *S. S. Céfalu*.

The ship was newly painted, comfortable, and had an air-conditioned dining room and lounge. My cabin had two big electric fans. From the portholes of my cabin, early in the morning of June 21 I could see nearby islands as well as cloud-draped mountains on the Honduran mainland. By morning the ship was tied up at the wharf in La Ceiba, Honduras, and I was searching the crowd for someone who might be looking for me. After awhile I saw a little blond boy and a man behind him wearing a sun helmet, with a camera slung over one shoulder, and carrying a brief case. It was George Miller, who with his family had opened the mission work in Trujillo in 1950. The little blond boy was his son, J. Mark.

It wasn't long before the immigration officials came on board and checked and stamped my passport and I walked off the *S. S. Céfalu* onto Honduran soil for the first time. The pier was crowded with barefoot, dark-skinned Carib men. George led the way to a combination bakery/inn operated by a Greek woman, where we had a breakfast of corn flakes with hot milk, fried eggs and ham, toast, and coffee. Then we walked up the sandy streets to visit Betty Brown and Don and Leora Ackerman and their eight-month-old son, Larry. The Ackermans and Betty taught in the United Brethren Mission School, which had one hundred pupils.

After picking up the three suitcases that had come with me on the *S. S. Céfalu*, George, J. Mark, and I went to the airport and boarded a little two-motor plane that had room for about 20 passengers and some freight. As we flew, low and not too fast, along the coast line, George pointed out Utila, Roatan, and the Hog Islands on the left. On the right were mountains. I saw several Carib, now called Garifuna, villages sandwiched between the mountains and the sea. From the air they looked like rows of cardboard cartons with thatched roofs.

Truck at the Trujillo airport.

The Trujillo airport was just a grassy field and a tiny wooden building. A truck with a home-made look backed up to the plane and the baggage was transferred to it. A little black and white goat that looked like a wind-up toy barked and ran around and climbed up over the roof of the building.

The six-mile road from the airport to town had once been a railroad track. Most of the road was just sand, but in some places there were still railroad ties. A two-rail bridge took us across a pretty lagoon. Before long we were driving up a steep cobblestone street past a jail, hotel, school, church, and then around a corner onto a grassy stone street to the Millers' home.

I was so tired I could barely hold my eyes open during the noon meal and took a two-hour *siesta* (nap) in the afternoon. After supper I was eager to talk with Grace, but again soon felt so desperately sleepy that I went to bed early. I must have gone into a deep sleep at once because it seemed only minutes before I found Grace beside my bed asking, "Did the shooting bother you?"

It was four in the morning and there appeared to be some kind of disturbance somewhere in the area. I got up and we went to the door. Swiftly-running figures slipped by in the half dark, and we heard drums beating and music playing in the distance.

Too sleepy to care, I soon headed back to bed and slept soundly until time for breakfast. Later in the day we discovered Trujillo was honoring John the Baptist, the town's patron saint, with a procession which included the shooting of firecrackers. The celebration continued all day with men, women, and children slowly parading through the streets.

Procession heading to the Catholic church. Note the park to the right, and the mountains behind Trujillo.

I was introduced to a new way of grocery shopping that first day in Trujillo. Soon after daybreak, Carib women started coming to the door. On their heads were containers which looked like dishpans or large basins. When they were lowered for inspection, I discovered they might contain anything from golden pineapples at seven cents each to *caracoles* (shrimp) for our lunch potpie. Once we purchased a watermelon that came to our door in that manner.

That evening I met up with my first tarantula. Just after family worship, George killed a big, furry-legged spider with a face like a monkey, on the kitchen floor.

Wall and entrance to the cemetery.

My first Sunday was full of new experiences. George, Grace, and I walked past the cemetery facing the jagged mountains, turned toward the sea, and continued down a cobblestone hill to Cristales, a Carib village of approximately 2,500 people. Many of the houses were of mud and sticks with palm-thatch roofs. None had windows with glass, just openings in the walls.

House and some residents of Cristales.

Fishnets drying in the sun in Cristales.

Note – thatched-roof house in the background.

About 30 children came for the service we held in Spanish. The two benches filled quickly and the chocolate-colored legs of the children who sat on the dirt floor soon showed a liberal coating of tan dust.

We sang songs together, read some Bible verses, and told a flannelgraph-illustrated story. That was followed by a short message by Pedro, a trusted Christian inmate on release from the local prison.

On the way home we stopped to visit a 13-year-old girl in a body cast. Grace took her a little package each week when they went to Sunday School. We stopped at another little mud house to visit a sick woman and promised to send aspirin each day for her pain.

Before the end of our walk, which included returning up that steep hill, the sun grew hot and I was glad for my umbrella. Lunch was ready for us when we arrived back at the house and after that I was ready for a *siesta*.

A second service was held in mid-afternoon in Trujillo, again mostly children were present. Shortly after it was over people from other towns came to join in a Catholic procession. Banners and even a life-size statue of John the Baptist were carried through the town and to the nearby villages.

Walking home after a third church service in the evening, I looked at the stars and thanked the Lord for a happy day. The North Star was not visible, nor was the Southern Cross, possibly because of the high mountains so close by.

Next day I was shown a house that could be rented for living space and a clinic. The front door opened on a large living room with a dining room behind it. On either side of the living room was a bedroom. One had a bathroom and closet space, and the other had a small room nearby which I immediately saw as a treatment room. The partitions were plaster and didn't reach to the ceiling, which was tin, an asset in termite country. A separate kitchen and porch at the back, and a gate in the side wall all pleased me. The *patio* (yard) had several mango trees, as well as breadfruit, papaya, and other fruit trees.

When the deal was closed to rent the property, I praised the Lord, but there were other things I had to do before I was ready to open the clinic.

♔

As promised, the mission board honored my request for training in tropical disease identification and treatment by sending me to the Moravian Mission Hospital in Bilwaskarma, Nicaragua. The Moravian work in Bilwaskarma was 50 years old, and further down the coast had been going on for over a hundred years—started in 1849 by German Moravians and taken over by Americans at the time of World War I.

I probably didn't set a record, but it took me nine days to reach Bilwaskarma. I waited three days in Tegucigalpa for a one-hour flight to Managua, and five days there for the two-hour flight to Bilwaskarma.

My trip began in Trujillo by doing a reverse of my entry. Down the cobblestone hill, then the six miles over the old railroad bed, followed by a plane ride to La Ceiba. Traveling is hard on suitcases and by then I already had two that were almost beyond repair. The little plane followed the coast most of the way, with the mountains on the left and coconut palms beneath us. From above, the palms looked like many-pointed stars or perhaps green daisies on long stems. After a stop at San Pedro Sula we flew south and crossed mountains. My destination at that point of the journey was Tegucigalpa, the capital of Honduras, where I went to the Central America Mission home of Mr. and Mrs. Cyrus Robinson. Mr. Robinson was to get the permit for me to enter the country as a missionary.

The next morning I went to market with Mrs. Robinson. We walked among beggars and people who apparently didn't bathe every day. The market was up a pair of dirty steps into an area where women had fruit and vegetables spread out on the floor. Afterwards we went into the cathedral, Catedral de San Miguel, completed in 1782. Its bells were from Spain and the inside front was a panel all covered with gold.

I was glad I wasn't alone when we went for a walk in the evening. The street lights were few and very dim. Mrs. Robinson said she always carried a flashlight when out at night and even so, she almost stepped on a drunken man lying on the sidewalk. Rooms of the houses opened right off the sidewalk and we could easily see and hear the people inside.

I asked if this was the worst part of the city, but Mrs. Robinson replied, "It is all like this."

The services on Sunday, both morning and evening, were in Spanish and I understood almost every word. On the way home from church in the dark that evening we got into sticky mud. I was so thankful for my plastic boots. I do believe that the day before several hundred Hondurans saw plastic boots for the first time—almost every person I passed on the streets turned to look at them.

Mr. Robinson got my permit to leave the country, and I took a taxi to the airport for a plane to Managua, Nicaragua.

I never imagined a country could have so little level space. There were countless hills and valleys. Everything was a vivid, living green and most beautiful in the brilliant sunlight with white clouds and blue sky above. Before long I had my first glimpse of the Pacific Ocean. After landing I went through immigration and was directed to a hotel to buy my ticket to Bilwaskarma.

It was then I discovered I needed to wait five more days before continuing my journey and once again needed to accept help from the hands of missionaries. I called Dr. Pixley, a total stranger, at the hospital run by Baptists, and he sent his wife to pick me up. The meaning of the Bible verses about showing hospitality to strangers became very important and real to me, and I hoped I would never forget the lessons I learned from the receptions with which I was greeted in the various homes. Dr. Pixley, a missionary doctor there since 1932, even got me an invitation to a party all the Americans were attending at the embassy.

Not only was I given room and board, but when I visited the hospital, Mr. Salter explained how to do blood counts and several other things I could put to use in my clinic work.

A group of missionaries including my hosts had planned a fourth of July trip to the Pacific, and I was taken along. It was a beautiful 50-mile ride, first into the mountains and then down to the shore.

High, rough waves were breaking on the broad beach, and every one had fun. We were told of an active volcano south of the area we visited that belched poisonous gasses, and we noticed trees along the way that were blighted.

Finally I arrived in Bilwaskarma. One of the first lessons I learned was why it carried that name. *Bil* means snake, *was* means water, and *karma* means neck or throat, so in the Miskito language Bilwaskarma is *snake water neck*. A creek running to the river was probably the *water neck,* and it was easy to believe the *snake* part. During the first two weeks I was there I saw a harmless five-foot green one on the

Snake on an iron pipe on the Moravian compound at Bilwaskarma.

Notice the bulge which indicated the location of a frog it had just swallowed.

Many of my black and white photographs were totally destroyed by termites. The white spots on this and a few of the other pictures in this book are the result of termite activity.

wall beside our house, a poisonous coral snake was killed near the reservoir, and Miss Martin and I walked over a Tommy Goff, another poisonous one. We always took flashlights when we went out at night, but we didn't see the Tommy Goff until we were stepping over it. Miss Martin told me she had once seen a boa constrictor between 20 and 30 feet long and at least ten inches in diameter hanging from a palm tree. The Miskitos kill boas whenever they see them because the snakes catch their cows.

A very welcome first letter from home caught up with me in Bilwaskarma. It reported that cherries were ripe, Summer Bible School was going well, my folks were having the house wallpapered and had attended a family reunion, and revival meetings were being held in Lancaster, Pennsylvania.

The first evening in Bilwaskarma I was invited to a welcome-home-from-school party for Dr. Thaeler's three children who had returned from school in Bethlehem, Pennsylvania, and Pastor Stortz's 20-year-old daughter who had just completed 12 years of schooling in the United States. During the party, a rat ran down a window frame. Almost without a pause in the game we were playing, a student nurse jumped up, grabbed a stick, killed the rat, and rejoined the game. One of the boys asked, "Was that part of the game?"

Dr. John David Arnold, an army doctor from Illinois, was at Bilwaskarma getting a malaria program under way. The natives called him the Mosquito King.

In July the Stortzes celebrated their wedding anniversary, and in November they celebrated 25 years of service in Bilwaskarma. The baked ham for their anniversary dinner, to which I was invited, came from Puerto Cabezas 100 miles away. The ingredients for the salad—lettuce, tomato, avocado, and cucumber—came from Managua, as did the potatoes for scalloped potatoes and fresh green beans. The meal ended with rolls, refrigerator ice cream, cake, and coffee—quite a treat for folks who didn't have such things often.

Our menu usually included rice and beans twice a day. Meat was cheap and we had it once or twice a day. Coconut milk was made by pouring water over grated coconut and squeezing out all the goodness, leaving an almost tasteless fiber, which was fed to the chickens. We used the milk to boil rice, and sometimes red beans left over from the day before were cooked in the milk, which resulted in a dish that tasted like coconut. We also used the coconut milk in cooking cereal—sometimes oatmeal, but more often ground rice. Bananas, plas, and plantains were on the menu every day. Ripe plantains were baked. Boiled green bananas tasted a little like potatoes. Desserts were usually puddings or baked goods, with a frozen dessert on Sunday. Mrs. Thaeler always made attractive meals with whatever food she had available. On the big wood-burning cook stove at one end of the kitchen she prepared meals daily for about 60 people with assistance from only two or three Miskito girls. When the clinic was closed on Saturdays I helped in the kitchen.

I was given a room on the mission compound, sharing a small house with Beulah Martin, a nurse from Frederick, Maryland. It was about 100 miles from the coast, and a mile from a river that went by three names—Coco, Wanks, and Segovia. In addition to the house Miss Martin and I used, the community was made up of the clinic, hospital, laundry, and church, and houses for the families of Dr. Thaeler, Pastor Stortz, Pastor Befus, and the native nurses and teachers. There were pine, coconut, citrus, and flowering trees on the grounds.

The electricity came from the mission's own power plant run partly by water power and partly by diesel fuel.

The climate was hot and humid and there was mold everywhere. I almost lived in my plastic boots and wished for the galoshes I had left at home, and I seemed to be using my handy collapsible umbrella all the time. The first night I woke up with pain in my joints—even the bedding seemed damp. As a reminder that I was in malaria country, I slept under a mosquito bar. This was a netting cage or tent suspended over the bed by string loops hooked over nails in the wall. The sides hung down and were tucked under the mattress all the way around. After you entered at a lapped-over opening you tucked that in as well. During the night I heard a tiny chewing sound, and, fearing that roaches were in my clothing, I got up to check. The sound stopped but resumed as soon as I was back in bed and quiet. I wondered if it might be wood worms, but it was probably termites.

Dr. Thaeler told me that only waterproof watches would last because of moisture, and I could well believe it as I saw my leather bedroom slippers, suitcases, straw hat, and even my pocketbook inside a suitcase become covered with mold. The floor boards in the house were painted and every week we rubbed them with a wax made from a mixture of melted candles and kerosene. For several days they looked nice, then gray mold started showing up between the boards and around the edges, and it was soon time to wax them again.

At first I hung my uniforms in my room at night, but I soon discovered that by morning they were soft, wilted, damp, and crinkled. Keeping them in plastic garment bags until I was ready to wear them was the only way to keep them crisp.

Moisture and dampness wasn't the only thing I had to learn to cope with in Bilwaskarma. Mother had a rash before I left home and I advised her in a letter that she should be in Nicaragua where it wasn't bad form to scratch. The itching there, however, usually came from mosquito bites, or bugs in the grass. The ones in the grass got on me and climbed to my waist or shoulders where my clothing was the tightest. There they dug in and big welts like hives showed up and provided plenty of violent itching for about a week. I usually had a dozen or two at a time.

Several hundred people from neighboring villages attended the Miskito service at 9:30 my first Sunday morning in Bilwaskarma. Pastor Befus preached in the morning service. He also did evangelistic work in the villages. At 12:30 a Sunday School was held and Parson Stortz had more than 100 children in his class. An English message followed with 35 to 40 people in attendance, and then I was invited to *coffee* at Stortzes.

About half of the 14 lay pastors Pastor Stortz was training to go out and minister to their own people were married and lived in a group of little split-bamboo huts thatched with coconut palm leaves. That afternoon the lay pastors were singing for the patients in the hospital. They sang in Spanish, then in Miskito. One song was “Must Jesus Bear the Cross Alone?” One Sunday afternoon I heard the tune of the German song *“Gott ist die Liebe,”* a carryover from the time the German Moravians had the mission.

♔

I started working in the clinic in the mornings and spent afternoons in the lab. As Dr. Thaeler saw patients with malaria, yaws, and carate, as well as diseases I had seen in the United States, he explained his treatments to me. The graduate nurses showed me the lab and allowed me to do white and red blood cell counts, differentials, and stool examinations. I was eager to do malaria slides.

On July 24, Elva, one of the nurses, asked me to accompany her to a village to give the daily dose of medicine to malaria patients. It was an interesting walk—no road, just a path over low hills. We went through a bit of dense jungle and crossed three streams. The bridges over the streams were three logs, not very wide, laid side by side. Some were chipped flat on top, but some were still round and hard to walk on. One bridge ended ten feet short of the bank. We walked to the end of the logs, stepped down several steps, and waded to the bank.

People were gathered at the church in the village to receive medicine, which someone took to them every day. They brought tin cans or calabashes of water to wash down the pills. Elva took 32 smears, and I filled out cards with names and ages. When I asked their age, the people replied, *No apn* (There isn’t any). A man helpfully started giving me ages in English, but since he stated a small child might be eight, and a much larger child four, I soon started guessing for children and listed all grown-ups as *adult*.

The houses in the village were on stilts and had thatched roofs. The walls were boards or split bamboo. Windows were an opening with just a wooden shutter for security. The furnishings usually included a very crude table, benches, and maybe a bed. A bed was a box which reminded me of a sand box, only the bottom was split bamboo and there wasn’t any sand. The stove was the same type of box but it was lined with zinc and filled with earth about six inches deep and stood on 24-inch legs. A wood fire was started on top of the earth, then a piece of tin or iron was placed on logs about two feet apart over the fire. There the women cooked their beans and rice, green bananas, or plantains.

The people bathed and washed clothes in the rivers, and also used the river water for drinking. One hundred percent of the people had hookworm and usually other kinds of parasites. About 35 percent of them had malaria according to the army survey. It wasn't long before I could recognize malaria and hookworm on slides. Once when I was doing slides for parasites the nurse said, "There are no negatives."

♔

Mrs. Stortz planned a trip down the river to visit some of their churches, and I was invited to accompany her, her daughter Margy, and 14-year-old Mary Thaeler. We started one Wednesday evening. First we heard the boats coming, and quickly ate supper and got ready to leave. Then as we hurried down to the river bank, I heard the unmistakable sound of boats leaving, but we weren't the only ones left behind. It appeared that all the passengers from our area were still on shore—the barge had been full.

We went back to the house and someone mixed up a cool beverage. Pastor Stortz decided to pop some corn while we waited for the next boat, but when we suddenly heard more boats arriving, he rushed to the shore to check if it was one we could board—and he forgot to put the lid on the popcorn kettle. When he got back, there was popcorn all over the veranda!

Two boats had arrived and the other passengers all boarded the first one. Mrs. Stortz, Margy, Mary, and I boarded the commissary boat which was like a store for the people living along the river. The crew set up our cots in the store room and we put up mosquito bars. Shortly after I went to bed I heard scratching and running sounds—rats. During the night a rat got into Mrs. Stortz's bed, but she just held up a corner of the mosquito net and let him out. In the morning I found a rat in a can beside my cot.

Although we had taken our own food, the captain announced breakfast was prepared for us. I noticed the cook rinsed the dishes in a pan of river water, but I couldn't offend our host, so I swallowed my squeamishness along with the rice, beans, eggs, and coffee.

At 7:30 in the morning we arrived at Twibila without seeing much of the river, which was high and fast because of the rainy season. Parson Isaac Lewis met us and introduced us to Jane Wedman, Loretta Tillet, and Lassie Watson, a Creole woman who was a perfect hostess during the short time we spent there. At 10:30 we left again in a dory or dugout canoe with a motor.

The river was level full, so the banks were barely visible. The mysterious-looking jungle foliage on both sides was so thick at places it looked as though nothing could penetrate. As we approached a huge tree, I counted 36 hanging nests in its branches. They were 12 to 18 inches long and made by Oropendula birds.

At Cape Creek we turned left into a creek about ten feet wide and later passed though a green meadow where cranes streaked their whiteness against the verdure or the blue of the sky. Other birds were there too, one a pretty little bird of gold and brown. At some places the creek through the meadow was only slightly wider than the dory.

We passed several villages of bamboo houses with thatched roofs. When the people heard the motor of the dory, they came to the bank to watch us pass. Boys up to eight or ten years of age were naked, but the girls were all clothed. All the villages had coconut palms and banana trees. At most of them I noticed cows and always several unbelievably bony dogs.

Every Indian man has his own dory or pit-pan and a machete. The dory is a long canoe made of a hollowed out tree trunk spread open to accommodate passengers and cargo. The machete is the long sharp knife that cuts everything.

After passing through the green meadow the creek entered real jungle with tangled mangrove roots and trees reaching 60 feet above us. Vines and creepers wove everything together and *that's where the snakes live,* someone said.

Under vegetation so thick the sun couldn't reach us, we chugged along in eerie semidarkness rounding one bend after another. In unison, we ducked our heads as we passed under a low footbridge. As our boat entered a lagoon, it got stuck on a sandbar, but after some pushing it was maneuvered free and headed toward a village we saw in the distance.

The houses, built on stilts, were of split bamboo with thatched roofs. Beside a little weather-beaten church was the parson's home where we had a dinner of chicken, rice, beans, boiled breadfruit, and cake.

Early afternoon found us headed back through the lagoon. Plowing against the swift current our boat created our own private rainstorm and we were all glad for our raincoats. We slept that night on our cots in the mission house in Twibila. Much of the village was under water, and we walked around on raised board walks. Lassie served us breakfast before we prepared for our return to Bilwaskarma.

We boarded a barge which was used to transport bananas. A load of 4,000 stems made a trip profitable, but this barge was carrying only 3,000. We shared cot space with onions and cheese and cartons and bales of other merchandise. The eight other passengers, with their bags and machetes, were given space on the open deck.

A tug pulled our barge and another one up the river. The other barge was open except for a roofed area and was loaded with livestock. I never forgot Klupki, a small village on the right side of the river. It was perhaps ten bamboo houses all sitting on their props in six to ten inches of mud. Children, older people, cows, pigs, and dogs all clopped around in the black mud. The people looked fairly clean except below the knees. I wondered what the houses looked like inside.

A bull with a rope around his horns was driven over a pile of logs until he was near the barge. He was then shoved off the bank where he plunged, sputtered, and entirely disappeared. Using the rope, someone pulled him alongside the barge. Another rope was put in front of his back legs and he was hauled up over the side. He didn't have enough fight left in him to cause any trouble.

Next a woman boarded with a machete in her left hand, a chicken in her right hand, and a baby on her hip. A little girl with a tiny dog, and an old woman with just a piece of cloth for a skirt and an old rag around her shoulders for a blouse were next. The little girl made several trips back and forth bringing a sack of something, a stem of bananas, a pot with a lid, and some calabashes. When she finally got on with her last load, a kind man lifted a bucket of water from the river and poured it over her feet and legs.

The mother, baby, and little girl settled themselves cross-legged on a shelf-bed against the wall opposite us in the open part of the barge. Under the shelf were the bags, bananas, machete, kettle, and a rag with the dog on it. The old woman sat on her haunches on the floor. The baby was about a year old, plump, laughing, and bright-eyed. Sitting beside her mother she had easy access to her breast, and it seemed as though she was sucking half the time. Mrs. Stortz talked to the mother in Miskito and asked when the child was born. The mother, however, didn't remember what month she had had her child.

I watched with interest as the little family opened the kettle and dipped out *wabul* into the calabash. *Wabul* is a thick white liquid made from boiled green bananas. The whole family, including the baby, had some. Later they ate the ripest bananas off their bunch. For supper a plate of rice and beans and a bun arrived from the kitchen and the baby ate most of that with her fingers. The old woman peeled some green bananas and put them in the *wabul* kettle, added some river water, and had it taken to the kitchen to be cooked.

Just before dark the baby began to whimper and was given another calabash of *wabul*. The mother undressed the baby and used the little garments to flick away mosquitoes. The baby's round shiny protruding abdomen reminded me in size and shape of the watermelons given us at Twibila. It wasn't long before she went to sleep lying on her mother's crossed legs.

All afternoon our tug pulled us up the river. We passed a few more villages, and saw many dories hurrying somewhere, usually in the possession of two women with a bunch of bananas or plantains. The woman in the front end poled and the one behind rowed. I noticed that when they left their dory on the bank, they pinned it to the ground by thrusting the pole through a hole in the front end.

I spent part of the time reading *An American Doctor's Odyssey*, but the scenes along the banks and on the river itself claimed my attention quite often. Twice I walked the deck to see what was happening on the second barge. Our accommodations were "A" deck compared to their steerage. Near the front of that barge were three cows tied side by side. In front of them were a dozen or so chickens each tied fast by one leg. The rest of the barge held a pile of poles and groups of people and their belongings. At the back were several wood fires where people cooked their meals. Whenever the boat stopped, people jumped off with their machetes and came back with arm loads of firewood. Under the eves of the roof I noticed someone had made a bed with some bamboo. Dories were tied to the end of the barge.

We went to bed, when it got dark, to escape the mosquitoes and bugs. The storeroom as well as our cots reeked of onions—we couldn't smell the good ones because the bad ones smelled so strong. The other people, out in the open part, lay on the shelves and on the floor. I expressed concern about those on the floor with no barrier between them and the river. Mrs. Stortz said that on one of her trips a mother and child were near the edge, and in the morning the child was not to be found. It had rolled off during the night. All the mother could do was to go on without it.

During the night there were numerous stops for people to get on and off, and to unload cargo from around us. I guess none of us slept too well even though there weren't any rats. The baby and dog family was gone in the morning.

For breakfast we ate the bread, pineapple preserves, cheese, cookies, and cake that we had taken along and were served coffee from the kitchen. I liked the white native cheese made in Klopke if it was fried, but I didn't like it raw. After each meal we stacked the dishes and Margy or Mary washed them in river water. Personally, I'd have preferred each one just keeping her own plate unwashed. Mrs. Stortz had a gallon of our own good rainwater along for drinking and it tasted wonderful.

Before we reached Bilwaskarma shortly after noon, the girls had a good time in the sun. They ate the sea grapes that the people in Twibila had given them, and also had a private supply of green mangoes from Lassie's tree. Mrs. Stortz and I spent the time getting better acquainted. I thought the return trip was unusually hot, but after I got home I discovered I was running a temperature of 102°. The flu!

♔

The beginning of August 1951 brought pleasant days of brief showers and cooling breezes to Bilwaskarma.

August 12 was Miskito confirmation Sunday. Before that service began there were three weddings. Pastor Stortz conducted two and Pastor Befus one. The pastors were always glad for these weddings because they considered the civil ceremony not binding in the eyes of God. Many of the couples had the civil ceremony first and waited for a church wedding until they were able to afford the expenses of a feast and a long wedding dress.

Five hundred people filled the church, and it was quite a sight because nearly everyone was in white for the afternoon communion service. The girls and women all wore something white on their heads—a handkerchief, a white piece of material, or a little white doily.

The 26 waiting to be confirmed that morning sat up front. Both ministers officiated, each taking two at the same time. They read a verse and the name of each person, then with their hands placed on the heads of the persons being confirmed, said a short line in Miskito. The choir then sang a stanza of "Just as I Am." That was repeated for each set of four. The baptism of a woman and a girl followed.

The service was over by 11:15, and Miss Martin and I went home with the Stortzes for dinner. The food was delicious—meat, riced potatoes, green beans, watermelon pickle, and pumpkin pie served with coconut ice cream. The pastors had worn white surplices for the morning service, and during dinner Margy asked her father if the rubber bands held. Pastor Stortz was a big man and he explained that his surplice would not reach around him so he had put rubber bands through the buttonholes.

We returned to the church for afternoon Sunday School and communion. The people sat in two rows of seats then left an empty row where the ministers passed through with the bread and cups. Pastor Stortz gave out the hymns, which were sung throughout the service, and Pastor Befus and Dr. Thaeler served. The service was in Miskito but seemed reverent and not much different from the ones I was used to in our own church. People knelt in prayer after the bread and wine and stood for prayer preceding it. I truly worshipped and thanked the Lord with all my heart for His broken body and His blood shed in my behalf.

Following the service I was invited to Stortzes for coffee. Mrs. Stortz roasted her own coffee beans; the coffee was delicious.

For supper I went to Befus' home. They were another lovely family. After supper their children, Ruthie and Jerry, showed me their little hospital.

Ruthie explained, "This doll has a broken arm and that one has fever." She went on to tell me, "We had 100 patients in clinic this morning. About six of them had fever and about seven of them had—is there something like DDT?"

I suggested, "TB?"

"Yes, seven of them had TB."

"How could Jerry take care of so many?" I asked.

"Oh," came the swift reply from the little girl explaining the efficiency of her brother, and probably remembering the confirmation service of that morning. "He took two at a time, that's what he did."

After the evening song service, Dr. Thaeler stopped me and put a crisp little roll into my hand. "Here's something for your work," he said. "If you can't use it this way, let me know."

When I got home and checked, I found it was a 20 dollar bill—worth a great deal more in 1951 than it is now. I was overwhelmed with knowledge that my Lord is good and this was just one more demonstration of His love. I knew I was unworthy of all His gifts and miracles, and it made my heart overflow with humility and a greater desire to pour out myself in service for Him. It wasn't always like that. I was aware that in between times of thankfulness I often forgot, was selfish and cold and negligent of my place at His feet. *Lord*, I prayed. *Forgive me again and help me to appropriate Thy grace for victory.*

♔

I left Bilwaskarma Monday, August 13. Mrs. Thaeler told me she had prepared my morning snack and left it in the kitchen. There I found a special treat—a banana split made of banana, ice cream, honey, and cashews. Everybody went to the airfield to see me off, and when I looked back from the plane it looked like 100 people. Perhaps many of them were there with a double purpose. Thelma Good from Bluefields on the coast was coming to teach in the school, and I think many of them were there as much to greet her as they were to see me off. Whatever their reason, I left with a warm feeling in my heart.

On the plane I had several interesting contacts and at least two Catholics read eagerly from my Testament as we discussed my beliefs and reasons for being in Central America.

I arrived in Managua, Nicaragua, about 2:45 and received immediate permission from Immigration to leave the country. I started to rejoice that my return trip to Trujillo wouldn't be as lengthy as my trip to Bilwaskarma, but as I turned to leave I was told that the visa office was closed. I went to the TACA airline office and made a reservation. Then I tried to complete my business at the Consulate, but it was also closed. Once more I had to rely on the hospitality of Christian friends. I took a taxi to the Pixley home and was warmly received.

Tuesday I visited the boys' school, saw someone about having Miss Martin's dogs immunized, and was entertained by Mr. and Mrs. Wyse until Mrs. Pixley came and took me downtown when she went to market. I got the visa and took it to TACA. Then I was told I needed one from the consul also, and also must get *timbres* or stamps from the *Banco Nacional*.

The bank was eight blocks away, and when I got there it was closed for a holiday. By the time I got back to the consulate my legs felt weak. When I told the consul about the banks being closed he said, in Spanish, "O, this is the day of the Japanese peace. If I had thought of that I wouldn't have worked today either."

There was no other place to get the *timbres*, and I resigned myself to another day's wait. By then the morning and all my strength were gone. I went to the market, bought a watermelon, and went back to the Pixley home to rest until lunch time.

I finally got as far as Tegucigalpa by Thursday. Mrs. Robinson invited me to lunch, and then I took a taxi to the *Sanidad* or The Department of Health. There I was told I didn't have to register or obtain a permit to open a clinic in Trujillo, I could just go to work. I also went to the embassy to register as an *extranjera* or alien.

At San Pedro Sula I got off the plane and knew that once again

Henry Garber, Stoner Krady, and Paul Graybill.

the Lord had timed my trip just right. Henry Garber, Stoner Krady, and Paul Graybill had just arrived from another direction. I had known they were coming to Trujillo for special meetings and had feared my delays would make me miss a portion of their visit. A second blessing was that my lodging in San Pedro Sula was automatically taken care of with theirs because a missionary, Harold Auler, was there to meet them and invited me to join them. A third blessing was that I needed authorization to buy medicine in San Pedro Sula for the clinic and Bro. Garber could handle that for me.

Mr. Auler drove us to his home, where we left our bags, then took us downtown and showed us the market and some of the churches. I registered with the American consul and put in my drug order.

Getting back to Trujillo was like going home. The Lord gave me joy and a song in my heart. I knew beyond the shadow of a doubt that He had called me to that place.

Sunday morning Don Pedro, the man from the jail, gave a fine testimony at the service in Teodora's house. Approximately 60 persons, including a number of adults, were present. The room was filled for the afternoon Spanish service, and in the evening it was overflowing. Bro. Graybill gave a doctrinal lesson first, then Bro. Krady followed with an evangelistic message. Each morning of the men's visit, Bro. Graybill gave us missionaries a study from I Timothy.

I could feel the Holy Spirit's presence during the meetings, but there were no decisions to accept Christ, and I was concerned—if the lost souls didn't accept the Lord then, I was afraid they never would. I was convicted that I was not spending enough time in prayer, and I asked the Millers if we could have times of prayer together. Two days later we held our first prayer fellowship. It was a blessing and I hoped it would never lose its sacredness and become routine. I prayed we would grow in our knowledge of the Lord and of prayer, and that His Spirit would have increased liberty to use us in effectual prevailing prayer. In myself, I praised the Lord for all He had taught me of Himself and of life in Him, but I knew there was much more He could teach me, and I wanted to be in the place where He could do it.

Bro. Garber was my first patient in the new clinic. He got sick during the meeting Sunday night and spent the next day in bed. Then the drug order arrived and I had a lot of fun unpacking and arranging the items on a shelf. A bottle of Chenopodium had leaked and the odor could be detected even outside the building. Next, I came down with Bro. Garber's bug and wasn't able to attend meetings for two nights.

The three visitors joined George Miller and Clinton Ferster in checking out sites for a church and a clinic. Meantime, we were experiencing a lot of wind from a hurricane passing near Haiti.

Although there were still no confessions at the meetings, some people attended the Friday service who never came any other time. Some of Trujillo's residents were from the Bay Islands and spoke English. The house was full as Bro. Graybill spoke on baptism and after the meeting I asked Pearl how she was with the Lord.

Her eyes filled with tears and her face flushed as she replied, "Not as I should be, Miss Dora." I asked her if she would like to talk to me sometime, and we set the next morning for our talk.

In our talk, she told me she had only one problem. "It's my patience," she said. "I'm ready to give up everything else. I've wanted to be a Christian so long, but it seems I can't give that up."

I gave her an illustration of a young man who never married the girl he loved, because he was afraid he couldn't support her for the next 50 years they might live. Pearl saw the point of my illustration; after we read some Scripture together, she accepted the Lord. We knelt and she prayed a beautiful prayer of penitence and submission and asked the Lord to help her grow in grace. Then she prayed for her family. It was a beautiful first prayer for a new Christian. She gave a short testimony at the meeting the following evening, and her face was absolutely beautiful with an inner radiance. I spoke to her grandmother, but she said she hadn't decided about accepting the Lord yet. Satan certainly blinds, binds, and deceives people. Just the next day Pearl looked as miserable as she had looked happy the day before. Her peace, joy, and assurance were gone. It was the beginning of a long struggle for her.

After the Sunday evening sermon on the "second coming," Hessie was in tears but still torn by indecision. She decided she was not ready to yield yet. The meetings ended and many people were still on the wrong side of the salvation decision.

By September the attendance at our Wednesday evening Bible studies usually numbered about 25 people, plus at least three dogs, and the black puss-in-boots that caught moths.

Maybell and Clinton Ferster had served in Tanganyika, Africa, where Clinton had done building. His assignment in Trujillo was to build a church. The Fersters and I looked at a house and then moved in using a few pieces of furniture the owner, Mr. Glynn, loaned us. More furniture was obtained—a buffet, several chairs, four rockers, and a table—all in bad condition and full of roaches. However, there was also a lovely bureau and an old wardrobe.

A few days later a stove arrived on the *Julia*, but we didn't have stove pipe. We continued getting our meals at Millers. When the stove was finally set up, Maybell and I cleaned the kitchen and started to *live* in our house. There was a stack of wood in the kitchen and when we needed more we bought it, a headload at a time from Carib women who brought it to the door. Grace Miller loaned us dishes and cooking utensils until mine came. Maybell baked bread and I made a cinnamon flop. We canned 16 jars of pineapples and five of syrup.

Women carrying wood up Conventillo Hill. Notice the pattern of the cobblestones street in the shadow of woman at right.

Until James and Beatrice Hess came from language school with an electric refrigerator, and gave us their kerosene one, we used clay pots to keep our boiled drinking water cool. The pots were porous and evaporation from water seeping through cooled the contents. I never expected to have ice cream cones in Trujillo, but a man known as Old Black Jim made it in a freezer and trundled it around in a wheelbarrow with the cones in a tin cracker box.

Even though my shipment had left New Orleans a month before and still hadn't arrived, my heart was bubbling over with joy and gratitude to God. My living arrangements were pleasant, and I appreciated the companionship of Clinton and Maybell. Although I could not start the clinic work until my supplies arrived, I decided the Lord was granting me the extra time for recovery from my bout with the flu. As I felt better, however, it was harder to be patient, especially when a baby came that needed penicillin and I didn't even have a syringe.

We prayed about the shipment in our little prayer fellowship, and I knew it was on the prayer list back home. I longed for the beds, the medical books and my medical bag, and the Aladdin lamp and sprayer and spray would have found immediate use, but it was the jar of peanut butter I wished for most. After suffering through some impatient frustration, I committed the whole situation to the Lord, and He took away all my anxiety. The luggage was in His hands and would arrive according to His schedule. Actually the beds didn't arrive until the end of December.

Meantime I worked on some stories for *Words of Cheer*, a Mennonite weekly Sunday School take-home paper for children.

At 8:30 one evening a man came and requested I go with him to deliver a baby. In the house my eyes burned from the smoke that came from a little concrete stove, and the tiny lantern they supplied gave very little light. I silently thanked the Fersters for the flashlight they had loaned to me. Soon after I arrived, I delivered a healthy six-and-one-half-pound boy.

My first baby with his mother.

A little girl was asleep in the bed with her mother and never woke up. The bed was an old iron one with just a poor mattress and no sheets. One leg of the bed was in a six- or eight-inch hole in the ground floor. After I had the mother fixed up I asked if they had any clothes for me to put on the baby. The father

Grace and Philip Miller and Beatrice Hess on a street in Trujillo. The first house on the right was where I delivered Sara's baby.

handed me a little cap made from a nylon stocking top gathered at the edge, and with two little strings to tie it under the baby's chin. The mother, whose name was Sara, said babies wear them for two or three months. That was the only item she had prepared for the new baby. The father finally found a little blouse. I asked about diapers, but they replied, "*No hay* (there aren't any), Dorita," so an old shirt had to substitute. When I checked on them next morning, the father was cooking beans for breakfast and mother and baby were doing fine.

After I had delivered more babies, I wrote home about all the exercise I was getting doing follow-up visits and Mother suggested I buy a burro to ride. When Clinton heard the suggestion, he laughed and said, "Going down Cristales hill you would slide right over his head, and coming back you would slide off his tail." Needless to say, I didn't buy a burro.

Even without my supplies, patients started coming to the clinic. A sick baby was brought in, and a neighbor needed a splinter extracted from a finger, and almost every time I treated someone a way opened for me to speak about Christ.

One Wednesday in mid-October a man came to the door with a message. "Big boxes and trunks at wharf. Too much heavy."

By Saturday, although my beds and one crate had not arrived, my home and clinic were getting into shape. The things borrowed from Grace were being returned as fast as the supplies were unpacked. Maybell said, "I believe this is His time," and immediately we had guests.

Reina and Terry Borden, two girls from Coxenhole, Roatan, one of the Bay Islands, arrived before their telegram. Trujillo's governor, Ephrain Pineda Zacapa, came with them and stayed to show them around. He had been governor of Roatan before he came to Trujillo. I showed him the clinic, and he urged me to notify him if I had any opposition. He sent up a cot and pillow and Clinton used it while the guests used the double bed set up in the living room. A few days later we invited the governor to dinner. After dinner we walked downtown and had *frescos* (soft drinks). I believe he knew he was a sinner and had also found out that the pleasures of sin did not satisfy. My thought was, *If only he knew the Lord Jesus and how He satisfies.*

Reina, Maybell, and Terry.

Before Terry and Reina left, several of us, including the governor, went for a walk part way up the mountain to the dam which was the source of Trujillo's water supply. We heard bird songs and saw beautiful climbing vines, flocks of parakeets, and armies of red ants carrying pieces of green leaves. Above the dam was a waterfall, and then the water tumbled over huge smooth boulders below the dam where the jungle closed in on both sides. I was quite aware that I was picking up travelers as we went along, and as soon as we reached home I took a bath. Perhaps it helped because I had only a few itching red bug bites.

As He Leads was proven true once more when a smiling Arab girl of 11 came to the clinic on October 27, and I pulled my first tooth, after injecting twice. A Christian dentist in Philadelphia had given me some instructions on extracting teeth and provided me with a basic set of forceps and elevators.

The tooth I pulled for the Arab girl was a lower first molar and badly decayed. I sighed with relief when it came out in one piece. I didn't enjoy that part of the work as much as, for example, midwifery, but I was glad I could give relief to many suffering people who had aching teeth that needed to come out.

By December 7, I had pulled 34 teeth. A few were so rotten they just crumbled and the patient had to go to La Ceiba to a dentist to have the roots cut out. I told myself the first hundred would probably be the worst, and sometime later discovered I wasn't disliking the job as much as I had in the beginning.

The clinic opened officially on November 4, 1951, with seven patients. If people arrived before 8:30 and attended the little Scripture reading and prayer service, their consultation was free. Those who came later were charged 25 cents lempira or 12½ U. S. cents for the visit. All paid a small fee for medicine. I usually worked until noon except on Wednesday and Sunday and, of course, I worked whenever an emergency arrived.

The second morning two patients arrived for the service and I had a total of nine patients for the day. Another morning I pulled two teeth and had a total of 16 patients. One patient was a little girl about nine years old who weighed only 36 pounds. Her father had brought her in a *cayuco* or dugout boat. Her lips were pale and the flesh under her fingernails was white. When I stuck her finger for a blood count the blood was watery and her hemoglobin was only 20 percent of normal. Her father said she had had malaria several weeks earlier and

Patients outside the clinic in Trujillo.
Tilda is the last person on the right in the second row.

was still getting chills and fever every day. I could tell both her heart and liver were enlarged. I gave her Aralen for the malaria, some iron pills, and a liver shot, and told the father to take her to the hospital at La Ceiba.

I developed a deep love for the people who came to the clinic. I wanted to put my arms around them and take them to Jesus, but I knew it wasn't that easy. I knew I needed a greater love and passion for their souls and should not allow the medical needs to crowd out time for prayer.

Heavy rain fell in mid-November. The bridge over the Rio Negro was washed away, and people had to take the *Julia* to get to the airfield. Letters from home usually arrived within five days, but that week the rain intervened and mail arrived only once instead of twice.

A fellowship meal was served at Millers' home on the United States Thanksgiving Day. Thirty-five people from the church were there and everyone enjoyed the get-together. Personally, I spent some time rejoicing in the Lord's goodness that year, and for His sweetness and love to me. Thinking things over, I discovered I had found out just how much it helped to thank the Lord when things seemed hard.

Soon it was Christmas, but temperatures were in the high 80's, and in the land of *palm trees and vine* none of the traditional customs was there to remind me of the season. The preparations among the local people consisted of buying a new outfit of clothes, laying in a supply of firecrackers and *guaro* (fire water), and practicing for processions through the streets. I hoped that some of the people who celebrated it in that way would by the following year have the joy of keeping it as the birthday of their Savior.

For that day at least, beans were replaced on the menu with a turkey James and Beatrice Hess had brought back with them. Maybell roasted it and took it over to Millers. She also unpacked home canned lima beans, applesauce, and pickles. The meal was complete with filling, gravy, mashed potatoes, cranberry sauce, ice cream, cookies, and coffee.

1952

The new year started off with good weather, noisy celebrations, an unruly patient, plus fever and pain.

The cool breezes started in the evening and cooled off the hot rooms in the house. The New Year celebrations lasted all night and kept me from sleeping soundly. In fact, for several nights the sound of drumbeats formed a monotonous background to what I considered screechy dance music. The rattle of castanets made from cans filled with shells filled in any gaps where quiet might have reigned. During the day, children in old clothing and brightly colored, hideous masks paraded the streets beating homemade drums.

The unruly patient was a young Carib woman who wanted an infected tooth pulled. I told her it was unwise to pull it at that time, but she insisted, because she was in pain. Then as I prepared to give a penicillin injection to offset more infection, fear got the better of her and she started grabbing my hand and arm. I said I would not treat her unless she agreed to keep her hands off and allow me to work unhindered. Reluctantly she agreed, but just as I began to pull the tooth, she grabbed my arm. She didn't let go, I didn't let go of the forceps, and the forceps didn't let go of the tooth, so out it came.

The woman was not the only one with fever and pain. I didn't feel really well for at least a week before I decided I must have malaria. The Aralen I took didn't seem to help and the fever continued. I couldn't bear the thought of eating. I took more Aralen, still with no noticeable change in my symptoms. It was then that a suspicion entered my mind that it might be tracheobronchitis—the cause of my having to leave Tampa several years earlier.

For the first week of this illness I had no chest pains—just extreme tiredness and weakness from not being able to eat. I remembered the letter "Mrs. S.," superintendent of nurses in La Junta, had written advising me not to go to Central America because of the climate and my bout with that virus in Tampa. I remembered also how I had prayed until I had assurance from the Lord that it was His will for me to go and that He would surely keep me.

When the chest pains started, I was no longer able to deny the cause of my illness. With prayer and Scripture verses, I battled not only physical illness, but also spiritual questions. I believed the Lord could have prevented the illness, but had allowed it for a reason. I turned to the eleventh chapter of John and read about the raising of Lazarus. In verse four, Jesus said, *This sickness is not unto death, but for the glory of God, that the Son of God might be glorified thereby.* I meditated on how God had been glorified when many of the people believed on Him after seeing and hearing about the raising of Lazarus.

As I suffered in pain and weakness, I considered requesting the elders of the church to come and anoint me with oil for healing. Perhaps God wanted to be glorified through the people's seeing a healing. I wanted, however, to be very sure that it was God's will, and as I prayed my eyes were drawn to verse forty, *Said I not unto thee, that, if thou wouldest believe, thou shouldest see the glory of God.* At that moment I realized that my greatest doubt was whether God could give me back my appetite, but immediately Genesis 18:14, and Matthew 19:26, impressed themselves in my mind, *Is anything too hard for the Lord? With God all things are possible.*

Maybell and I discussed my desire to be anointed. She encouraged me with Mark 11:24, *Therefore I say unto you, What things soever ye desire, when ye pray, believe that ye receive them, and ye shall have them.*

"That's it!" I said, and after we had prayed together, we agreed she should ask George Miller to come over that evening to arrange for an anointing service.

As George encouraged and prayed with me that evening, I felt the Holy Spirit was very near. Together we decided to have the anointing after the Sunday evening church service with everyone invited to attend. I was so exhausted I could hardly wait for George to leave, but tired as I was I was too sick to rest and I remember saying, "Lord, You are going to heal me anyway, can't You do something now?" But He didn't. I had faith that I would be healed and was puzzled over why He didn't do it immediately.

By Sunday, although the pain had eased slightly at times, I still couldn't eat and was losing weight. I decided Satan was doing his best to shake my faith and my belief that God would heal me. Once again I drew rich truths from John 11. As I meditated, I wondered if Lazarus ever stopped giving God glory for raising him back to life. I thought about how Jesus waited until Lazarus was dead before answering the call of Mary and Martha, so that later they glorified God. Jesus even said He was glad He wasn't there in time to keep Lazarus from dying because the people who saw and believed in Lazarus' resurrection gave glory to God. Jesus made sure that Lazarus was raised from an already stinking tomb so that no one there would later be tempted to deny the miracle. With that last thought came knowledge that I would get no better until I had been anointed so that I could never say, "Well, I was getting better anyway."

Sunday evening after supper the pain was worse and caused the same sick feeling I remembered so well from before. A hot water bottle helped a little, but after fifteen visitors that afternoon, I was totally exhausted. With weakness of body came fear that just when I needed it most, my faith would fail. Again the Holy Spirit encouraged me in my thoughts with the words from Luke 22:32, *I have prayed for thee, that thy faith fail not:* followed by Isaiah 26:3, *Thou wilt keep him in perfect peace, whose mind is stayed on thee: because he trusteth in thee.* Curiosity followed—I was sure He would heal me, but I wished I could know how and how soon.

When I figured the evening church service was about over, I got up and dressed, then went to lie on the bed in the living room. Thirty people came to witness the anointing service. Following a time of testimony and prayer, Clinton anointed me with olive oil and George prayed, and then we sang a hymn. Except for a beautiful calmness and joyful confidence that I would be healed, I felt no different.

Everyone had left when I noticed a craving for a grapefruit. I realized the Lord was starting my healing with what I considered the most difficult part. Maybell, Clinton, and I rejoiced together as I ate.

I slept well all night and when clinic time arrived in the morning, I was ready to open the doors. Thirty people came early enough for the Scripture reading time. Never before had more than ten arrived for the morning devotions. Twenty-one of the patients needed treatment and I worked until almost noon, marveling that I felt no more tired than I had the week before after seeing only four patients.

Dinner tasted good to me and after an hour of rest, I unpacked books and arranged them on my new book shelves. Next I saw a couple more patients, cleaned the clinic, went outside and planted flower bulbs, and could hardly wait for supper.

I dried the dishes, wrote a long letter, and before bedtime, my stomach was again calling for food. The sick feeling was gone and strength was fast returning. *All glory and praise to God!* I wrote in my journal, and wondered as I had before if I would ever doubt Him again.

I remembered how the devil caused opposition toward Jesus after the raising of Lazarus, and I wanted to be on guard so the work I was called to do would not be hindered. I didn't have long to wait for the first attack. I was awakened during the night with hot seething pain in a heavy chest, and knew I was learning a new lesson in walking by faith—not by sight or feelings. By morning the pain had died down a little, and by faith I could say, "The Lord is keeping His word." I saw 17 patients that day and had no trouble eating. The pain was there, but like Job 13:15, I could say, *Though he slay me, yet will I trust in him.*

Within a week, I had gained back my strength and had spent many hours dwelling in the presence of the Lord and reading His precious Word. The clinic work was a joy to me. I knew I was where the Lord wanted me to be, and I knew I was doing the work He wanted me to do. As I sat one day listening to the rain beating on the tin roof, sometimes gently and other times drumming heavily, I thought, "This is the music of my Honduras home!" I wondered if I could be any happier if the Lord had given me certain desires of my heart which I had once felt were necessary for my happiness.

♔

Deep contentment filled my days, and praise filled my heart. The opportunities to witness to patients sent me to prayer many times a day. Some young men refused our invitations to the morning Scripture reading, but one old man with a terrible sore on his foot hungrily read one of our Bibles while waiting for treatment. He said he had once belonged to a church, but they didn't allow the common people to read Bibles and he wanted to buy a Bible for himself.

Days were full of work and I felt better than I had for many weeks. The day came, however, when I was extra tired and immediately Satan used it to get my eyes off the Lord and onto myself. Clinton and Maybell stood in the gap with prayers for me at that time of discouragement and I was soon believing that the Lord makes no mistakes. I filled my mind with Scripture verses and quoted John 12:38; *Father, glorify thy name . . . I have both glorified it, and will glorify it again.*

The end of January the *Julia II* went to Puerto Cortez to pick up a new electric plant for Trujillo, and Clinton and Maybell went along as far as Cayos Cochinos to visit Hessie Griffith. On the return trip, however, high seas prevented the *Julia II* from stopping at the island. Mr. Griffith came to tell me of the reason for their delay and invited me to return on the *Julia II's* next trip for a three-day vacation with them. Cayos Cochinos, or Hog Islands, is a group of small islands and keys belonging at that time to Hanno and Hessie Griffith, owners of the *Julia II.* The Griffiths had a house and coconut grove there.

Tilda, my good clinic helper, agreed to watch the clinic and the chickens, and at 6:30 when I got on board the *Julia II*, a sunset was lighting the western sky behind coconut palms. In awe I watched the spectacular display as reflected light glorified the mountains to the south. I continued to watch as red sky faded to pink and then into a golden glow that spread all around. Dusk fell rapidly and stars came out, but I remained on deck watching the sky and the shoreline. At the Carib or Garifuna villages of Santa Fe and San Antonio all I could see were lights at the base of dark mountains. We stopped at Santa Fe and waited until two dories brought a box of freight and some passengers. One dory was tied on behind and the passengers rode the waves in the *Julia II's* wake.

I took a short nap, but before midnight was again watching as we passed islands and keys. As the sound of water softly lapped the shore a dark mountain grew and took shape. Dim lights silhouetted bowing and swaying coconut palms, and just as the first drops of a rain storm splashed on my hand I stepped ashore at Cayos Cochinos to be greeted by Clinton. On the porch of the Griffiths' house Maybell welcomed me with open arms.

Clinton Ferster

Everyone was concerned about the storm and when we went to bed, Hessie Griffith stayed by a window watching the rising waves. At 1:30 she woke the men and they hurried out to pull the skiff and two dories out of the water and away from the crashing waves so they wouldn't slam against each other or break loose. The men pulled them onto the beach, set them on logs which they rolled, moving the skiff and dories one by one up the slope away from the sea.

In the morning when the sun came out I walked the beach and noticed that the *Julia II* had drifted eastward in the wind, but had safely weathered the rough seas of the northwester. How good the Lord had been to bring us into a safe place before the storm struck.

I saw a red-billed hummingbird with changeable green-black feathers and marveled at the variety of trees and fruit. I identified almond, papaya, fig, orange, lime, rose apple, soursap, banana, plantain, and avocado trees, as well as pineapples and sugar cane. The soursap fruit looks like a five-inch green strawberry. At lunch time we had a soursap drink.

The coconut grove had trees as tall as 100 feet. One was all twisted like a snake. Their annual yield was 175,000 *cocos* (coconuts). To make copra or dried coconut the thick husks were split off, the cocos cracked open, and the pieces laid out to dry. After eight hours in the sun the coconut meat came out of the shell easily. It was dried another eight hours to complete the process.

The storm-scattered coconut leaves and other debris were cleaned up by the men, and the Governor Plums brought down by the storm became jam to eat with hot coconut-flavored rolls.

Coconut and coconut oil were used in many ways. When we visited a sick neighbor we were served syrup cookies made from a half cup of coconut oil, a pint of cane syrup, a teaspoon of ginger, and three cups of flour. The beef at supper was fried in coconut oil. Even the potpie was made from a coconut dough.

To make coconut oil, the coconut was grated, covered with water, and allowed to soak overnight. The next day the thick *cream* that had accumulated on the top of the container was skimmed off and boiled down.

Clinton, Maybell, Hessie, and I walked around the east end of the island one day with several other people, but when we got to a rocky cliff, Maybell and Hessie turned back. The rest of us kept on to a little cove I called Shell Cove because of the piles of shells washed up on the shore. We waded in the warm water to get to the cove and then climbed to the highest peak above. Far below, the sea was a beautiful shiny green. We hiked on across a cliff to the north coast and were able to see the big island and seven keys.

When we returned to the cove, the tide had come in and we had to climb up the cliff to get home. None of us could resist picking up shells and pieces of coral. I learned that coral turns into pure lime when burned, and that when the men had burned the coconut leaves and debris from the storm, the heat was sufficient to burn into lime

Discarded conch shells. The conchs were used for soup.

some coral they had thrown into the fire. Coconut palms planted in coral-enriched soil bear fruit in four years rather than the usual six to twelve years.

After we got back to the house, a northeaster followed a land wind, and the temperature dropped to 74°. I put on a sweater, then added a jacket, and finally draped a blanket around me as we sat on the porch that evening. A windy 74° felt cold after days of 86 to 90°.

On another hike the following day we climbed along the east coast and over a steep hill. From one point we were able to see La Ceiba, 22 miles to the west.

As always, vacations end. The sea was still rough for our return to Trujillo, and the boat seemed to want to go in several directions all at the same time. I got some sleep, but after the boat stopped at Santa Fe, I stayed outside watching the scenery. By then the sea had made a complete change and was so calm that only the flying fish ruffled the surface of the water. They flew along, dipping to touch the water, eight, ten, and even fifteen times before diving back under the surface. The ripples they created reminded me of those caused when someone skips stones across the surface of a lake.

We were landed at the second pier in Trujillo because the storm had broken off the end of the first pier. Another result of the rain was an overabundance of mosquitoes.

The storm also provided me with my first suturing job. During the storm a cabinet had fallen, cutting the arm of an 80-year-old woman. The tendons at the wrist were exposed and the cut went around her arm in a half circle. Although she didn't complain, I gave her an injection for pain immediately, and then put in 13 stitches about three-eighths of an inch apart.

The end of February brought more storms. The *Julia II* was damaged and had to jettison 400 bags of rice, and all the rest of her cargo got wet, but no lives were lost. The *Higueral* was caught near Cuba and also damaged, and the *Los Cayos* was beached. Mr. Griffith hoped the engine could be salvaged, but the boat was beyond repair.

March brought hot weather that reminded me of Tampa—oppressive heat and humidity. A wild wind blew one night banging shutters and rattling the zinc fence across the street. Mangoes, small and too green for good eating, fell from the trees in our patio, and I woke up from a hot, restless night far from rested.

When the humidity was high, I discovered it was almost impossible to slip out of dresses or uniforms that needed to be taken off over the head. Depending on the material, I had quite a struggle and decided all new ones from then on would open most of the way down the front.

Clinic work slowed during March and I was able to complete and catch up on book work and correspondence. An inventory of clinic records showed I had treated 212 patients in November, 217 in December, 326 in January, and 396 in February.

Toward the end of the month I had four deliveries in one week. George and Grace Miller's baby girl, Miriam Joyce, arrived at 11:02 p.m. on the 13th. On the 15th José David Madrid came feet first, and on the 17th another boy arrived that my records show only as Baby Boy Guardado. The fourth baby must have come with little or no fanfare because I didn't record name or date in my journal, just stated I was grateful that all four arrived safely and without complications.

After several nights of strong, wild land winds, a night of total calm followed. Only crickets and other night insects sent a steady hum through the evening quiet. Even the card players who usually spent the evening under the street light were missing. It was during the last night of the wild winds that the *Julia II* was lost. Seventeen of her 60 passengers were reported missing. She had been carrying 60 barrels of gasoline and all the equipment for the Brookwell gold-mining expedition. Mail bags from La Ceiba went down with the boat as well as drugs I had ordered from San Pedro Sula.

Two weeks later I did get some of that mail and a week later I heard they were still trying to salvage her. Sand was sifting into the wreck, however, and all they recovered that time were bottles of soft drink and beer.

♔

Every month brought a new adventure or experience. April's was an iguana dinner. George caught the iguana, a big lizard, in their yard; Clinton tanned the 42-inch skin; and we ate the tender, moist meat that I thought was better flavored than chicken.

When I made a medical visit to Cristales one day, I was shown where fire from the dump had spread into the cemetery. The woman who showed me the damage said she was sad because the spirits in the little houses must have become very hot. The little houses were above-ground tombs.

Her words gave me an opportunity to witness. "The Bible tells us that only the bodies are there," I said, "and that when people die the spirits go to be with either God or Satan." I told her the reason I was in Trujillo was to tell her and other people about the love of Christ, and I explained how she could be saved and go to be with Him when she died.

I discovered other superstitious customs that Satan used to keep the people in bondage. One patient came to me with painful feet and told me she got her feet wet crossing a creek the day after ironing clothes. When questioned why she gave that explanation, she patiently explained to me that it is well known that getting one's feet wet after ironing day always causes foot pain.

Even Holy Week had its share of superstitions and traditions that had little to do with the death and resurrection of Christ. Somebody said it would rain most of the week, *because they always catch the Holy water on Good Friday*. Sure enough it did rain a lot that week. One other year, though, I saw the priest filling the children's water bottles from a spigot at the side of the church.

Silent processions started the Thursday before Palm Sunday. Good Friday's parade centered around three life-size images—Christ on the cross, John holding a cup, and Mary holding a handkerchief. A priest followed the images, and a girl dressed to represent Mary walked in front.

The evening procession was more impressive, with lighted candles and ten little girls sitting on high chairs each carried by four men. The girls were dressed as angels with waving wings. A glass casket containing an image of Christ followed and everyone looked mournful and sad. The music was also mournful and played in a minor key. Easter morning's procession centered on a statue of the resurrected Christ accompanied by angels and joyous music.

April was the time of ripening mangoes. At first we searched eagerly for the few that fell under the wide spread of the tree's laden branches. As the season progressed, however, the daily yield increased from one or two to one or two dozen and finally to an abundance that filled two or three dishpans. Among the creations Maybell and I experimented with were mango sauce, orange and mango jelly, and mango and spice jam.

In May I took a short vacation in La Ceiba. At first all I wanted to do was catch up on sleep, but after a week I was ready to do something else. One morning I bought a second-class ticket and rode the narrow-gauge train to Tela to visit the hospital there. The open-air coaches gave an excellent view of the mountains the first couple of hours, and later of the thick jungle. For someone on foot and without a machete, the jungle we passed through would have been impenetrable.

The passengers talked and drank *frescos* (soft drinks) which were brought around in buckets by two boys. At Masica women and girls with strange hair styles boarded the train with trays of cooked rice, comida, plantains, and cheese tortillas. Squares of banana leaves were used for plates. Buckets full of *helotes* (corn on the cob) were also brought aboard for sale. I bought one of those because I was always conscious of sanitation and they had been boiled in the husks. I also bought a tamale with pork and red sauce. It was wrapped in banana leaves and boiled and was delicious.

At one stop a woman and a little girl got on the train, and a short time later discovered their dog was with them. The girl was afraid they would have to pay fare for him. Everyone joined in the conversation to offer advice. The problem was solved when the conductor dropped him off at the next stop without collecting a fare.

At Tela I toured the hospital and the commissary and visited veteran Plymouth Brethren missionaries, the Ruddocks, where I was given a warm welcome. The Ruddocks were friends of the Plymouth Brethren in Trujillo and had at one time owned the building where we later had our clinic.

I was advised it was safer to travel first class, so I bought a first-class ticket for my return trip. The seats were more roomy, but I had less opportunity to talk to other passengers than on the second-class ticket.

Back in Trujillo Pedro told me that it always rains on the 13th and 14th of May. Whether it was a superstition or not I do not know, but sure enough those days brought heavier rains than during the rainy season. Our whole lower patio was a lake, and the Rio Negro bridge was washed out. It was good little J. Mark didn't break his arm until the 16th, because he had to be taken to Tela by the MAF (Missionary Aviation Fellowship) plane and it couldn't have landed in the storm. Another patient with appendicitis was also taken out with J. Mark. Hoby Lorentz was the pilot.

Two days later I had another emergency. Mrs. Donnell nearly died. The Donnells were from Texas. Mr. Donnell was out in the jungle with some Hondurans cutting mahogany logs. I spent most of the day with Mrs. Donnell, but during the evening she began hemorrhaging. The pharmacist, two neighbors, and I worked to save her life. We started I.V.s of dextrose and plasma, but at times her pulse was too weak to count. Twice she went into severe chills. A telegram was sent to Tegucigalpa for a doctor and a plane, and when they arrived they carried Mrs. Donnell on a cot to the airport.

I had prayed for the Lord to spare her life and had an assurance from Him that she would live. That assurance sustained me through many long, tense hours as I used all my nursing skills with few visible results. Ten days after she was taken to Tegucigalpa I was notified she was doing well. I still treasure the gift of a watercolor scene she painted for me.

It seemed I could get through the difficult situations like that one with faith that God had heard and would answer prayers, but only days later I discovered my private prayers were not so freely given. As I searched for a reason, I wrote the following words as the cry of my heart—a surrender of my stubborn will:

Dear Lord, through Thy great Son, we give Thee thanks
For His (our) power to do Thy holy will.
For wondrous love poured out in drops of blood
'Neath olive trees and high on Calvary's hill.

For Thy great love to fill our hearts we plead
To overflow to reach the lost with truth.
This man of intellect who knows Thee not,
These bright-eyed children, lovely eager youth.

Not only them; Lord, give us love to love
The warped, the dull, the strongly unperfumed,
The leering, grasping, those who beg our bread,
The hopeless—till by heavenly light illumed.

Prostrate beneath the olive trees we fall
And yield our wills to Him, to self to die,
Accept in faith Thy victory and life,
Go forth to serve—Thy Name to glorify.

To help remind myself of my need to love more, I decided my motto would be, "The second mile the second year." Only by God's grace could I live those words.

♔

New missionaries, Eldon and Jessie Hamilton and their children, who were going to open work in Tocoa, arrived the last of May with quite a load of baggage which included a Jeep pickup with four-wheel drive. Their son James arrived with German measles.

The first week they stayed with us George Miller, Pedro, and Clinton Ferster went with Eldon to take baggage to Tocoa in two trucks. To avoid 13, either thrilling or frightening, high bridges that were only a few inches wider than the rear wheels of the trucks, they went through several miles of jungle. It took them close to eight hours because they had to cut their way through jungle growth at places, and also took turns pulling each other's truck out of the mud several times.

A week later they went again, to repair and clean the house the Hamilton family would use. That time they went in the Jeep and made the 51 miles in five hours.

It was during their visit I met my first *madre culebra*. When looking out the clinic waiting room window, I noticed what I first thought was a twig stuck on the screen. On checking closer I realized it was an insect that reminded me of what I knew as a *walking stick*, but much larger. Tilda, however, informed me it was a *madre culebra* and much more poisonous than a tarantula.

"You better kill it," was Tilda's advice.

I called Fersters and Hamiltons to see it, and before long a crowd had gathered. I handed Eldon a medical instrument to pluck it off the screen and as he did it curled its tail end around much as a scorpion does. Two quick blows from a rock ended the creature's power to strike and poison.

Walking back from Cristales a few days later, I came upon a group of boys with a five-foot-long dead boa about two and a half inches in diameter with black and tan markings over the back. It had been found trying to capture a young chicken in one of their homes.

The Lord certainly protected me when a few months later I noticed something on the wall of my bedroom just before getting ready to go to bed. I called Clinton and he said it was a black scorpion. He was able to knock it into a can of alcohol and I had a fine, uncrushed specimen to examine and keep. The next morning I found a dead tarantula on the bathroom floor. I am sure the Lord protected us many other times when we were not even aware of danger.

June was a time of fresh fruit and good eating. The mangoes continued to drop in our back yard by the buckets full. We ate them fresh, and we cooked and preserved them. Mango jelly and jam, mango sauce, spiced mangoes, and mango pie appeared on the table. We even made mango vinegar. To make that, about a tub of mangoes was beaten and mashed by Clinton and squeezed through a burlap bag. Maybell then added yeast and *raspadura* (a coarse brown sugar made from cane syrup boiled down and solidified in round cakes) to the juice to begin the activity that would result in mango vinegar. Three weeks later Clinton announced the mixture was vinegar.

Bonaco pineapples also ripen at that time and we thoroughly

enjoyed that tender, sweet treat. Maybell canned some and made jam from them also. Of course, we always had bananas, but in June we were getting extra large ones that were picture perfect.

Victor Borden, a man who had a *platanal* (plantain plantation) couldn't get rid of all his *platanos* (plantains or cooking bananas), so he brought a load to Trujillo. Clinton got a dozen. They were huge—two to three inches thick—and one was 12 inches long and weighed two pounds.

The good eating started to show. I slowly gained weight until I reached 135 pounds and my clothes started feeling tight. Just then an epidemic, with symptoms like what we used to call *the grippe* struck. For a whole month I suffered chills, fever, a full-blown head cold, and later a congested chest with lots of coughing and pleurisy on the right side. At one time I had 30 patients suffering from the same ailments. After all that, my clothing fit more comfortably.

A June letter informed me that my parents had moved to their new house south of Morgantown, Pennsylvania. My sister Joyce and her husband Melvin Mast lived on a farm adjoining their property, and when my sister Muriel and her husband Noah Mack returned from 13 years in Africa, Noah set up medical practice in Morgantown. Years later my brother Glenn and his wife Catherine also moved to Morgantown, and my sister Lois and her husband Wilbur Erb built a house beside Mother's.

Just as I had had to seek the hospitality of mission workers in various places as I traveled, so I was able to extend hospitality to persons traveling through our area. Two men from Pennsylvania stopped in one day on their way to Tocomacho to make gospel recordings for Atwoods' ministry. Ralph Zeager knew my sister Lois and her husband and brought a recording from them. It was a great treat to hear the voices of my dear family. Melvin Schultz, the second man, was from the Strasburg, Pennsylvania, area.

In July an exciting time began for the missionaries and church in Trujillo. Clinton and George spent three days in La Ceiba buying building materials for our new church. A house for the clinic and Fersters and me had also been purchased and men had been doing preliminary repairs and renovation work for some time. It was an old colonial house with a porch 109 feet long in the front, facing the plaza, or *Parque Colón*. We hoped to move in by October.

After enjoying the abundance of fruit from the patio where we lived, we wasted little time in getting our own trees started on the

Our house and clinic.
A corner of the plaza can be seen on the left.

new property. Early in the summer, Clinton, Maybell, Pedro, and I planted 21 papaya trees, two avocados, and several mangoes. Later we planted bananas.

I chose the spot for the first avocado, but before Clinton had the hole deep enough to plant a tree, he struck something solid. Pedro cleared the area a bit more and discovered a flat well-made brick surface. He suggested it might be an old well, or a big box filled with money, which according to an old story was under the *Cuartel*, the soldiers' barracks next door. I suggested it might be part of the legendary tunnel that was supposed to run from the sea to the Catholic church. We abandoned the spot, but Pedro said whatever it was it belonged to me. I said that after the house was finished and we were living in it, he was invited to come sometime and we would dig for buried treasure.

Picking papayas from a tree I planted.

We forgot about it, but years later after I came back from furlough in Pennsylvania, James and Beaty Hess, who were living in the "L" part of the house at that time, told me a lady came from Tegucigalpa one day and asked if she could dig in a certain part of the patio. The spot she pointed out was under a shed where James kept his chickens. He agreed she

Mr. July

could dig, provided she replaced the dirt and left it as she found it. She hired a boy to do the digging, but sadly they replaced the soil without finding buried treasure. I told the Hesses I knew where the treasure was, but we never did try to dig it up.

Even without the buried treasure, the new property grew more fascinating every day. We had chosen our rooms in the house, and one day Maybell and I went to pick out the locations for electrical outlets. The patio already looked nice, and we hired Mr. July to cut the grass. That was done using his faithful machete. Mr. July was from Jamaica and his skin was pure black, not at all like the people native to the area. He spoke English and his sense of humor was a source of entertainment at times. Ten years later he was still doing this job for us. Once while he was resting and eating a fallen mango James Hess cautioned him that he'd better watch out for worms.

Mr. July's reply was, "Those worms can watch out for themselves."

Well ahead of schedule, we moved into our new home on July 31, even though the stove and sink were not installed or kitchen shelves built. For paint, we bought red and yellow ochre and mixed it with whitewash. If we wanted blue walls, we mixed bluing with whitewash.

Portion of the *Cuartel*. Cannons shown on the next page can be seen under the tree in the center of the picture.

Old cannons facing Trujillo Bay.

I wanted green walls in my room so I mixed bluing with yellow ochre—blue and yellow make green, right? For some chemical reason I was ignorant of, my mixture turned out a pale gray. I couldn't throw away two buckets of whitewash, so I had lovely gray walls. To brighten things up I mixed a little red ochre with a small amount of whitewash and had a light rose color for the arch and doorways and was quite pleased with the results.

My new pink and gray room with a 12-foot ceiling was so large my furniture looked lost. There were no windows, but a pair of big double Dutch doors with a few bullet holes in them allowed me to open the top halves and enjoy east breezes and a view of some old palace ruins. Another set of double doors and five steps up separated my room and the Fersters'. The doors had 12-inch HL iron hinges. On the other side of an archway six feet high and eight feet wide was the "L" where the Hesses later set up housekeeping. The walls were 28 inches thick and the floor was smooth, cool concrete.

When we explored the nearby ruins one Sunday afternoon, we discovered features similar to our house. Some doorways were squared off, some arched. The walls were about the same thickness and the layout was almost identical. Mr. Hode said the building went back to the old Spanish days and was the Castillo de Santa Bárbara, the home of the *encargado* (man in charge) of all Central America for the King of Spain. Above a door in our house, under many layers of whitewash, we had found the words, *Casino Mercantil* (Mercantile Casino), leading us to believe it had once been government property.

When the Mission Board was looking for a place to build our church, they settled on a property with old walls of a house built only

Ruins of Castillo de Santa Bárbara.

to the top of the window openings. Mr. Hode said the walls had been built of stones and bricks robbed from the palace ruins by a *Comandante*. When the *Comandante* died a sudden death, the people considered it was his punishment. At the time the Mission Board purchased the property from the heirs, Señorita Nina's primary school students had a garden inside the walls, which were known as *Las Tapias*.

Creatures of all kinds lived among us. Iguanas ate some of our new papaya trees, so Maybell and I continued to plant trees and other plants in our patio. Rats were everywhere doing damage, and I wrote home a request for rat poison. One day I saw an iguana about two feet long in the patio and so bright green he reminded me of a child's drawing of a dragon. He even had spines down the back of his head. One of the patients said, "Cut off his head."

"But how do I catch him?" I asked.

"Just grab him by the tail and hold him up," she said. "He can't do anything to you then."

One evening I heard a rumpus among the chickens and rushed out to investigate. One of the chickens was crying like a baby, and I found what I thought was a huge rat sucking blood from the chicken's neck. While all the other chickens cackled and flew around me, I grabbed a box and killed the creature. I discovered it was a *watusa*, with a baby in a pouch in its chest. The chicken was too far gone to save, so Clinton killed it and we had it for dinner the next day.

♔

Records indicated several babies were due all at about the same time. One night I was called out at 11:30, and was back home by 12:15. That birth was quick and easy compared to the one I had had a few days before. The first mother was in labor for 78 hours, then had a perfectly normal delivery. Through that delivery, I met the new doctor for our area, Dr. Jorge Gasteazoro, a Honduran who had worked in a laboratory in the U.S.A. and was sent by the government to work in Trujillo as a practitioner. He set up in the building we had vacated.

A few days later I had two women in labor at the same time. I had spent most of one night with one woman, but when things weren't progressing, I went home only to discover the son of another woman waiting to guide me to his mother.

Before either delivered, I had a third call. Around 11:30 that evening the third mother had a little girl. I spent the following night with the second mother who delivered at 5:30 in the morning. Finally, the first mother had her little girl after another all-night vigil.

Four tension-filled nights with little or no sleep and a lot of stooping left me with muscles that simply refused to relax. Even though I was exhausted, the sheer misery of an aching back kept me from sleeping. Only after Maybell gave me several back rubs was I able to sleep.

♔

Elias Kulp, Grace Miller's father, visited Trujillo in September. The Fersters, J. Mark Miller, and I took him on a trip to Tocoa. Upon return, his evaluation was, "I wouldn't have missed it for a good bit, but I wouldn't give five cents to do it again."

We started out at 8:45 one morning and arrived in Tocoa at 4:15. The road was what was left of the old United Fruit Company railroad bed. I began the trip in the back of the pickup truck, sitting on a folding chair. Elias joked that I looked like the governor of the province riding along in style. At the turnoff near Puerto Castilla, the chair and I became airborne when the truck hit a bump. I landed with only a jolt, but the chair suffered a broken leg brace. Elias then insisted I sit in the front of the truck while he made a seat on some of the bundles we were taking to the Hamiltons.

The railroad bed was built 10, 20, and even 30 feet above the surrounding jungle floor, but vines and creepers bound the trees together into an almost solid green screen so that often we had no idea how high up we were driving. It was impossible to see ten steps into the jungle, and at times branches and trailing vines reached out and brushed both sides of the truck as we passed. The rails had been narrow-gauge, so the road wasn't very wide—in many places just the width of one railroad tie. The ties were gone in some places and there we drove on the ground. In other areas, the ties were piled up to fill dips or muddy depressions. It was easy to believe the road became impassable during the rainy season.

Many of the old railroad bridges were still being used. In fact, between Trujillo and the Aguan River we crossed 29 bridges. They were anywhere from ten to 250 feet long. We also forded 11 places where bridges had disintegrated or washed away. When we came to those places, we had to drive off the high road, down to the river bank, and through the stream. Originally there had been 86 railroad bridges in the 51 miles between Trujillo and Tocoa.

When we came to the Aguan River, we drove off the high road and across a meadow to the river bank. Everyone except Clinton got out of the truck and watched as he drove it over two planks onto a ferry. Both truck and ferry dipped and tilted, but nothing slipped. Then we boarded and the ferryman pointed the ferry slightly down stream. Two ropes with pulleys attached to a cable high above the water guided us across the quarter-mile-wide river. Minutes later we were safely landed on a muddy bank and ate our lunch under a tree with a huge spreading trunk and root system. We weren't aware of it at the time, but we entertained guests at our picnic. Shortly after lunch we all started itching from tick bites.

We crossed 27 more bridges in the remaining 20 miles, and within the first two miles were the 13 famous high ones. Crossing those 13 was especially thrilling. Some of the bridges had ties laid side-by-side on the rails and were only one-tie wide—with broken edges. If two or more ties were broken at the same spot, Clinton and Elias would search by the side of the road for pieces of other broken ties to fill in the gaps. Planks over the track rails provided the roadbed of other bridges. At times the men had to get out machetes and hack away jungle growth so they could see the approach to the bridges.

When a bridge looked especially narrow, Elias got out, looked under the truck, and directed Clinton onto the bridge. At one four-plank-wide bridge just four miles from Tocoa, Elias reported that both front tires were bulging out over the edges and that the right back tire wasn't going to be lined up properly with the bridge. Clinton maneuvered the truck slightly to the left, and then Elias said, "Now

Checking a bridge. Note the by-pass road used to reach the ford. The flat stone in the lower right corner is used as a washboard by women who do their laundry in the stream.

those wheels aren't going to make it." The back wheel-spread was wider than the bridge!

A woman walking along the road had stopped to watch and declared it was *peligroso* (dangerous). After watching Clinton maneuver the truck, she reported, -*No cabe.*- "It doesn't fit." She then took off her shoes and walked through the river and went on her way. A man on horseback rode by and also forded the river, and then while Clinton drove the truck down the bank and through the water the rest of us walked across the bridge.

We saw lots of lizards and birds and one dead alligator. When we came upon cows and horses grazing on the grassy roadbed, they had to run ahead of the truck until they came to an opening in the jungle big enough for them to get off and allow us to pass.

While in Tocoa we took part in the Hamiltons' church services. I had a lesson for the children and interpreted for Clinton. In the evening with about 30 present I gave another lesson and interpreted for Bro. Kulp.

Jessie Hamilton took Maybell and me to visit four families in the afternoon. The houses were built of sticks and clay with thatched roofs and ground floors.

When we drove back to Trujillo we took along a woman, her five children, and probably all her worldly goods—a cot, four cardboard boxes, and a suitcase. Maybell and I commented that she owned less than we packed for a trip of a few days.

Before Bro. Kulp left we had services for several evenings in our almost-completed new church building. I was especially praying for several people I knew who were under conviction, but none made a public confession. Many people, however, were strengthened in their faith and commitment.

Our church in Trujillo.

I knew that at least Juana, who had helped us move into our new house, and had recently had a baby, had accepted the Lord earlier. She and her family were English-speaking Negroes. After her conversion, her father, Mr. Jackson, told Clinton, "Juana change up plenty."

Mr. Jackson often amused me with his expressions such as when I nearly ran into him and said, "Excuse me."

His reply was, "You are quite excusable, Mam."

When he was painting in the clinic, I took a chart off the wall and he requested, "Will you take the sounding trumpet too?" It took a second to realize he meant the stethoscope.

While getting supper one evening, I noticed Mr. Jackson and

several men gathered at the door in the patio wall. All were looking toward the sea, so I called out to ask what they saw. They replied they were watching a waterspout. I pushed the skillet to the back of the stove and called to Maybell to come and look. Coming across the bay were two tall narrow funnels reaching up to dark clouds. Water was being drawn up from a huge circle of foaming water below. When it drew closer, I could see the dancing water as it spiraled upward in several interweaving columns. After awhile the waterspouts moved on along the coast and we went back to our cooking.

The rainy season, babies, and emergencies all arrived in mid-October. One day a real northwester blew in with howling winds and slashing rain. The sea roared and breakers broke over the pier. The temperature dropped to 74°. That was the first time since June the temperature was lower than 80°, and only the third time since March it was lower than 79°. It felt cold!

The next day a school teacher arrived with a boy who had nearly cut the end of his finger off with a pocket knife. I was still suturing when I got a call to go to deliver a baby, and then before I got off a boy came to request that I take care of another delivery. Out into the storm I went to check the first patient first, and then went on to see if the second woman was ready, but she had already delivered so I only needed to finish with proper care of the mother and child.

I returned to the first mother and stayed all night. The little boy, delivered in the morning, never breathed. That was the second baby I delivered that didn't live. The other one had been at Preston Maternity Hospital while I was in midwifery training, and that was an abnormal and premature child who was dead when the mother came to the hospital.

I got home that morning after nine o'clock and found a man waiting to take me to see his wife, who had suffered a bad fall. Another man was waiting to have me lance a huge boil on his arm. The following day there were 23 patients in clinic, but most of them only needed injections. In addition to my clinic patients, I was seeing several others at the request of Dr. Gasteazoro who was off somewhere fighting a yellow fever outbreak.

The Fersters were leaving for furlough and we wondered if the air strip would be flooded, but the storm passed. I was supposed to start off with them for a two-week vacation in San Pedro Sula, but had been too busy to more than gather a few things together. I had halfway planned to go home for four weeks, but after learning that several class reunions would be held the following year, I decided to request a six-week vacation at that time so I could attend and still have time for family.

Just when I thought I'd have time to pack a bag, a little boy, Pablo Hernandez, fell on some rocks while carrying a glass butter dish and the wife of the British consul, his neighbor, rushed in the door yelling, "His tripes is out."

Pablo was there holding his side and I guided him in and laid him down. Sure enough the peritoneum or membrane lining the abdominal wall was sticking out from one of several bloody, dirty cuts. I knew immediately he needed to get to the hospital in La Ceiba, but the only way to go was on the boat that evening. I gave him several injections, cleaned the dirt from around the wounds, wrapped the part sticking out in sterile gauze and kept it wet with normal saline. I had to give him a complete bath and was so rushed I could only hope I had forgotten none of my own luggage for vacation.

Pablo's foster father, Antonio, and I took Pablo aboard the *Carlton P.* at 6:00 that evening and placed him in a bunk suspended on chains from the ceiling. I thanked the Lord that the sea was calm because I didn't want Pablo to get sick and vomit. Whenever I went to check on him and wet the dressing on his wounds, I had to step over the legs of sleeping people. Every available dry space was occupied by other passengers. The only unoccupied space was a table with a lantern sitting on it. It wasn't totally unoccupied either because in the dim light I saw roaches running over it all the time. The longer I looked at that table, however, the more inviting it became. Finally when Antonio came to check on Pablo I mentioned I would like to use the table for a bed, and he tied the lantern in a hook on the ceiling and found me a blanket and a sheet.

We anchored in the harbor at La Ceiba around 3:30 in the morning, but it wasn't until 6:00 that we disembarked into a dory, which landed us at the bottom of a series of steps we had to climb to reach the pier. We took Pablo to the hospital immediately and he was soon in surgery.

During the long night I searched for a reason the Lord had allowed the accident to happen to Pablo and was convinced it was to create an opportunity for me to tell the salvation message to him and Antonio. Pablo was afraid he would die, and I was able to tell him the old gospel story. He accepted Christ and prayed his first prayer. Although it was not the first time Antonio had heard the gospel message, he did some serious thinking and asked many questions.

Antonio took me in a taxi to the Camerons, the Methodist missionary couple in La Ceiba. The Fersters were due to arrive on the flight I had also expected to be on, so I walked out to the airport to meet them. Maybell and I ate lunch in a park while Clinton took care of baggage and saw Mr. Cooper of the Fruit and Steamship Company.

The next day we took a little train to the pier, and with prayers and my blessings the Fersters steamed away for their furlough. My two-week vacation and the desire to check on Pablo helped to keep me from feeling totally alone. I wasn't able to see Pablo but was told he was doing well. Antonio hired another taxi and took me to the airport for my flight to San Pedro Sula, where I was graciously received by Rev. and Mrs. Auler, Reformed missionaries in Honduras for 30 years. It was a pleasure to share their comfortable home and eat meals I didn't have to plan.

The Reformed Mission had grown to the extent that the Aulers were acting mostly as administrators. They had a large primary school, a secondary school, and were training their own teachers. At the time I visited they were also operating 23 Sunday Schools, and had 12 native pastors and many parish workers. I attended a Sunday School with 169 lively attendees Sunday afternoon and services in the big church of several hundred members in the evening. Mrs. Auler played the Hammond electric organ and a native pastor preached.

Mr. Auler invited me to go with him to a wedding he had to perform in Cofradía, a small town about 18 kilometers from San Pedro Sula. On the way he taught me how to recognize various trees growing beside the road. The wedding was in a small church decorated inside and outside with palm fronds. They created beautiful designs and shadows on the whitewashed walls. The floor of the church was strewn with pine needles, which gave the building a pleasant scent. The palm leaves were especially for the wedding, but the pine needles were replaced weekly for regular church services.

People packed into the seats, but quite a crowd was unable to get into the church. After we waited nearly an hour, the groom, a tall, bashful young man, and the pastor came in a side door. Soon the pale bride in white, on the arm of her father, followed a little flower girl and her escort to the front of the church. The groom was a believer, and the bride had been a leader in the Catholic church until just a few weeks before.

After congregational singing, a solo by a girl, and a duet by two men, the ring wedding ceremony was performed. Mr. Auler gave a short sermon, and then everyone left the church. The windows and doors were barred and locked, and a procession escorted the bridal couple to the home of the bride, which was a clean, white adobe house with a tile roof.

Guests crowded into the house, and other people from the town gathered outside and looked in windows and doors. After a short program of songs and recitations, the bride and groom cut the cake. The wedding had been postponed a week because some official had refused to sign the papers, and I suspected the cake had been prepared for the earlier date. My first bite tasted like pure mold, but everyone seemed eager to have a piece. Along with the cake, soft drinks were served in little glasses. I assumed the family had only ten glasses because they served ten people and then the glasses went back to the kitchen before the next set of ten guests was served.

My delightful stay in San Pedro Sula ended, and Mr. Auler suggested I go overland to Tegucigalpa and visit the evangelical hospital in Siguatepeque on the way. Mrs. Auler packed me a tasty lunch, and I took a train to Potrerillos, where I ate my lunch while waiting for the *Empresa Dean* (the Ford truck/bus) for the trip to Siguatepeque. It was a beautiful drive beside Rio Lindo where the river flows in a series of *lindo* (pretty) cataracts. About 3:30 in the afternoon we started climbing, and soon I felt cool enough to want a sweater.

I had seen switchbacks in Virginia, the Rockies, and the Alps, but compared to those the ones on the way to Siguatepeque went every-which-way and reminded me of the story of some pigs and a fence so crooked that every time the pigs tried to escape underneath they came out on the same side. On the road to Siguatepeque, I was never sure if I was coming or going. All the big peaks were surrounded by lesser peaks and the bus wound up and around and around. The elevation of Siguatepeque is 3,500 feet, and it is situated in a beautiful valley.

Upon arrival, I went to the national pastor's house. He was from Belize and spoke English. His wife brought out a special treat for me—a dish of peaches and cupcakes. They had bought them for their baby's birthday the following day, but they wanted me to celebrate with them. I felt honored and humbled.

Ruth Raws, a nurse at the hospital, came for me, and I gained this impression of Ruth: she was a lovely person to look at, to listen to, and to watch at work. I also met Nancy Norman, a technician from Cedar Bluff, Virginia, and nurses Verna van Wingerden from Ohio and Beatrice Aguilar, a Honduran, who showed me their lab and pharmacy.

Dr. McKinney and his wife, Helen, were leaving for furlough in a few days, but everyone did his best to entertain me and give me useful information, tips, a few supplies such as eye droppers and bottles, and even slips to start new plants when I got home.

The hospital was on a hillside among pine trees, overlooking the valley and town. The town was mostly adobe or adobe brick houses with tile roofs. There were no paved streets, and although the whole area reflected a lack of wealth, it was no worse than other places.

On a tour of the San Juan United Fruit Company's experimental farm I was given celery, lemons, and some Ecuadorian fruit. I also went to the workers' prayer meeting one evening.

The nights were damp and cold—57°. I slept under a double woolen blanket and couldn't get my feet warm for quite awhile. The second night I borrowed woolen bed socks from Verna and slept better. A wood fire was kept burning most of the time.

Five days later *Empresa Dean* came for me at 5:00 a.m. for my journey on to Tegucigalpa. Immediately after we left the valley we climbed into the clouds. I had never been able to see the top of the mountain from the hospital because it was always in a cloud cover.

One of my fellow passengers took it upon himself to act as tour guide. He informed me the peak we were climbing was the highest between Siguatepeque and Tegucigalpa. He also said the mountain water looked milky because the ground had something in it like starch which made it very good for planting yucca.

While the driver delivered mail in Comayagua, the former capital of Honduras, I visited the cathedral and walked around the town a bit. The narrow streets, patios, walls, old trees, and beautiful flowers reminded me of an old-world city.

As we continued our journey the driver made another stop to buy a long-billed bird from a girl along the road. My *tour guide* informed me the bird is a pet much like a cat or a dog. He said if you keep it in your house ten days it will never leave, and that long before you know it is going to rain the bird tells you by making a certain noise.

We descended from the 5,000-foot peak on curves my *tour guide* described as worms, and were soon on a plain. Rather poetically he had described the adobe houses of Siguatepeque as *a flock of white doves in green grass*. He praised Ruth Raws and said she was a *pajarita* (little bird). We crossed the plain and again climbed up and down and around and around. The views were stupendous!

Along the way our driver did more shopping. In one village he bought an unusual clay water pot with an animal snout on one side and a spout on the other. In another village he stopped to buy a hen *guaranteed to lay*. When we bought some round, flat, hard, cornmeal cakes for lunch, he bought some to take home for his family, and later when passengers boarded the bus with pork tied up in a cloth, he purchased some ribs. Apparently there was no schedule to meet because he stopped frequently to talk to drivers headed the opposite direction. Just before entering Tegucigalpa, he stopped to wash the truck. Cans of water from a stream were splashed against the sides and underneath and the truck was wiped with cloths. He finished the job by pouring water over his shoes and wiping them clean.

Upon arrival in Tegucigalpa I registered at Boarding Central for $2.50 per day room and board. Walking around the city I noticed that the houses looked like many I had seen in Europe. The streets were steep, and some were steps like those I had seen in Paris, France. Supper was a tamale, fried potatoes, steak, and cold coffee, followed by quite a long talk with the proprietor of the boarding house. Our discussion gave me an opportunity to point out to him, from his own Catholic Bible, the reasons I believed as I did.

The next morning before going to Pentecostal services I spent some time on the balcony of my room, where I could enjoy the chiming of the bells in the cathedral two blocks away. As I watched, the hot sun burned the mist from the mountain peaks and reflected like a flood of light over the tile roofs below me.

In the evening I went to services at the Central American Mission, where 200 people were in attendance. Loudspeakers reached many more outside. First a wedding was held, then an anti-alcohol program was given with several poems, recitations, and skits. An adorable little girl started a recitation but got confused and started over—four times. After sitting down until someone else said a poem, she got up, apologized and started again. Three more times she started over, but finally had to give up and read her part from a book. The bridegroom gave a good testimony about how he had found the Lord a year before and was also saved from drinking. The pastor's stirring sermon gave Christ the credit for victory over sin and over drinking problems.

A friend in Trujillo had asked me to deliver a package to her sister, and when I did I was invited to a birthday party the next day for their two-year-old daughter. The big family of Arabs welcomed me warmly into their midst. On the porch I watched Ruthie and her blindfolded friends beat a swinging piñata with sticks until they slashed it open and claimed the little prizes. The adults talked and visited while the children shrieked and ran around. A huge meal was served amidst family jokes and a lot of ribbing back and forth.

All twelve of us then packed into a jeep and went to the home of the visiting relatives. The children were put to bed and the adults shared more stories and family reminiscences. Since it happened to be the thirteenth anniversary of that couple, more cake and ice cream were served—and that was the way I celebrated my forty-second birthday.

The day before my birthday I had a spell of great weakness come over me while going to the market. I was also sick most of the night after *my big birthday party* and most of the next day. I couldn't diagnose the illness or the cause but felt cheated out of my last vacation day. After I got home, I found out I had picked up endomeba histolitica.

♔

A plane returned me to Trujillo in three and a half hours, but that was far less interesting than the two-day overland trip to Tegucigalpa. It, however, was the roughest plane ride I ever had, and my not-quite-settled stomach was close to revolt. I discovered that because of rain no boats had left Trujillo since the one Pablo, Antonio, and I had left on two weeks before.

It started raining again before I got to the house, and during the night we had an earthquake that made quite a rumble but no noticeable damage. Above the din of the rain on the tin roof, there were other sounds in our house. Drips and drops sent me hurrying here and there as new leaks became apparent. The clinic ceiling leaked and water ran in under two doors. The dining room ceiling showed a wet spot and rain came down the chimney. Next I discovered water running down inside the can cupboard, but my bedroom was the worst. I heard drops on my bureau and before I finished, I had moved most of the furniture around and there were five containers catching water.

The rain also brought mosquitoes, and the clapping sound that rang through the house wasn't from joy! I killed almost a dozen while writing in my journal one evening, and in the morning a lot more were on the window screens and buzzing around. As an escape and a safeguard we slept under mosquito nets, but occasionally a mosquito managed to get inside. A much nicer welcome home was a note and an alarm clock Maybell and Clinton had left for me as a birthday present. Early in the evening the first day I was home the lights blinked—the signal they would go out in 15 minutes. They usually blinked at ten o'clock, but since no boats had been able to bring in fuel because of the rain and flooding, the electric plant was conserving energy.

Eight-and-a-half-pound baby Ethel Idalia arrived with no complications on my father's birthday, November 18. Otherwise my work in the clinic wasn't heavy, and I was able to get things back in shape after being away for two weeks.

Once more we celebrated Thanksgiving day with church services and a meal with friends. Personally, I thanked the Lord for the joys of the past year, for the joy of serving Him, and for how He revealed Himself to me in new ways and taught me of Himself. That year I was especially grateful for the blessings of a home and the new church building.

I got up as usual on December 4, never thinking it would be the last time I got up for several weeks. That evening, a Thursday, several persons, including Bob Atwood, the missionary from up the coast, gathered at the house to make a recording in Garifuna for use in evangelistic work. I began to feel strangely tired and went to my room to lie down. When they were ready to leave, I went out to say good-night, and after that I suffered a chill that shook my whole body. Pedro went to get Dr. Gasteazoro, and Claudia, the young black woman who worked for me, went for George Miller, and he and Bob Atwood returned with her.

George had worked in a mental hospital for his Civilian Public Service (CPS) and had some medical knowledge and experience as an orderly. He brought a cot and set it up in the dining room right outside my door, and even in my sickness I realized that was the worst spot he could have chosen because a rat had died in the wall, and the smell of that and the creolin we poured in was strongest right there.

The doctor was with a dying patient and didn't arrive until around midnight and by then I was too sick even to pray. He drew blood and left. When he returned, he said it showed the white cell count was high, there were falciparum malaria parasites, and mentioned bacterial endocarditis and pneumonia as possibilities. Falciparum or malignant malaria can be fatal. He gave me three Camoquin pills and left.

Between the terrible chills, rising fever, aching, and shortness of breath, I didn't get a moment's relief all night. Never before had I suffered that way. In my pain and confusion I asked, "Lord, how did this ever happen?"

He answered so clearly, *This is the Lord's doing; and it is marvelous in our eyes.*[1]

I asked, "But why must I suffer like this?"

What I do thou knowest not now; but thou shalt know hereafter.[2] was the reply.

"I'll probably be awhile getting over this," I thought, and again words entered my mind—*My times are in thy hand.*[3]

Those words comforted me during the next two days and nights when I longed and even pleaded for sleep, which didn't come. I reminded myself it would come *in His time.* I don't know how I would have stood those long painful hours if I hadn't felt the presence of the Lord. He was so precious that it made the suffering worthwhile, and I was able to praise God for permitting me the experience.

Toward morning I was so short of breath that I called George. He got Claudia to go for the doctor, who arrived about six o'clock. Meantime I got worse and worse and wondered if I was dying.

I don't remember what George and Claudia were doing, but I told the Lord, "If You want to take me, I am ready to go." Once again He very clearly gave me an answer, *I shalt not die, but live.*[4]

Upon arrival, the doctor asked, "What is the matter?"

Because the Lord had given me assurance that I would live, I answered, "Nothing."

He put a capsule in my mouth and poured in some water. I sputtered and almost choked and when he dropped in the second one, he said, "Try not to spill water all over the place this time."

He warned me the quinine injection he was going to give me would hurt. It did! Forty-seven years later my right arm is still weak and awkward, and the deltoid muscle is atrophied.

I was only vaguely aware of what was going on around me, but I was aware of the presence of the Lord. In a very loving way He brought things to my attention and filled me with His Spirit. For years I had longed to be fully His, but during those hours He showed me areas I had not surrendered. He blessed me as I released those areas to Him. I realized the money in my bank account was a reservation, and I gave it all to Him. I had long sought release from a craving to be noticed, and as my Lord and I communed, I saw that it was simply by trusting Him, and not by trying, that the victory would come. I became aware that I was being given a genuine love for people, especially the people in Honduras.

After that, things grew worse. Disconnected words floated through my mind and a terrible ringing started in my ears. I was gasping for breath and every breath was a groan. The pain in my chest was terrible. George and Bob were with me, and I saw them look at each other and shake their heads. Other people came into the room. I began speaking words the Lord put into my mouth; they were messages for certain people.

Once again I committed my life into the Lord's hands, but this time I had no assurance I would live, so I started saying good-bye to the people around me and gave messages to be given to my family.

Dr. Gasteazoro returned sometime during the day and sat by my bedside. I asked him to take the Lord as his Savior, and he said he would, but I could tell he was uncomfortable. I then added, "And trust Him."

He replied, "Who doesn't?" I found out later he believed all religions were equal in gaining salvation.

I asked George to read the twenty-third Psalm, and the words held precious meaning for me—*Yea though I walk through the valley of the shadow of death I will fear no evil for thou art with me,* and then in my mind there followed *O death, where is thy sting? O grave, where is thy victory*?[5] George prayed and I felt stronger immediately. In fact, whenever George prayed, all through those days, I was strengthened.

Three or four times that day I had severe, body-shaking chills. Once when I felt one starting, I cried out to God, "O Lord, not another chill." That time His answer was, *There hath no temptation taken you but such as you are able to bear.*[6] The chill came and with it, *Fear thou not; for I am with thee . . . I will strengthen thee. . . .* [7] It was enough!

Claudia's presence and help were beyond measure. My weakness was so great I couldn't even raise an arm to brush the hair out of my eyes. Her actions were gentle, she anticipated my needs, and she cared for me most lovingly through the most distasteful tasks. She even held my head when I vomited because I was too weak to hold it over the pan.

Although that night was a restless and long one of suffering, yet I remember more the sweetness of the Lord's love in the words He gave to me. When I wished for morning to the endless night, new meaning was given to the words, *One day is with the Lord as a thousand years, and a thousand years as one day.*[8]

I found I could say, *My soul waiteth for the Lord more than they that watch for the morning: I say, more than they that watch for the morning.*[9] After awhile, however, I began to wish the Lord had taken me home—it would have been so much better than the pain and baffling weakness, and the constant distress for air.

With Paul I said, *For I am in a strait betwixt two, having a desire to depart, and to be with Christ; which is far better.*[10] But like Paul I was ready to *abide and continue.*[11]

Songs came and sang themselves in my mind, "All the Way My Savior Leads Me," and "Why art thou cast down, O my soul, and why art thou disquieted within me?"[12] I remembered that joyous, exulting tune that we used to sing in Ladies' Chorus. The words lifted me up and I was glad I knew Him *who gives songs in the night.*[13]

Another time when I was too sick and weak to allow the wrinkled sheets to be changed, these words came to me, *He will make all thy bed in thy sickness.*[14]

Once when my back hurt so much I thought I couldn't stand it any longer, I cried to the Lord and immediately it felt as though something was gently moving under the small of my back. It may have been the muscles twitching, I don't know, but then words came again, *Underneath are the everlasting arms,*[15] and I felt such relief I cried out to myself, *-¡Milagro milagro!-* ("Miracle, miracle!")

That same night I sensed a presence over the bed. I opened my eyes and saw the mosquito netting rippling in a slight breeze. Immediately the words came, *He shall give his angels charge over thee.*[16] If the words had come first, I might have thought that it was only imagination that I had heard and felt what I believe was the presence of angels.

After all those experiences and others, I was just bubbling over with joy and rejoicing in the wonder of it all. I said, "Lord, how precious are Thy thoughts unto me. It seems You answer my every thought."

Thou understandest my thought afar off,[17] followed.

I said, "It seems that You have a promise for every need."

And He said, *There hath not failed one word of all his good promise,*[18] and, . . . *exceeding great and precious promises,*[19] and then, *My meditation of him shall be sweet,*[20] and, *How sweet are thy words unto my taste, O how love I thy law!*[21]

I said, "And it's so wonderful how You just give them to me as I need them."

His reply, *The Holy Spirit . . . shall bring all things to your remembrance.*[22]

"O, Lord, I love You so much."

I have loved thee with an everlasting love,[23] He answered.

The days and nights were filled with unrelenting chest pain and aching through all my body. Breathing was labored and sleep was fitful. When the doctor arrived, I told him about how the Lord had comforted me with knowledge that I would not die.

He said, "There was an ecstasy about your delirium that I have never seen before." Later he said, "You had a long conversation with your God, didn't you?"

One time Grace was sitting with me and I asked her what day it was. She said it was Saturday afternoon. For two days I had been off someplace with the Lord and everything else was incidental. Although I was back to awareness of my surroundings, He was still near as He had always been but closer and more real.

Sunday morning Claudia and George lifted me onto a cot while they changed the bed. Then they left to get ready for church, but before long I realized I was dying and sent Tilda to get George. By 10:30 I was very cold, as though all heat had left my body. My arm was blue, and cold perspiration was pouring out of me. I got colder and colder. Twice I felt myself slipping off—I knew death was imminent. George sent Tilda to get the doctor, but he was otherwise occupied and didn't arrive until a long while later.

I was not afraid to die because I knew my sins were covered by the blood of Christ, "but I must go alone," I thought. George was on one side of the bed and Tilda on the other, fanning—"they cannot go with me." Then my Lord gave me this: *Yea, though I walk through the valley of the shadow of death, I will fear no evil; for thou art with me.*[24]

I asked George to take my hand in his as I prayed, "Lord, I'm ready to go if You want me to, but I don't think You do, do You?"

Go home and tell,[25] He said. After that, I told George I wasn't going to die.

George said, "When you first got sick, the Lord gave me John 11:4, *This sickness is not unto death, but for the glory of God.*"

I was sure the Lord had given me that verse as a promise of life, and when George confirmed it, I became aware that Satan was the one attacking me. I did not see him, but I truly felt his presence. I knew he did not want me to go home and tell, and I knew he was the one I had to fight against for my life. Then it was as though I was the nurse standing beside the patient in the bed.

George began to rub my cold hand and it started to feel warm. I said, "Get towels." Then they rubbed the other hand and my feet. My whole body was sore and the vigorous rubbing Tilda gave me was more than I could bear, so I asked her to fan me so I could breathe better. George continued to rub my arms and legs and then I suddenly got pain in my left chest area and thought, "I guess that's my heart."

I was still cold and perspiring and was afraid I would chill so I sent Tilda for a hot water bottle. Gradually I felt a little warmth returning. Then my left arm began to tingle—circulation returning?—and my breathing began to come easier.

The doctor arrived about that time and because he had been called away from his personal activities, he reacted with rough words and actions. He told them to change my wet sheets, and when I was too weak to move, he flopped me over and jerked out the bottom sheet. I cried out in pain and said, "Oh let George do it; he can do it gently."

Immediately the Lord encouraged me. *Consider him that endured such contradiction of sinners against himself. . . .*[26]

I knew the doctor was not saved; therefore, it was Satan using him to destroy my life. I told the Lord I would gladly suffer it all and more if it could lead the doctor to salvation. I have wondered many times since if he is saved.

Sunday night I had my first good sleep, except that I was wakened for medicine every two hours. (Dear Tilda slept on a cot beside me at night, and during the day she kept the clinic running. I can never repay her.) Once when I woke up, I was gasping for air and fear passed through me that if I went back to sleep, I might stop breathing. Again my Lord comforted me with: *When I awake, I am still with thee,*[27] and I was able to go back to sleep.

Monday morning I couldn't talk above a whisper and didn't see how I could start a new day. I asked George for prayer, and before he prayed, he gave me this precious thought, the Lord's mercies . . . *they are new every morning.* That promise from Lamentations 3:22 and 23 encouraged me, and he added, *As thy days so shall thy strength be,* from Deuteronomy 33:25. It was precious!

I was being given streptomycin, terramycin, and penicillin, and I began to suspect the terramycin was partly to blame for the nausea and vomiting. In spite of the doctor's advice, I stopped taking it and Tuesday I was able to eat the mashed potatoes and eggs Claudia brought me.

I gained strength very slowly, but all the while I had peace in my heart. *I learned, in whatsoever state I am, therewith to be content,*[28] and *Godliness with contentment is great gain.*[29] After ten days I sent Tilda home at night and welcomed a few visitors, who had been forbidden by the doctor the first week.

As I lay there in bed rejoicing in how good God had been to me, I could recall every one of my cries to Him and His answers to me in the exact order they occurred just as though they were typed out in black and white. Then I began to realize that all His answers were verses from the Scriptures—except His promise to make my bed in my sickness. When I was strong enough to handle my Bible, however, I found almost the exact words in Psalm 41:3. I didn't remember ever having read it, but since I had read the whole Bible numerous times I know I had.

Gradually I regained strength, but the first time I tried to stand I went right down as though my legs were rubber.

Christmas Eve Grace Miller brought Tilda and a few of the Carib girls to sing Spanish carols outside my door. Pedro and J. Mark were visiting me and we enjoyed the singing.

I was taken to Millers for Christmas dinner but found out I was weaker than I knew.

[1] Psalm 118:23
[2] John 13:7
[3] Psalm 31:15a
[4] Psalm 118.17
[5] I Corinthians 15:55
[6] I Corinthians 10:13
[7] Isaiah 41:10
[8] II Peter 3:8
[9] Psalm 130:6
[10] Philippians 1:23
[11] Philippians 1: 25b
[12] Psalm 42:5a
[13] Job 35:10b
[14] Psalm 41:3
[15] Deuteronomy 33:27
[16] Psalm 91:11
[17] Psalm 139:2
[18] I Kings 8:56
[19] II Peter 1:4
[20] Psalm 104:34
[21] Psalm 119:103 and 97
[22] John 14:26
[23] Jeremiah 31:3
[24] Psalm 23:4
[25] Mark 5:19
[26] Hebrews 12:3
[27] Psalm 139:18b
[28] Philippians 4:11
[29] I Timothy 6:6

1953

Strength came back very slowly and we knew it would be a long time before I could work. On January 10, I had some kind of attack. When the doctor came, he said my heart was dilated, had a murmur, and was going at gallop rhythm. When he left to work in another area the following week, he said I must either go home or to Siguatepeque. After much prayer and soul searching, it was decided that my brother-in-law, Noah Mack, a medical doctor, would fly from Pennsylvania to take me home.

It was not my desire to leave Honduras. The Lord had taken me there and I was very happy in His work. But He was taking me home and I would be just as happy there. AS HE LEADS is joy.

Sunday, February 1, was my last day in Trujillo—for how long I didn't know, but it was all in the Lord's hands, and His hands are loving hands. Actually, those two months of sickness were a wonderful time of learning to know Him better and coming to love Him more. *How unsearchable are his judgments, and his ways past finding out!* (Romans 11:33). Noah allowed me to attend the last part of the morning church service even though I had to be carried into the church.

I have no idea how I would have ever gotten ready to leave Honduras if it hadn't been for Grace. She sorted and packed the things in my closet and on shelves to take with me, to be given away, or to be sent on to the United States if I was unable to return. I tried to do some things for myself, but soon the bed was piled full around me and I was too weak and tired to concentrate on what to do next. Finally Tilda just gathered it all up and plunked it into my suitcase, and I could lie down to rest.

I certainly found out how friendly, appreciative, and courteous the people of Trujillo were. Getting a bath and packing had to be done in installments between visits. Saturday at least 25 persons dropped in, and the visits began again at 7:30 on Sunday morning. When we got to the airport Monday, a crowd of at least 30 people had walked out through the hot sun to see us off.

They tried to get the Missionary Aviation Fellowship plane to take us to San Pedro Sula, but it was in Tegucigalpa being painted, so we flew to San Pedro Sula on TACA and spent the night at the Reformed Mission. Noah had brought a mattress and a stretcher, and I wasn't too uncomfortable on the floor of the plane. It was a smooth trip, but I felt extreme tiredness, and until after we left La Ceiba I was short of breath.

We left San Pedro Sula on a Braniff plane the next day and had a compartment all to ourselves. We thought we might have to spend a night in Miami because of the close connection between our arrival and the flight to Philadelphia, but the pilot of our plane out of San Pedro Sula radioed that he had a stretcher case and mentioned the connecting flight in Miami and was given a through flight.

A cabulance (taxicab/ambulance) met our plane in Miami to transport me to the National Air Lines' DC-6 Star. I spent about 45 minutes in the cabulance while Noah took care of luggage, customs, and public health papers.

While I was waiting, Mother's cousin, Daniel Wright, came with a dozen lovely carnations. Mother had met him at a funeral in Ohio the week before and had mentioned that I was being brought home. He had contacted the consul of Honduras, found out when I would be passing through Miami, and had requested permission from airport authorities to come out on the field to greet me. When I arrived at the hospital in Philadelphia a few hours later a nurse remarked, "Not many people bring their own flowers." I don't think I ever explained.

Somebody carried me, wrapped in a quilt, up the long flight of steps to board the plane. I was loaded as *baggage*. The backs of two window seats were folded down for the stretcher. The stewardesses were helpful and my meal of steak, green beans, cake, and piping hot coffee tasted delicious. All along the way I felt loved and cared for by people I had never met before. The cabin of that plane was pressurized and I had no difficulty breathing as we flew above the clouds to Washington at 15,000 feet, and at 7,000 feet the rest of the way to Philadelphia.

Twelve hours after leaving San Pedro Sula we landed in Philadelphia. An ambulance was waiting to take Noah and me to Hahnemann Hospital, and the driver seemed to consider it his duty to entertain us. Tired or not, I was quite amused at his colorful descriptions of the sights along the way.

How I appreciated my brother-in-law, who had traveled all those miles to care for me on my flight home. He had taken responsibility for every detail of the flights and entry into the United States.

On the ninth floor of the hospital I shared Room 959 with another woman. I couldn't help comparing the stale smoky room that looked out on a courtyard facing the solid wall of another wing with my big airy room in Trujillo that had a view of the mountains and the ruins of the old palace.

Immediately upon my arrival nurses took blood tests, a TB test, chest x-rays, and an electrocardiogram; a doctor withdrew bone marrow. Later another doctor took my medical history and informed me that my heart was not damaged.

One of the joys of coming home was visits from family and friends. The first morning Noah and Muriel arrived. When my sister Joyce brought Father and Mother in to visit, I was reminded that when I had been close to death I had been assured by the Lord that I would see my parents again.

My brother Glenn and his wife Catherine came next, and in the days that followed Eunice Graybill, Etta Horning, and Ruth Peachey, who was in medical school. Titus Lehman called and later walked over from the University where he was studying psychiatry and sociology. Before he left, my sisters Joyce and Muriel arrived to tell me Mother and my other sister, Lois Erb, and her new baby were in the lobby waiting to see me. My heart overflowed with gratitude as cards and letters arrived, and as I saw how everyone was looking out for my well-being.

After a two-week stay at Hahnemann I was discharged but needed to see the doctor at his office two days later. I decided to stay in Philadelphia for the two days and accepted an invitation to stay at Preston Maternity Hospital, where I had taken my midwifery. A friend there even took me for the doctor appointment, where the report was that I definitely had had falciparum malaria, plus a long list of complications. I could only rejoice at how the Lord had brought me through that often-fatal disease and at how wonderful it felt to be better.

Looking back I am amazed at the cost of my hospital stay—$350.72. The medicines cost $77.35, and Dr. Thompson did not charge for his services because I was in mission work. The entire cost for the excellent care I received would not cover one day in a hospital now, 46 years later.

Joyce and her husband, Melvin Mast, came to Philadelphia to take me to the new house Father and Mother had built south of Morgantown, Pennsylvania. As we pulled up outside, light streamed through plant-filled windows, and the boxwoods on the lawn were a reminder of Father's hobby at our old home in Malvern. Inside, the familiar furniture quickly had me feeling I was truly home.

Love is a wonderful thing; family, friends, acquaintances, and neighbors showed it in many ways as they visited, called, and sent greetings. Everything from cinnamon buns to invitations for meals arrived at our door.

I thought of my roommate at Hahnemann who complained that her brother should at least come to visit, but when he called to say he was coming she told him he didn't need to bother. While in the hospital, I had wished I could do something for the people around me for I saw as great a need in Philadelphia as I had seen in Honduras. In Trujillo it was shooting and *machetando* (slashing with machetes), but in the United States I encountered harsh words and calloused hearts.

Since I was feeling so well and had recovered so fast, it was a shock when Dr. Thompson sent advice through Noah, that I should not return to the tropics. He said with depressed bone marrow and tropical anemia such as I had, another attack of malaria could be fatal.

Noah and Muriel told me they were sure the Lord would lead me to the right decision, but Mother advised me to follow the doctor's suggestion. For myself, it was a great disappointment even to consider not returning to Trujillo, but doing the Lord's will was my highest joy and deepest aim, and I knew He would make it known.

During a visit with Glenn and Catherine, who still lived in Lederach, I had an encouraging visit from Catherine Lederach, a missionary for 24 years. She told about experiences before she left China and wonderful things of how the Lord had led her.

Attending a mission board meeting, however, very poignantly renewed my disappointment if I could never return to Honduras, but I trusted in the Lord's grace to be able to rejoice in whatever He allowed. "He has not turned the page of the future yet," I reasoned, "and I am satisfied to wait."

In mid-April I went to La Junta, Colorado, for my five-year class reunion. As I reviewed those five years—a year at La Junta in obstetrics, school nurse for a year at Eastern Mennonite College, followed by midwifery training at Preston, the time spent in Honduras, and finally my return home with the future unknown—I discovered that the sweetness of trusting in God was greater than ever before.

Attending an alumni meeting, a tea, and our class reunion dinner brought back many memories and renewed acquaintances. All too soon it was time to return home. I had gone to Colorado with friends by car, but returned by the *El Capitan* train to Chicago, and from there by *Greyhound* bus to the Morgantown exit of the Pennsylvania Turnpike.

The end of April was "Homecoming" at Eastern Mennonite College, and I remembered how a year before I had saved vacation time so I could attend. When "The Holy City" was sung, it meant far more to me than ever before, because only six months before I had been so close to going to that holy city.

Life in the new Morgantown house was pleasant, and I helped family and friends when I could. I accepted quite a few invitations to speak in Sunday Schools, churches, and at youth meetings, and I tried to make every day count for the Lord. In May my niece, Mary Lois Mack, invited me for an African supper, along with her Aunt Mary Mack and her Franconia school friends from Grace Bergey's class.

Meantime my senses were bombarded with spring sounds and colors that were unknown in the tropics. The white and pink dogwoods competed with a riot of colors in tulips, lilacs, bleeding heart, and iris, and the dozens of shades of green in the opening leaves. Bluebirds built a nest in the box Father put up, and birds everywhere sang their spring songs in competition to the spring peepers and the drone of farm tractors.

Straight rows of tomato plants were set out in Joyce and Melvin's fields which joined our property, and Mother and I planted garden and enjoyed and froze fresh asparagus.

At General Mission Board Meeting in Harrisonburg, Virginia, in June, I was among the 60 persons consecrated for service. I believe the Lord allowed me to attend that meeting because my faith was strengthened by the speakers. Bro. Joseph Graber spoke of the hardness of the missionary life, the need for sacrifice of ease, family ties, fellowship, and perhaps even life itself. He cited the time David, in II Samuel 24:24 said, . . . *Neither will I offer burnt offerings unto the Lord my God of that which doth cost me nothing.* My desire was to return to Honduras, but my prayer was to know if it was the will of God. I was torn between the faith I had that He could and would take care of me and the advice of the doctor.

Home mission work presented itself only a mile from my door when neighbors Moses and Rhoda Stoltzfus opened their home to Spanish children from New York City tenements. In groups of ten, *Fresh-Air* youngsters spent three weeks each on the Stoltzfus dairy farm. The four boys in the first group slept in the farmhouse, and I lived in a cabin in the woods with six girls.

The children helped weed the garden, set the table, wash dishes, and wash and iron their clothing. They loved taking horseback rides and playing with the collie dogs and the nanny goat and her kid. They learned a lot about life on a working farm, and they fished and swam in a creek, and hiked in the woods. We also had a Bible School for them where, perhaps for the first time, they heard about the Lord.

One girl asked me, "Do you get paid for keeping us?"

"No," I replied, "just getting to know you is reward enough."

"Well!" she said, "I don't see how you can have so much patience."

Only the Lord could have given me the grace to deal with the problems two of the girls in one group created. They had never learned to submit to anyone and to keep peace and harmony within the group, I needed to rely on prayer for strength and wisdom.

As she was ready to leave one girl said, "I didn't know before that you could pray to God and He will do it." She had lost a quarter and a nickel somewhere in the barn or on the lawn. When she told us about the loss, I suggested we pray about finding the coins. A week later, Moses found the quarter in the hay behind a cow in the barn, and the last week of her stay another girl found the nickel in the grass on the lawn.

When the *Fresh-Air* children were all back in school, I substituted a few weeks as nurse in Dr. Paul's office in Honey Brook. I was again invited to speak about Honduras at sewing circles and other church meetings around eastern Pennsylvania.

Family dinners and gatherings were so precious as I got reacquainted with nieces and nephews. Once while a group was playing hide and seek, I heard little Paul call out, "Ready? If you're ready, don't answer. Are you ready? Huh?"

♔

I'm afraid it wasn't with very good grace I said "Yes," to the Lord about working at Philhaven Hospital, a Mennonite mental health center founded in 1952 at Mt. Gretna, Pennsylvania. I had been asked to consider a short fill-in position there, but I fervently hoped I wouldn't get a definite offer. I knew I'd be happy if it was God's will because I was always happy when in His will, but of everything I could think of, that was the thing I least wanted to do. I agreed to try it for a month, and when the time arrived for my first day on the job, I felt as well as I ever had felt. I worked with a fine group of staff members, and the work itself was a valuable experience. When the month was completed, I even agreed to stay an additional three weeks. In fact, I liked it there . . ., but Honduras still called . . ., and the Lord *in His timing* was preparing the way.

The mission board contacted me about returning, and Noah agreed to my going if another nurse shared the assignment. I then discovered the Lord had been quietly preparing Jean Garber for that position. For almost a year she had felt a conviction for Honduras—even before I got sick!

Vera Jean Garber

The year 1953 drew to an end in a flurry of activity. My commitment at Philhaven finished, and I was home for Christmas, when all my family was together for the first time in 15 years at the home of Noah and Muriel.

1954

Father declared, "Mother and I have been married 43 years and we never had roast goose on our table." To remedy that deficiency, goose was the main course on our menu for New Year's Day, 1954.

I began the year reviewing my blessings—health, a comfortable home, happiness in knowing the Lord, consciousness of His leading, and the promise of a return to Honduras. *God giveth us richly all things to enjoy.* (I Timothy 6:17). I chose *Third the Third Year*, as the motto for my coming third year in Honduras. Christ first, others second, and Dora third.

Although painting and wall papering was tiring work, to see the new house looking prettier after each job made the work enjoyable.

I spent a week at Preston Maternity Hospital for a refresher course. I delivered two babies and watched several other births, including a forceps delivery by Dr. Hirst. He also took time in clinic to explain things and allowed me to watch some repair procedures.

Tickets were purchased for March 9 for Jean Garber's and my departure to Honduras, Suddenly, there were many things to do. Jean's father took us to Philadelphia for our yellow fever inoculations, and then the very next day I became sick with a virus infection.

The virus hung on and I had to agree with Noah that I couldn't go to Honduras if I wasn't going to be able to work when I got there. On the other hand, we both knew the Lord could prepare my body if He wanted me to go.

My times are in thy hand. . . . Psalm 31:15, was a verse I clung to through the disappointment and uncertainty until I got peace that what happened was God's will and not my problem.

Noah decided to take me to the Foreign Missions Council in New York to get a second opinion on whether or not I should return to the tropics. Meantime, he advised me to cancel all speaking engagements and rest until my appointment, and although I felt fully recovered for a time, the day of my appointment I was in bed with chills and fever.

The Mission Board canceled Jean's and my reservations, and rescheduled Jean for April 13, with time to go to language school in Costa Rica. Noah suggested she and I spend that extra month studying malaria and tropical diseases at his office, but then, during that time, Jean's x-ray report came back showing her lungs might be diseased.

Attending Mission Board meetings in March lifted our spirits as we listened to talks and testimonies. But only days later, after more tests at the Ephrata Hospital, Noah called me and asked, "If you are passed in New York, would you go to Honduras alone?" and then informed me that Jean's sedimentation rate was 35 and he was much concerned. It should have been in the range between 10 and 15.

In a wordless prayer, I cried out to the Lord, and after a few minutes I found myself almost joyfully asking, "And now what is the next thing You want us to do, Lord?" How wonderful to have and to know the tender Lord who is so gentle and gracious. The future was unknown, but I was not downcast. Instead, I was ready to believe that perhaps He was going to work a miracle. Whatever He did would be well!

My appointment in New York resulted in the verdict that I wait a year, and then if bone marrow studies were normal I could return to the tropics. I was disappointed, of course, but I accepted it as the Lord's will for my life at that time. Although I had made commitments to the Mission Board and had hoped to deliver babies for both the Hess and Hamilton families, I could not apologize for what the Lord had brought about. The question that remained was whether Jean's tests would allow her to go before me, and then I heard that Grace Miller's x-rays indicated the possibility of tuberculosis.

When I lay just one step from death in Honduras in 1952, the Lord had said plainly to me, "But Satan doesn't want you to live," and with all these negative physical reports, I couldn't help wondering if Satan was attacking the work by attacking our bodies. Since the Lord permitted it, however, we needed to seek God's will and ask to be shown what He would have us do.

Two months later Jean was in Costa Rica in language school, and Grace was packing drums to leave for Honduras. After further tests and more x-rays, both women were told that what the x-rays showed in their lungs was no threat to their health.

The Lord had been just as good to me. He gave me such happiness that when I said good-bye to Jean, I was as happy as if I were the one going. Also, just after my disappointing report in New York, Noah asked me to work in his office. It was a wonderful arrangement, and we were soon wondering what he would do for a nurse when it was time for me to leave.

I had suppers with the Mack family between afternoon and evening office hours. One evening my little niece Elsie came in for supper and gleefully told her mother she had been swimming.

"But, Elsie," Muriel said, "you didn't have your bathing suit, did you?"

"Oh no, Mother," Elsie replied. "We just took off our clothes so they wouldn't get wet."

Muriel asked, "Did you take them all off?"

"My friend left her panties on, but I took mine off because I knew they would get all wet." Elsie's merry laughter rang through the house as she finished with, "Oh, it was so much fun!"

At the supper table only minutes later Noah was telling us things he had seen while making house calls that afternoon. "I saw a family of three boys and a girl having a good time this afternoon," he said. "They were playing in the water wearing only their underwear. I guess their mother didn't know." Little did he know that his own little girl had been having an equally refreshing time that very afternoon—not in her underwear.

When he heard the details later, he said, "You can see that she lived in a primitive country (Africa)."

♔

The end of August Norman and Grace Hockman left for language school in Costa Rica, and George and Grace Miller embarked from New York for La Ceiba. I felt confident I would be going by the end of the year, and Noah was arranging an appointment for my reexamination.

My Spanish, meantime, was being put to good use again. In August I agreed to teach two classes of Puerto Rican migrant farm workers in Brethren in Christ churches near Elizabethtown, Pennsylvania—at Conoy during the Sunday School hour and at Mt. Pleasant during the church service. Someone drove to Morgantown for me each Sunday and someone else took me home. Around 30 men attended, and it was a privilege and joy to see the Holy Spirit take these men from complete ignorance of the Scriptures to acceptance of His Word. Ten of them made commitments to accept Christ as their Savior.

In my *spare time* I processed in tin cans the abundant produce from garden and orchard to take to Honduras. Gratefully I watched my inventory grow until it showed 82 quarts of beans, 8 corn, 50 applesauce, 16 carrots, 8 Swiss chard, 6 tomato puree, 3 yellow tomatoes, 21 beets, 17 pickled beets, and 14 pints of seven-day pickles. Shortly after my baggage arrived in Trujillo I sampled some and found them well worth the work and time that went into preserving them. In fact, my pantry shelves held treasures.

I returned to New York for my appointment, this time alone, but the reports they gave me were not encouraging. All the tests were within normal or acceptable limits, but the doctor did not recommend my return to the tropics.

When I met with the Mission Board Executive Committee, however, it was decided I would return to Honduras and I was grateful for their willingness to try me again. I definitely felt the Lord was opening the way, and His reason for me to remain in the United States for that period of time had been fulfilled.

In my heart I hoped I would be able to return and work without interruption or illness, but if the Lord allowed it, I was willing to die there.

1955

Time to pack! In our basement, surrounded by empty drums and a variety of items, Father and I began the job. Some of the things had been ordered by or were being sent to other missionary families, a lot were things various church sewing circles had donated and/or made for the clinic, and the rest were my belongings. The tins of food I had preserved almost filled one drum. A sewing machine donated by my brother-in-law's mother, Minnie Erb, took up most of the space in another drum.

It was the second trip to Trujillo for one item—the small mattress Noah had taken with him to bring me home on on the plane when I was sick. I later had a chest built by a carpenter in Trujillo, and with a cover I made for the mattress we had a comfortable, attractive couch in the living room, which doubled as a bed for guests. After treating the wood against termites, we appreciated the extra storage space the chest provided.

How wonderfully the Lord worked. He gave me the desire to go back to Honduras and He opened the way. Even though several doctors at various times said I shouldn't return to the tropics, yet I had no doubt the Lord wanted me to return. I was sure I would be able to handle the work with His help. I had asked Him to lead and He did, step by step, and I am glad I never ran ahead of Him.

The Sunday before I left, a meaningful farewell service was held at the Frazer Mennonite Church with many friends and relatives present. Noah had the morning sermon, Bishop Mahlon Witmer gave a missionary message in the afternoon, and Bro. Henry Garber told about the work in Honduras. I gave my testimony and Bishop Witmer gave the charge. In the evening there were more testimonies and another inspiring message.

Two years to the day that I flew into the United States on a stretcher, February 4, I boarded a train in Paoli, Pennsylvania, and by evening was aboard the *S.S. Contessa* in New York harbor ready to return to Honduras. The 340-foot-long ship was built in Glasgow in 1930. An older couple from New York, who called me the saint of the *Contessa*, and a man from New Jersey were the only other passengers, so we all ate at the Captain's table.

During the first night I was awakened several times when the tossing of the ship caused me to roll from side to side in my bed. At breakfast someone asked, "Is this rough or very rough?"

The Captain answered, "This is smooth."

The sea got rougher all day and by the time we were opposite North Carolina, the bow of the ship was constantly rising up on waves and then dipping down into troughs leaving the stern high in the air with the propeller out of the water.

February 8, we passed Miami with its white hotels shining in the sun and saw the bridges to the Keys. From there we continued on toward Cuba on a calm Caribbean sea. The cold winter weather of Pennsylvania and New York were only a memory as I strolled the deck without a coat or even a sweater. Sixteen times around the promenade deck equaled a mile and I put in a mile twice a day. I also played shuffleboard with the other passengers and wrote a lot of letters. After passing the tip of Cuba, we saw only water, beautiful flying fish, and a flare marking a submerged submarine. At breakfast the morning of February 9, the Captain reported that the ship was, *Goin' along like a scared cat*, and that we would dock at La Ceiba the next morning.

I could hardly say I was on dry land after docking, because it rained, and IT RAINED, and IT RAINED! In four days and five nights the storm dumped 34 inches of water. The airport turned into a lake, and the last plane able to land at Trujillo had left La Ceiba the morning we docked. The telegraph lines were down so I couldn't even inform my friends in Trujillo when I would arrive. They later told me that groups of people went out to the airport to greet me at least four times.

The Ackermans opened their home to me in La Ceiba, and other missionary families invited me for meals as day after day the rain fell and planes didn't fly. My baggage hadn't been shipped on the *S.S. Contessa,* so with the rain delay I decided I might as well forego the first plane that did go to Trujillo and wait to see my things through customs when the next ship arrived from New York. By the time that ship was unloaded and I discovered my baggage wasn't on it either, I had missed the plane to Trujillo.

I noticed that more stores in La Ceiba had American goods than when I first shopped there four years earlier, but the city still had only one paved street and very few sidewalks. With pleasure I looked into brown faces, listened to the plaintive music and the songs of native birds, and it all made me realize how much I loved the people and the country of Honduras.

I finally reached Trujillo February 19, just in time for the annual celebration of the Christian victory over the Moors in Spain in 1492.

Those representing Christians dressed in blue and white, and the Moors in bright colors and flowers. Most of the participants were women. Each side had a band, a mock army carrying wooden swords, a general on a horse, and a little ten-year-old queen. The procession marched through the town and the opposing sides finally confronted each other in Cristales at the foot of the steep hill. To the sounds of the bands, the beating of drums, and shouts of *Viva la reina Mora* and *Viva la reina Cristiana* they fought their mock battle. After the Christian side won, their little queen tried to splash water on the Moorish queen. Sheets were held up to protect the Moors' queen, but if any water reached her she was considered to have been baptized a Christian. It was a startling idea to me that the people made a play of becoming a Christian, and even more startling that they did it without knowing what it really meant.

How good to be back at work, this time with Jean, who had finished language school in Costa Rica. We hired a boat to take us to Santa Fe

Beaty and Danny waving adiós to Jean and James as they leave for Santa Fe.

for weekly clinics. One man poled the boat while two others paddled. Santa Fe was an idyllic spot of mud huts with thatched roofs, garden plots of pineapple, coconut palms, and cassava. On the way home from our first clinic, the flying fish were out and one jumped into the boat and swam around in the water in the bottom. Jean and I had taken our shoes off to keep them dry. The sea was calm and blue and the air so clear the mountains seemed higher and closer than usual.

We decided to take six-week turns holding clinic at Santa Fe unless I was expecting a delivery in Trujillo. James Hess always went along to hold a service there and sometimes went on to the neighboring villages of San Antonio and Guadalupe. To cut down on travel time as well as the expense of hiring a boat with three men to paddle and guide, the mission soon bought a cayuco with a motor and named it *Caridad* or Love. When we discovered how temperamental it was, we jokingly threatened to rename it *Perversidad* or perversity. We later learned it was previously called *La Consequencia* or the Consequences.

There were so many things I had forgotten about Trujillo, such as the beautiful tone of the church bell striking the hours of the day and the whistling back and forth of the *Cuartel* guards doing their rounds at night. Their whistles let each other know they were awake and on-the-job.

One morning four girls from Santa Fe came to visit. On their heads were pans filled with malanga root—a starchy vegetable. Because of all the rain we had, I asked about the water level in the rivers they had to cross. Three of the girls indicated it was up to their shoulders, but the smallest one, the daughter of the believer where we held clinic, held her hand about two inches over her head. To keep their clothes dry, they had taken them off and carried them in the pans on their heads.

Termites had eaten their way through many of the things I had left behind; the curtains were in shreds and the rugs destroyed. Many of my books and papers which had been stored in a suitcase were a total ruin, including my *Mennonite Community Cookbook*; Mother gave me another one for Christmas in 1960. Most of my pictures were ruined or partially damaged, so the majority used in this book are taken from slides. Although all my books suffered damage, only one medical book was beyond use.

Later in the year I discovered termites in the medicine closet in the clinic. I decided roaches, ants, spiders, mosquitoes, and even scorpions did not compare to the mess termites created. They ate into the wooden shelves, chewed up the medicine boxes and labels, and created a dirty jumble, with every bottle and item needing to be cleaned. James and George made repairs and painted the shelves and wall with Coppertex. It was almost a week before everything was neatly back in place. Thereafter we thoroughly inspected the closet every week. I learned to keep a check on my bedroom closets also. The walls were painted with a solution that was to discourage termites, but they loved to get into dark places and eat their way through clothing, wood, or paper. Nothing was safe, Millers even had a calendar destroyed while it was hanging on the wall.

The Vesper family.

Tegucigalpa missionary Arthur Vesper had attended a conference in Trujillo and returned for vacation with his wife Doris and their children, Mary Jean and Philip. I went along with them on a cayuco trip starting by moonlight at five in the morning. We saw blue, gray, and white egrets and herons when we turned from the sea into the lagoon. Doves and many other birds flew among the coconut palms, mango, and other tall trees, and I had the pleasure of seeing all these sights anew through the eyes of the thrilled Vesper family.

One afternoon a group of us went swimming out near the new Trujillo airport. The sun was warm, the water just right, and the beach clean, wide, and sandy—as nice as any beach I had seen in Florida. Thick bushes provided private bath houses. Nelda was the only one not swimming because she had ironed clothes the day before. As mentioned earlier, getting wet the day after ironing was thought to cause body pains.

That same day in clinic I had explained to a patient with an breast abscess that microbes had probably entered through a crack or cut in the skin. She said, "Yes, at night when I didn't see them"!

A man from another village had come for treatment of a sore hand. It appeared to be getting better, but when his wife died, he insisted his hand was much worse. We discovered that the people in his village were also sure they had to wait two months after getting an injection before entering a house where a person had died or they would die.

It was good I hadn't waited in La Ceiba for my baggage to arrive, because it didn't clear customs until the end of March, and while it was tied up Mr. Vesper was able to get it approved for duty-free entry. Duty could have been as much as 100 percent of its value. One woman Mr. Vesper knew had to pay over $600 duty on her shipment, and everything she brought had been dumped out of the containers, itemized, and then dumped back in. Anything that didn't fit easily was piled in cardboard boxes; some things were lost or missing.

Part of my shipment was a stove for the Hesses' new house, and Jean and I were waiting for a washing machine and my sewing machine. I was confident the Lord would see my things got through at the proper time, and perhaps the delay was His way to get the regulations straightened out. It wasn't until July that I got the final bill for the extra shipping and *aduana* or custom house charges. My share was less than I expected, only $120.74, and left me with enough money to take Spanish classes in Costa Rica during my vacation.

The *Suyapa* finally brought everything to Trujillo on Wednesday, April 6, and on Saturday it was hauled to our yard. The drums went into my big bedroom, and Jean and I started unpacking. By evening my bedroom looked just like the basement had looked in Pennsylvania before I started to pack. It was a month before I found the last item I had feared was left behind—a tin box of lavender-scented talcum powder in a drawer of the sewing machine. In May when I had three patients in labor at the same time in different parts of the town, I opened the clinic for inpatients, and we certainly appreciated the bed sheets, crib sheets, canvas bassinets, bed pads, shirts, and diapers made and/or donated by various sewing circles.

Jean and I had to stop in the midst of our work and fun of unpacking to answer a call to deliver a baby in Cristales, and were more than a little tired when we got back to the house at five o'clock in the morning.

That same evening a man from Cristales died quite suddenly. First he felt ill but soon was so sick he couldn't walk. Within three hours he was dead, probably from the same kind of malaria that had almost taken my life. He had been engaged to Claudia, the Miller's cook who had taken such good care of me when I was sick, and it was then my turn to sit and comfort her. Her questions about why God allowed such things to happen gave me a wonderful opportunity to talk about my understanding and experiences of trusting in God.

Several weeks later she became very sick one night and thought she was dying. It turned out to be indigestion, but the thought that death was close caused her to think seriously about accepting Christ. The Lord prepared her heart during the following days, and when I approached her once more to make a definite decision, she was ready. In her prayer she thanked God for taking evil thoughts out of her mind and told Him she was accepting Christ as her Savior. She asked Him to forgive her sins and to help her to live true to Him. When she was preparing a testimony to give in church, she came to me for help in deciding which Psalm to use. "There are a lot of pretty ones," she said, and I was glad she had made that discovery about God's Word.

♛

Good Friday evening as we were kneeling for prayer in the Hesses' home, Beaty noticed a four-inch scorpion just inches from George Miller's knee. She sounded the alarm, the scorpion was killed, and when we knelt again we had an extra reason for gratitude for God's protection from dangers seen and unseen.

Sunday evening as I was getting ready for bed among all the unpacking clutter in my bedroom, my left foot was suddenly a blaze of pain. Even before I glimpsed a scorpion as he dived under a pile of crumpled newspapers, I knew what had happened.

Immediately I felt sick all over, but I managed to hobble to the door and call Jean to quick bring *Merck's Medical Manual*. It said to inject Novocaine directly into the site. She got a cartridge of Novocaine that we used for pulling teeth and injected it. Although the pain was more bearable, I got weak all over, my breathing became light, and my tongue felt cold and stiff. Jean went to ask Dr. Rivera for advice and he prescribed Coramine orally and calcium gluconate by I.V.

During the night the pain got severe again and Jean injected more Novocaine. I went into chills and it took a comforter folded double to get warm enough to go back to sleep. For several days whenever I got out of bed I was weak and short of breath and broke out with perspiration. The doctor said, "O, you Gringos can't take anything," and prescribed Cardiazol-efedrina. The sting could be fatal to a small child, so I prayed often for safety for the babies born in the clinic.

Then I started hearing scorpion stories from neighbors. Amadeo, the carpenter, said he once put on his shirt and one was in it and stung him on the chest. He was in bed five days. Claudia was stung on a finger, Mary was stung at night while sleeping, and one got Eriberta when she was putting on a dress.

Beaty Hess killed a scorpion one morning on Danny's mosquito netting, and I tried to be more careful. As I reached into a dark corner for the dishpan, however, I stepped on something soft and discovered I had killed a scorpion without even trying. Beaty came over all excited one evening and said she had just killed seven little ones in James's study, and while talking she said, "There goes a big one now under the buffet!" It took only a few seconds for me to snatch off my shoe and whack him, only three feet from my chair. In the morning, James told me he had killed six while Beaty was visiting me and then another one after she got home. We all were careful to shake out our shoes before putting them on, and we carried flashlights after dusk. I must admit I was careful even when picking up my shoes for fear one would come out and sting my hand. Surely the Lord kept all of us many times from being stung and poisoned.

Niña (means little girl but is a respectful title for a spinster) Genoveva Mendoza, a woman about 50 years old weighing only 80 pounds and not more than five feet tall, was hired as cook and housekeeper. She had difficulty seeing even with the shaftless glasses she kept on her nose with a string around her head. She tried hard to learn our way of doing things. When Jean noticed her brushing the crumbs from the table onto the floor, she handed her the little crumb tray my niece Elsie had given me and explained its use. Genoveva understood the spoken instructions, but must have wondered about them because I later noticed her carefully tilting the tray to dump the crumbs onto the floor.

About the same time, Heriberta Laboriel replaced Tilda in the clinic. Tilda knew the people would show her more respect if she had hospital practice and left to work in the hospital at Tela. Heriberta, a Carib, had been a school teacher and had been in an English class I had had earlier. With Niña Genoveva in the kitchen and Heriberta in the clinic, Jean learned conversational Spanish, and at the same time Heriberta learned conversational English.

Helen Headings in Tocoa requested a prenatal examination and Jean and I found transportation on one of the Grasshopper Control runs. It was two and a half years since I had seen the Hamiltons, and I had never met Maynard and Helen Headings. Jean had never been to Tocoa and the trip was quite an adventure for her. We soon found out what George Miller meant when he said that although the road was much more traveled than previously and the trip could be made in only four hours, we would have the pounds bounced off of us. The driver of the Jeep drove as much as 40 kilometers (25 miles) per hour at times with abrupt slowdowns to avoid deep holes. He seemed to know the location of every rut and hole and slowed the Jeep just in time to avoid crashing into them at full speed. I wondered how the passengers in the back of the Jeep were faring, because it was rough enough on us sitting on the seat.

We got to Durango and crossed the Aguan River by ferry at sunset. To avoid the 13 thrillingly high bridges we followed a path that curved through the jungle and wound in and out and bumped up and down before finally emerging back onto the original road. Several more times we left the road and dipped down to ford creeks where bridges, were not safe to use. A tie was missing in one of the remaining bridges and a passenger riding in the back of the Jeep fished one out of the stream bed and placed it in the gap so we could cross.

The forest had been cut back so the trees and vines no longer reached out and brushed our vehicle as they had on my other trip. Once the Jeep came to a sudden halt and the driver snatched up his rifle as he leaped out to shoot at a fleeing deer. He missed it and we soon dashed on through the jungle, passing many iguanas and flying birds.

Just beyond Corocito a woman flagged us to a stop. Her son had fallen from a coconut tree and her husband wanted a ride to Tocoa for medicine. I suggested we might be able to help and by the light of pine tapers and Jean's flashlight we examined the boy in a little windowless two-room adobe home with mud floor and roof thatched with corozo palm leaves. He was suffering from bruises and was having chest pains and other aches. We gave him some medicine and saved him from the purge of castor oil they were about to give him. A dose of castor oil was the normal home remedy for falls and many illnesses and usually left the patient feeling worse instead of better.

As we continued our trip, the lights of the Jeep caught and reflected the red eyes of *Cucuyos* sitting on the road. With cries of "a-will, a-will," and the white spots on their wings creating circles, the dove-like birds flew up and away as we approached.

The temperature dropped to 60° that night and we saw that the fireplace being built of river stones in Hamilton's new house was a necessity. Sixty degrees was winter temperature and it was the month of May.

During the few days we spent in Tocoa, Jean and I examined and prescribed for Helen Headings, pulled a tooth for Alice Hamilton, and prescribed for "Uncle" Dan Shenk's cold and Jessie Hamilton's laryngitis. "Uncle" Dan and "Aunt" Nancy were volunteers working in Tocoa. We were also asked to go to Manga Seca, an area a mile outside of Tocoa, to see a 21-year-old man very sick with malaria.

Our return to Trujillo was uncertain, as many things are in Honduras. First we expected to return with the Jeep, but it was delayed. Next Eldon Hamilton discovered the bearings were burned out on a rear wheel of his four-wheel drive. Only two horses could be found for hire, and before a third one was located so Eldon could accompany us, he got enough grease in the wheel to be able to use the vehicle. We telegraphed to James Hess to meet us at the river, and he arrived there with several persons along for the ride. From the back of the truck, they filled the air with singing while someone beat out the rhythm.

We picked up several more passengers along the way—several boys with a chicken and a woman with a baby and a little girl. We also made some visits, including one at the lagoon Guaymoreto. Our friend's house there was of manaca palms. Even the doors were removable manaca screens. Back of the house the land dipped down to the lagoon, and across the lagoon stood Calentura in a twilight haze—a sight too beautiful for words. Calentura is the 3,000-foot mountain back of Trujillo that appears as though a bite were taken out of it. Tilda told me it is called Calentura because if you don't have *calentura* when you go up you will have it when you come down. Calentura means fever and in Trujillo fever means malaria. This was sensible because the cooler temperature at the top would cause the malaria parasites in the blood to break out. Meanwhile, the sand flies were feasting on our unprotected legs and kept us from going into a complete trance over the beauty. The people who live there outsmart the sand flies by tying their pant legs tight at the ankle.

A little further on we stopped to pick up three more boys and a dog, and shortly after that the truck got stuck in soft sand. As the wheels churned, the differential got hung up on the high grassy center of the road. Everyone except James got out to lighten the load, the boys pushed, and the truck slowly plowed through. As I walked behind, I tripped and fell flat on my face, but the sand was soft and I wasn't hurt.

♔

The clinic work and Jean and I entered a time of testing after I called Dr. Rivera, the doctor working in Trujillo at that time, too late to save the life of a breach delivery baby, and another woman miscarried who had had an (unrelated) injection at our clinic. Rumors also went around the town about our being the cause of another miscarriage, although as far as I knew the mother had never been treated for anything at our clinic. About the same time Dr. Rivera received a directive from the government that all clinics should be closed in areas where a doctor was practicing. We could still do deliveries and we were still free to go to Santa Fe because no doctor was assigned there. According to a census, Honduras had only 400 doctors for a population of more than one and a half million people.

I accepted the blame for the death of the breach baby and felt quite downhearted until I took it to the Lord, who restored my joy and gave me assurance of His love. With a blessed sense of His presence I was able to move forward with confidence as I delivered normal babies, and, in less than two weeks when the doctor was in another area, Jean and I were seeing more than our usual quota of patients in the clinic. It was an opportunity to put my nonresistant beliefs into practice and not defend myself during times of adversity, and it brought me closer to God once again. Several months later the doctor reversed his directive and we were again able to carry on as before, making it more convenient for the poor people.

For a period of time after that we had no sale of Bibles or Scripture portions. It was as though we were up against a wall of hardness. After we had prayed specifically for a breakthrough, a girl came to purchase a Bible, and shortly thereafter several other people asked for the Scripture portions. God had broken a gap in the wall of resistance, and we believed the power of His Word would not return void.

At 3:50 a.m., June 24, I woke up thinking someone was battering down our doors. It only took a few seconds to realize it was just a fusillade of firecrackers signaling the beginning of the festival in honor of the birthday of John the Baptist, Trujillo's patron saint, but by then my heart was thumping wildly. When I told Jean in the morning, she said, "Yours too?"

Because it was a holiday, we closed the clinic and went with Jorge, James and Danny Hess to San Antonio, a Carib village beyond Santa Fe. We used the sails going down and it was lots of fun. We saw only eight patients, but the house was full of people all the time, and we sang, read Scripture, and talked with them. I told Jean she made a pretty good preacher.

The sea got too rough to take the boat home, so Jean and I left our supplies with James and started walking. The wind fought against us on the beach, but part of the way we were on a path where the sand was only one or two inches deep and the sun and wind less strong. We tried to hire horses in Santa Fe, but the owner wasn't home. A lady offered to sell us coco cakes right out of the oven—a flat iron kettle with a fire of coconut husks on top. The cakes were heavy and filling. We were given mangoes and I ate at least four as we walked.

The rivers, Mojaguay and Rio Grande, only covered our feet, and after crossing we continued walking in the water at the edge of the sea which was easier than walking in loose, damp sand. San Antonio

Walking home from Santa Fe.

is two miles from Santa Fe, and Santa Fe six miles from Trujillo—or so they say; it seemed longer to me. Once Jean and I lay down on the warm sand to rest and just before sunset we were within sight of Cristales. James, Danny, and Jorge had changed their minds about staying overnight in San Antonio and came along in the *Caridad* and picked us up and took us the rest of the way home. They were completely soaked and said it was the worst trip they had ever made.

The following week the sea was just the opposite—so calm the surface in one area was as smooth as though it were oil, and at another place it had a fine pattern of ripples covering the flat surface like lace. I had no maternity cases due that week, so I went to Santa Fe instead of Jean.

The next week the motor on the boat needed repairs and Jean went for clinic in Santa Fe on horseback—her first riding experience! Genoveva brought out a chair to help her mount, and James gave her a boost. She was finally *up there* after several tries, and then the horse began turning around and around because she didn't know how to direct him. She caught on quickly, but after the two-hour trip to Santa Fe and another two hours coming back, she could barely walk the following day. Later in the week James said he made the trip walking in only one and a half hours. I teased him by saying he must have been trying to get there before he got tired.

He replied, "If I walk only my feet hurt, but if I ride I hurt all over."

Just days later the man who ran the ferry across the Aguan River brought the young woman who worked as cook for his family to our maternity clinic. She was 18 years old, less than five feet tall, and had previously had two stillborn babies. Her hemoglobin was so low it didn't register on our scale which only registered above 30%. The day after she arrived she delivered a normal six and three-quarters pound girl, and I was given the honor of naming her. Cristina was the name I chose. When the ferryman came to take them home 11 days later, the baby had gained 12 ounces, and the mother's hemoglobin was up to 50%.

♔

No one fell asleep in church that Sunday evening. From all over the building, the noise of clapping and smacking sounded. The showers of the past few weeks had produced a multitude of places for mosquitoes to breed. Beaty had a bout of malaria with chills that shook her bed, and Grace also took her turn being sick. Jean and I took Camoquin every two weeks, and the others took Aralen.

Jean left for her month's vacation in the States the end of July, but I didn't feel alone, with the Hess family living in the "L" end of the house. My work in the clinic was a pleasure, and I was given many opportunities to witness. I wouldn't have exchanged my work for anything else, and wrote in my journal, *As long as the Lord wants me here, I want to be here.*

The adults weren't the only missionaries. Little Danny Hess taught his friends some of the Bible verses he knew and sang hymns with them. He also visited with the soldiers guarding the prisoners working on a project in front of his house and took them drinks of water in his sand bucket. I often recorded the children's antics in my journal, and it says that when Danny's Grandmother Hess sent him a wristwatch for his fourth birthday, he woke his father at three in the morning to ask if his watch was still safe on the dresser.

♔

Mr. Solano who worked with the logging company, INSCO, was in the clinic one day in July. He worked under Mr. Griffith and was in charge of loading mahogany logs, 15 to 18 feet long and up to 150 inches in diameter, onto rafts to float down the Aguan River to a special log ship from Pensacola. I asked about his work, and he said that although they had 1,500 logs ready, rain was needed before the river would be deep enough to float the rafts. I said I would enjoy seeing the operation some time, and he explained the logs were loaded onto the rafts with chains and hooks and that the winches handled the heavy logs as though they were match sticks.

August was hot. When I went outside, I used my umbrella for shade from the glaring sun and was glad for any shaded area I passed. I waited until evening to work in the garden and flower beds, and I slept on a mat on the concrete floor some nights when the temperature didn't go lower than 86° in my bedroom. Beaty's gift of a flannel nightie was encouraging. She said I would need it in San José, Costa Rica, when I went in September to spend my vacation in language school.

While Jean was home on vacation people had asked her if Trujillo was hotter than Pennsylvania. She wasn't sure until she returned and then she knew her answer should have been "yes!" She had visited my family, and my sister Muriel had shown her the style of prayer covering the Christian women in Africa had worn. Jean had made several and presented them to the women in Trujillo who had become members of our church.

She had missed three deliveries, but when she returned there was one new mother and baby in the maternity ward and a brand new mother and baby in Cristales for her to take care of.

Shortly after Jean's return, and just before I flew away to San José, Costa Rica, for my vacation, Red Brown, a radio technician, came to install transmitters so we could talk by radio to Tocoa twice a day. That radio contact was a comfort to all of us.

A special treat during the flight to San José was a brilliant circular rainbow with a secondary bow outside. After the pressing heat of Trujillo, the climate in San José, at 4,000 feet elevation, was delightful and slightly on the cool side of comfortable with rain every day. I wore a sweater all the time and slept under two or three woolen blankets. The homes were stucco with tile roofs surrounded with luxurious plants. In surrounding villages, many of the homes were built of wood and painted all the colors of the rainbow plus many unconventional combinations. The house where I stayed was very comfortable and was furnished with Oriental rugs and lots of lamps, pictures, books, and even a piano.

I was amazed to discover that bus fare was only three cents a ride. My amazement, however, changed to frustration the first time I stood on a street corner and signaled for a ride. At least 15 buses, which all appeared to have every seat and all standing room filled, passed me before one stopped. Next I discovered that even a seat wasn't a great luxury—no springs or padding!

The streets and avenues of San José were numbered; I was sure I would have no problem finding my way around the city. I soon found out, however, that no one referred to street numbers, but rather gave directions by naming nearby landmarks. When I asked directions to the Honduras consulate, I was told it was in the Maryland apartments, across from the Jara Drugstore. I walked about eight blocks, keeping a sharp lookout for the drugstore. When I finally found it, I discovered it was right on the corner of Fourth Avenue and Third Street.

I enrolled in Phonetics, Grammar, Speaking and Writing Spanish, and Stories and enjoyed being a tourist during my spare time. In a leather factory in Morávia, I purchased a shoulder bag for my niece Mary Lois, whose name I had for the family Christmas exchange.

Virginia Allen, another student, and I took a 25-cent round-fare bus trip to Santa Ana. The ride through the mountains was beautiful. We walked around the little town and entered a Catholic church where a priest was baptizing two babies. I talked with one mother, and she said her baby was 40 days old and was named Margaret María de los Angeles (Mary of the angels). A sign over a collection box said the saint was asking for alms for the repair of her church. I took a picture of the confessional.

Confessional.
Note the oval grill which allows the priest to hear a person's confessions.

♔

Although I had been speaking Spanish for several years, I learned a great deal, especially in the grammar classes. As I listened to some of the first-year students, I wondered what dreadful or hilarious mistakes I had unknowingly made in my early days. One student solemnly stated, "All we like *fishes* have gone astray. We have turned everyone to his own *truck*." Another one while telling the story of John the Baptist said his feet were shod with watermelons, using the word *sandía* instead of *sandália*. A prize should have gone to the girl who went shopping for a salt shaker but asked for a *bachelor*, or maybe to the one who when a workman completed a job at our house asked him if she should *hit* him now or later (*pegar* instead of *pagar*, the word for pay).

One Saturday several of us students hired a station wagon for the

One of the famous painted oxcarts.

35-mile trip to Irazú, an active volcano. Since its elevation was 11,260 feet, the trip from San José at 4,000 feet was uphill all the way there and downhill all the way home. All around were mountains although at times the tops were hidden by clouds. We passed through several towns where we saw the famous painted oxcarts of Costa Rica painted in bright colors with intricate designs. Even their huge solid wheels and tongues were painted. Much of the land was cultivated and I saw oxen pulling plows in several places and potatoes and corn growing in some fields.

We climbed the volcano's one side amidst lush growth of flowers, evergreens, and six-foot bushes with berries, and looked down into a huge crater. Although the sun was hot, we were glad for sweaters and coats when now and then a cloud swept by and enveloped us and the whole mountain top in a damp fog-like mist. We drove down into the crater for a closer look at three deep holes, two of which had sulfur fumes and smoke coming out of them constantly. I guess the

Plowing a field with oxen.

Irazú, an active volcano.

thin air got to me because I was just too breathless to hike down into the one hole for a closer look. I was told that someone had dropped a rock and counted 13 seconds before it struck the greenish lava boiling far below. I felt awed before the great and powerful God who made it all but Who loved me so much that I could stand before Him with confidence and without fear. He gave us a good day, and it didn't rain until we were on the way home. Along the road we passed a little girl about four years old holding a huge leaf over her head as an umbrella.

♔

Doctor Señora Carmen de Torres, a converted nun, spoke in the language school chapel service and several other meetings around San José that I attended. One was in a church with at least 1,000 people in the audience. She always gave an invitation to accept Christ, and at every meeting there were people who made that decision. For myself, her testimony was a challenge to have greater faith in God's power and to be faithful in prayer and in giving out the Word which would convict sinners of the need for a Savior. Carmen was evidence that it worked.

She was born in Venezuela and at the age of 14 a blue-eyed missionary had handed her some tracts and said, "This will show you the way to salvation." Her friends said, "Oh, he is Protestant; let's stone him." The group of girls spit at him and threw stones, but Carmen noticed tears in his eyes and always remembered his words even though a priest had taken the tracts away from her, poured kerosene on them, and burned them immediately. He also got a broom and swept the ground where the missionary had walked, and then washed his hands to cleanse himself of the contact with a Protestant. He told the girls that whenever they saw missionaries they should stone them.

Señora Carmen de Torres

Carmen had married but soon found herself a young widow. She later entered a convent with a required dowry that equaled $3,666 American dollars and left her family very poor. She studied philosophy and science and got her doctorate degree, but all the while she was seeking holiness. Her order required the nuns to wear something on their foreheads that kept their eyes partly shut and something on their jaws to keep them from talking. To eradicate their own will and replace it with the will of the Pope, she had to lie on the floor and allow one hundred nuns and priests to walk over her. She was also required to kiss the feet of priests and make the sign of the cross on the floor with her tongue. None of these things or hours of prayer ever brought her the peace and holiness she sought.

She confessed in her talks that she was vain and proud of her degree and knowledge, and that she was also a liar and a thief because she had sold little scraps of embroidered cloth to the poor, claiming the virgin would forgive their sins if they purchased them. She did have slight Bible knowledge, but the priests told her she would go crazy if she studied the Bible. Finally one day she went out of the convent on some business and saw herself in a mirror—a thing she hadn't done for two years. Something happened inside as she looked at herself, and she decided to leave the convent. She got a teaching job and earned good money, but neither the convent nor her family would have anything to do with her after she left.

One evening she went to look for a student who had failed to show up for class that day. As she walked along, she heard singing, and the words *perfecta paz* (perfect peace) caught her attention. She hoped to slip into the building without anyone noticing, but the missionary was by the door and guided her to a seat near the front of the room. He later told her he had been praying for her for 32 years. Someone offered her a Bible which she coldly refused, but every word of the sermon was like an arrow piercing her heart. She recognized herself as a great sinner. When the invitation was given, she accepted the Lord. Immediately she had the perfect peace she had heard about in the song.

♛

Spanish mission in Orosi.

The last Saturday I was in San José several of us students rented a Taxi Metro, a little French car, and crossed the Continental Divide and went on to the Orosi Valley, also called The Enchanted Valley. A turbulent river rushes through the valley, which is surrounded by beautiful mountains. Most of the cultivated land was on the sides of the mountain, and one place there was a banana grove on an almost vertical slope.

In the town of Orosi is the first Spanish mission of Costa Rica, which is also the oldest church still being used. It dates back to 1565 and has a brick floor, tile roof, and hand hewn beams, pillars, and pulpit. One part is now a museum displaying old books, vestments, images, diaries, and chairs. A picture painted in 1642 by the Spanish painter, Morales, shows Jesus in shallow water with John the Baptist beside him pouring the baptismal water from a shell. We climbed up into the bell tower to take some pictures of the surrounding scenery.

On our way to the nearby valley of Ujarrás we traveled a narrow, twisting road with a view of the Orosi waterfall which tumbled 300 feet down the side of a mountain. The mission there was also built by the Spaniards in the 1560's, but it is in ruins and is now in the middle of a coffee *finca* or farm. The bunches of berries were just beginning to turn red on the six- to ten-feet-high coffee bushes that were shaded by trees planted among them. Harvest would begin in December.

Painting of the baptism of Jesus.

Bell tower at Orosi.

A stop at the Basílica of the Virgin of the Angels ended our outing. It is supposed to be one of the most beautiful churches in Central America. The floor is tiled and all the walls and pillars are painted in mosaic patterns. People approached this shrine on their knees beginning at the outside door and going up the long aisle past the statues, flowers, and candles to the main altar, topped by an angel. In a grotto downstairs was a tiny statue about two inches high of the virgin with the baby.

The virgin was supposed to have appeared August 2, 1624, to a *mulata* peasant girl gathering wood at a spot where a spring bubbled through a circular stone. After the virgin disappeared, the tiny black virgin image was found. Several times the image has been stolen, but it always mysteriously returns. The shrine was built to enclose the spring, and people were filling bottles with the sacred water, which is supposed to have miraculous powers. Display cases on inside walls exhibited little silver or gold arms, legs, heads, eyes, etc., which were consecrated offerings from those who had been cured in those body parts.

All planes out of San José were canceled the day I planned to fly to Honduras, and so once again I was delayed on a return to Trujillo—I arrived Sunday instead of Thursday.

I flew from San José to Tegucigalpa on Thursday and on Friday went on to La Ceiba. I immediately made my reservations to fly to Trujillo on Saturday and ordered a taxi to pick me up in time to get me to the airport, but everything worked to make me miss that plane. The taxi never came to pick me up. When the friends I was staying with took me to the airport, the plane had left—early! Then I discovered my reservation was never recorded, so they didn't know I was coming. I thought of Romans 8:28, *And we know that all things work together for good to them that love God, to them who are the called according to his purpose.*

His purpose apparently was for me to go on the *Suyapa*. The sea was calm, and I shared Captain Cooper's quarters with his aunt, Mrs. Powell.

Jean delivered three babies while I was gone, two in their homes and one in the clinic. The doctor had also delivered one in our clinic, and so Jean had patients to care for.

It was good to be back, not only doing clinic work, but also being a part of the social life of our mission group. Nicolás and Victoria, a Carib couple in Santa Fe, were married Saturday, October 15. They had waited a long time until they had enough money to pay the fee for the civil ceremony and other wedding expenses. Both were new believers soon to be baptized.

Don Emilio, a fine Carib believer, sent us his big cayuco with two

Don Emilio's family.

other believers to paddle it. It was 27 feet long and over three feet wide, hewn from a single mahogany log. James planned to pull it with our motor boat, but the *Caridad* refused to start, so James helped row. Two-thirds of the way to Santa Fe the sea became rough; water came in faster than we could bale it out. Within a minute we knew we had to abandon ship, and everyone got out and walked the last two miles. The men tied a rope to the boat and towed it along while walking on the shore.

James Hess with Nicolás and Victoria Morales.

The civil ceremony had already taken place when we arrived at the home of the bride's mother. Victoria was dressed in a long white dress, white low-heeled shoes, white anklets, and a veil I suspected had been made from a curtain. Nicolás wore the customary white suit and a pair of new work shoes the Hesses had given him as a wedding present.

James, who was to perform the Christian ceremony, had worn an old shirt, faded trousers, and the heavy work shoes he called his clodhoppers. Somewhere along our journey he discovered that the suitcase with his good clothing and Beaty's good dress had been left at home. George offered to stay in his old clothes and lend James his good coat and trousers. Since the men were not the same height, James wore the trousers low on his hips hoping to hide his badly scuffed clodhoppers. During the ceremony I realized his and the groom's shoes were identical in style, but the groom's were shiny new and several sizes larger. They were Nicolás's first pair of shoes.

Jean played her accordion; Jean, Beaty, and I sang several hymns; and James performed the ceremony. We took some pictures and were served cake the bride's uncle had baked, and green coconuts with their refreshing liquid and jellylike flesh. Victoria said they had twelve cakes and Coca-Cola, but the guests served before we arrived had drank all the Coca-Cola. The coconut water was better, anyway.

The sea was still too rough for the boat when it was time to return to Trujillo, so the men walked home. Don Emilio insisted Jean, Beaty, and I stay at his house for the night so we wouldn't get wet. We stayed but thought about the ice cream and cake Grace had planned to make for Ruthie's birthday that evening.

Most of the houses in the village of Santa Fe were made of mud. To build them, palm tree poles were put into the ground about four feet apart with thinner poles about five inches apart between them. Vines were used to tie bamboo poles crosswise about five inches apart over them, and the whole wall was plastered with mud. The finished wall was about six inches thick. Several tree trunks provided support inside the structure, and most houses had at least two rooms with a mud wall between. The roofs were high, steeply pitched, and made of poles tied together with vines and then thatched with palm fronds. The floors, like the walls, were finished off smooth with mud that looked like concrete.

The only nails I saw in Don Emilio's house were those hammered into the walls and used as hooks for kettles, pans, and other house-

Some of the houses in Santa Fe.

hold items. The furnishings were cots and a hammock for the baby in one room, and in the second room a table with a lovely embroidered and starched (with yucca starch) tablecloth, four chairs with embroidered pillows, and a side table. Around the walls hung kettles and dishpans, and the stove was a piece of tin set on four tin cans over a fire on the floor. Everything in the house was neat and clean.

Don Emilio's wife, Doña Marciana, made us dinner. Later a daughter grated six coconuts on a board about 30 inches high and 12 inches wide with sharp stones pounded into it. She covered the grated coconut with water and then strained it through a loosely-woven tray. Doña Marciana mixed the resulting coconut milk with about six pounds of flour, baking powder, and salt in a dough tray a yard across and six inches deep. The dough was shaped into biscuits about the size of a doughnut, and a little stick with a design cut into the one end was pressed into the middle and around the edges before each biscuit was ready to bake.

The fire, built on the kitchen floor out of the coconut hulls, heated a black iron kettle oven. After some biscuits were laid on the bottom and around the sides of the flat kettle, a big circle of tin was placed on top for a lid and burning coals scooped onto it. When she figured the biscuits were baked, Doña Marciana raked the hot coals from the tin

Doña Sergia baking in Trujillo, but Doña Marciana used the same method when she baked in Santa Fe.

with her machete and pushed them back under the oven. As fast as the biscuits were baked, one of the daughters took them out and sold them. Jean, Beaty, and I were each given one of the lovely browned *pan de coco* (biscuits) which were delicious.

A woman came to the house through the rain and asked us to visit a sick woman. Don Emilio went with us with his flashlight. The woman appeared to have shingles, and we promised to send medicine back with Don Emilio when he took us home. My bed for the night was a dark blue denim hammock, and I was surprised at how many positions I was able to assume in it. Since the night was cool, I folded the edges up and over me for cover.

Sometime after midnight Doña Marciana woke us to say the rain had stopped and the sea was calm enough for the trip home. We hadn't undressed, so we were soon ready to leave. The men pushed the boat halfway into the water; after we climbed in, it was pushed out to sea.

The night was clear and cool and from a sky full of stars we easily picked out the Southern cross. The good dresses we had taken along to dress up for the wedding were soon unpacked and put on as coats over our older traveling dresses. The sea was too smooth to justify the nausea I felt, and after my shoulders started aching I realized it was the same old thing again. While in San José I hadn't taken any malaria medicine, and it had apparently caught up with me.

We got home around 3:00 in the morning. As Don Emilio was getting ready to return to Santa Fe, he asked about an unfamiliar noise in our house. James told him the sound was running water—Beaty was taking a shower. Our Honduran friends did everything possible to avoid getting wet after nightfall and they never bathed at night, so after all the care Don Emilio had taken so we women wouldn't get wet from the storm, he must have pondered on our strange behavior. Another of our oddities was that if I ran out in the rain to the garden for something, I usually took off my shoes so they wouldn't get wet, but the Hondurans put shoes on to keep their feet dry.

Some time after we arrived home, it started to rain heavily and I had to move the furniture around in my bedroom to avoid the leaks. The men had painted the roof during the dry season, but it was soon apparent they had not sealed all the holes. A *lake* formed in the bathroom, a *puddle* in the dining room, and a *river* ran across my bedroom floor. The local people rarely discussed the weather, and I realized that even I had started to accept the constant mold the humid weather brought.

I spent the early part of my birthday, October 28, delivering a baby for a girl who had once worked for me. The home was one of the poorest I had seen—a mud hut of two tiny rooms. Two cots completely filled one room, and a cot, small table, folding chair, and a rickety stool filled the other room. The new baby, a man, three women, and three children lived there. A shed was used for their kitchen.

The baby was premature and weighed only a bit over four pounds. No baby clothes were provided, but I was offered a piece of a gray rayon skirt and some rags. I tore one rag for a band, and another for a diaper. The rayon skirt was a poor substitute for a warm blanket for the tiny baby girl they named Elga Emerlisa.

My birthday was celebrated with coconut ice cream and an angel food cake baked by Jean, more ice cream and a chocolate cake baked by Grace, greeting cards, and gifts Mother and my niece Mary Lois Mack had sent with Jean when she returned from vacation.

Nicolás, the bridegroom of a few weeks, and Jorge Flores arrived one morning at 7:30 with Don Emilio's cayuco to take us to baptismal services in Guadalupe and Santa Fe. In spite of the rainy season, the sun blazed down hot on us, and we were glad for the slight breeze which ruffled the water at times. I watched white clouds drift and settle over the rain forest on Calentura's summit, and out at sea, among the rocks we saw fifteen cayucos with fishermen. Several times we surprised schools of flying fish which entertained us as they fled.

Life was also stirring awake along the shore. Three times I saw women standing in the edge of the water scrubbing furniture, and in the inlets of several rivers women were washing their clothes and spreading them on the sand to dry. At one place about fifteen women, each with a tub, were washing clothes. One had piled up the sand and had her tub elevated to make her job easier. She had stripped to her half slip and was washing her own clothing along with her other laundry. At another place a man appeared out of the bushes and dumped a sack of coconuts into his cayuco, and another man walked along the shore towing his cayuco loaded with wood.

At Santa Fe we picked up Don Emilio and went on to Guadalupe where we put on our shoes and went to a home for refreshments. The woman there wanted to be baptized in a river, so we walked to Rio David where she knelt in the water while James baptized her. As we walked to the river, about 150 people joined us to witness the ceremony and hear the songs and Scripture reading.

Back at Santa Fe we gathered in Don Emilio's house for the baptism of Nicolás and Victoria, the bride and groom, and two others. It was a very precious time for us missionaries and the new believers.

Baptism day in Santa Fe.

George gave a message explaining communion, and nine believers and we three missionaries then observed that ordinance as well as the believers' first foot-washing service.

One woman gave her testimony in Moreno, and Nicolás spoke in Spanish stating that he had wanted to accept Christ for eight years, but only after Victoria had suggested it was time they do so had he made the decision. All expressed a desire to live for the Lord always, and the oldest, a sixty-five-year-old woman, expressed joy and a hope the Lord would give her a few more years so she could witness to others. Victoria told me privately that the *old Nicolás* that scolded her all the time was dead, and the *new Nicolás in Christ* was nice to her all the time.

Following that part of the meeting, James asked if they had been praying about someone to act as counselor for their group of believers as he had suggested. Unanimously they chose Don Emilio.

I asked Victoria how she had broken her smoking habit. She said she was sitting at the window of her house one day smoking when Don Emilio walked past and handed her a tract about tobacco use. He asked, "Why do you spend your money for tobacco? With this money you could buy salt and sugar and kerosene. Why don't you take your pipe down to the beach and throw it into the sea?"

She read the tract over and over for a week and then walked down to the beach and threw her pipe into the sea. She never smoked again.

White clouds were brilliant against a beautiful sky as we made our way back to Trujillo. The sun was hot until it sank behind the mountains, and then the sky turned a pale gold and even the water Jorge's paddle dipped up looked like liquid gold for a few seconds before it dropped its riches back into the sea. Jorge whistled hymns as he paddled, and once turned to say, "Next year I want to be baptized."

As we approached Trujillo we saw the clinic perched up on the bluff and the soldiers keeping their constant watch of the coastline from the thick ancient walls of the old fort at the *Cuartel*. Seconds later we heard, "Yoo-hoo," and saw Beaty and Jean in the chicken yard welcoming us home.

♔

Meantime, Grace Hockman was operating a clinic in their meeting house in Tocoa and had some questions she felt I could answer. So Paul Weir, an MAF pilot, picked me up in Trujillo on December 1, and flew me over. As it came in, the plane looked like a little yellow bird, but when we took off down the runway, it reminded me of driving in a car. We lifted off and circled out over the bay before cutting across the lowest part of the mountains. The rain forest was so thick the only place we could see between the trees was where a river cut a path. On the south side of the mountain range there were cultivated patches and an occasional thatch-roofed house.

Tocoa missionary families.
Jessie and Eldon Hamilton with children James, David, Elsie, and Alice.
Maynard and Helen Headings.
Grace and Norman Hockman with Larry and Dicky.

Tocoa mission buildings.

Paul kept me informed of where we were. When I saw the Aguan River, I just had time to wonder where Tocoa was before Paul pointed it out, and I saw the mission buildings and the landing strip the missionaries worked hard to keep clear of vegetation. Several people were scattered around the edges of the field, having just chased the

A soldier, pilot Paul Weir, and George Miller.

cows off so we could land. A trip that took anywhere from four to ten hours driving, depending on weather and road conditions, and almost a day on horseback had taken 15 minutes' flying time.

Before I even got to the house, a woman came to ask Grace and me to go to see her sick mother. We did, slopping and slipping through the mud that was everywhere in Tocoa. We held clinic hours both morning and afternoon the next day. In between patients I mixed up double recipes of cough syrup and ferrous sulfate syrup. Just as I was showing Grace how I prepared obstetric packs, we were called to a difficult delivery case. The mother had delivered one twin with the help of the local midwife the evening before, but the second baby was not coming normally. Finally it came in breech position, but it had apparently been dead for some time. The mother and the first twin, named *Dora Emperatriz* (Empress), appeared to be all right.

I thoroughly enjoyed visiting the missionary families and as always found the children entertaining. Hockmans' little son informed me that when he got to heaven he was going to get the moon and play ball with it. One evening we all got together to make fudge. We thought we were doing fine according to the candy thermometer, but we beat and beat and beat before giving up and putting the mixture in pans in the freezer. Before going home, we served everyone fudge with teaspoons. In spite of heavy rains and terrible mud, nearly 60 persons attended church services on Sunday.

The week I was there, the man cutting the Hamiltons' yard with his machete killed three deadly coral snakes, one a brilliant coral about two feet long, and he also found a dead Barba Amarilla. The cook saw a Barba Amarilla in the wood pile outside the kitchen door, and another coral was found in a pile of lumber. Both of those were killed,

Three of the deadly coral snakes.

but we heard that a woman in Siguatepeque had been bitten by a Barba Amarilla and lived only a few days. Once more the Lord kept us safe.

My time in Tocoa included a case that made me feel it was the main reason I was there. A little girl about three years old was brought to the clinic more dead than alive. She had been given worm medicine while already sick with malaria and had also had a bad fall and was having chest pains. Although I knew how much it hurt, I gave her an injection of a half dose of quinine one day, and when I discovered she was still vomiting and had diarrhea the next day, I gave her the other half. We had prayer for her and asked God to spare her life.

Later in the day someone came to tell me the girl was vomiting blood. After I entered the house, she sprang up wild-eyed in her bed and vomited blood again. I gave her crushed calcium gluconate, and in the morning she was better. I told the family to feed her some liver and I continued giving penicillin. I sympathized with her as she began to take nourishment, because I remembered the gas pains and discomfort I had experienced when I started eating after my own illness.

The home was like others in the village—mud house, mud floor, and thatched roof. The room with the girl's cot in was half filled with ears of corn in the husk.

Fruit and vegetables were more plentiful in Tocoa, and I was given some as gifts. I also made some purchases before my return to Trujillo. The family of the girl who had been so sick gave me two pumpkins, three papayas, and a bunch of flowers. The father, in gratitude for my services, sold me a stem of about 100 bananas for 25¢. The normal price would have been 37¢ or 38¢. I also bought a bunch of plantains at a cent each, 15 eggs, ten pounds of cornmeal, and five dozen oranges. All this food cost a total of $1.16. Because one of the Trujillo women who had been cooking for Grace Hockman was returning on the plane with me, I had to leave some of the bananas behind. The plane, in addition to the pilot, could carry only 425 pounds of passengers and cargo.

Stem of bananas before being cut.

♔

We landed in Trujillo 15 minutes after

lifting off from the little Tocoa flying field Eldon had cleared the year before when Jessie had to be air lifted out to the hospital. I was glad to help Grace, but it was good to be home for the next Sunday service on the beach at Cristales. Thirty people came for Jean's lesson from Isaiah 53. I played Jean's accordion. I had been teaching myself to play, and it was the first time I felt confident enough to play in public.

On the way home from Cristales, Flavia, the 16-year-old girl who helped us with our housework, told me people made fun of her for going with us Evangelicals. "Well," she asked them, "which would you rather see, me going with them or out in the streets with a man?" In six months Flavia never missed one of our Cristales beach meetings, and I believed she was sincere in her desire to love the Lord more fully.

The man we hired to run our boat after James left on furlough was different. He boasted of being baptized in 1937 in Jamaica, British West Indies, and that it was the happiest day of his life, and that he had once been Catholic, but now knew better. He constantly went around saying, "Praise the Lord," but his life didn't match his words. He had no testimony about any current experience with the Lord and was living with a woman who was not his wife.

As the year drew to an end, Jean and I once more had to remind each other that in spite of green plants, warm breezes, and sunny days, Christmas was coming up on the calendar. Jean was cook for Christmas week, and she baked five kinds of cookies to share with the mail boys, the garbage man, and friends and neighbors. We too received plates of tamales and other treats, and even a piece of pork from a friend who butchered a pig.

On Christmas Eve about 15 of us went caroling. One of the group was a believer who had fallen back into a life of sin. He expressed dissatisfaction with his current style of life but wasn't to the point of repentance. He had already been partaking of liquid spirits before he joined us, but I believe the Lord led him to go with us. When we prepared to sing outside the prison, he boldly led us in through the open door, out into the courtyard with its high stone wall topped with broken glass, and into another part of the building where there were two rooms with barred doors where the prisoners were locked in. We sang in a large hall between the two rooms. We also had the children give the parts they had prepared for the Christmas day Sunday School program.

After our caroling George received a letter from one of the prisoners giving us very effusive praise and signing himself

Gumercindo Diaz F., a humble prisoner. He had accepted the Lord some time before and was taking a Bible correspondence course.

We had spent several weeks practicing for the Sunday School program, and the girls in my class did well when they gave Luke 2:1-20 as a choral reading. Others sang and also gave readings, and everyone joined in carols. We decorated the church with poinsettias from our patio and used lamps on the window sills and candles on the pulpit to light the building. When the program was over, one woman said she could have listened for another hour.

By the time I received all my Christmas mail sometime in January, I had over 100 cards from back home. Never before had cards meant so much to me. In fact, they pleased me more than gifts, because by the time I would have paid the custom charges on gifts, they would have cost me as much as if I had bought them myself. By trial and error, I had gradually found out the best ways to have things sent. Books and letters had no charge, but unless gifts were marked "unsolicited gifts," I had to pay full value in custom charges the same as if I had ordered an item from a mail-order catalog.

I valued each gift I received from the missionaries and local people, but when I thought of the unspeakable gift of my Lord as compared to my giving of myself and my possessions, I was ashamed. As I allowed the Lord to search my heart, I saw my littleness, my selfishness, and the times I showed a lack of love. I knew I had been impatient at times with the babes in Christ, and unloving when they needed tender loving care. I prayed that my actions in those times of selfishness had not hindered anyone in his Christian walk and that God would use me for His glory to bring others to Him.

In my illness three years earlier, I had thought I would always live in an awareness of His love, but I discovered I forgot so often and lived according to my own desires. Only in Christ could I find forgiveness. His great gift to me was the forgiveness He gave as soon as I went to Him in repentance.

1956

The New Year began with a Watch Night service at Millers followed by a busy day in the Lord's work. Seven *señoritas* and four young men were in my Sunday School class in the morning. Only six persons attended the afternoon service on the beach at Cristales, where I played the accordion and Jean gave a flannelgraph-illustrated message. Most of the local men were in a political rally for the President of Honduras that day.

My Sunday School class.

At four in the afternoon we were invited to a service at the jail. Each year Don Salvador Hode had held a New Year's Day service at the jail and distributed treats to all the

Don Salvador, America (Meca), and Doña Florinda Hode.

Trujillo jail. Note broken glass on top of wall.

prisoners. His widow, Doña Florinda, and his daughter, America (Meca), decided to continue the practice after his death and invited George to give a simple message on forgiveness of sins. About 25 persons from our church went along; Jean played her accordion and we all joined in the singing. Meca asked me to help her hand out the treats, which were tamales, rolls, coffee, and a little pack of peanuts. In addition to the prisoners and our church group, we had food for other visitors and the guards.

The following day George received a letter of thanks from one of the prisoners, addressed to *Mr. Miller, pastór del Evangelio de esta Ciudad* which means: Mr. Miller, Pastor of the Gospel of this City.

Sunday evening the electric plant broke down, and it was a month before service resumed. When we went to evening services, a stranger might have thought we were having a religious procession. George walked along with a gasoline lantern; Grace, Jean, and I followed with our Aladdin lanterns all burning brightly. Besides lamps, the church was decorated with poinsettias from our patio.

Our patio was beautiful that year with a double pink hibiscus, a bright rose-colored single hibiscus, light pink oleanders, roses, purple bougainvillea, and poinsettias that reached the roof. The *civil* (Seville) orange tree produced sour oranges, good only for marmalade, sweetened drink, and flavor for the ferrous sulphate syrup we made for the clinic. The grapefruit tree, too, was a success—even the woodpeckers that lived down the hill in a palm tree without a top visited our patio to peck holes in the fruit. Although Mother wrote about icy roads and putting chains on the car, I suggested she tuck a few tomato seeds into her next letter. When they came, I planted them with cornmeal, which I hoped would attract the ants and keep them from eating the seeds before they sprouted.

Unusually cold weather arrived with the new year and lasted about two weeks. Temperatures dropped to 62° at night and didn't get above

Lorraine Roth

70° in the daytime. I slept under my quilt folded double but knew that many people had no blankets or extra clothing to keep themselves warm. The wind roared and drove the sea, even in Trujillo Bay, into white caps. The beautiful bougainvillea was torn down but not broken, so Jean, Lorraine Roth (a teacher from Canada who had been sent to open a Christian school), and I braved the wind to tie it back on the arbor.

Because we knew the owners and had used it at various times, we felt we had suffered a personal loss when we heard that the *Carlton P.* had sunk between Trujillo and La Ceiba. A small boat rescued the crew and passengers, but all the cargo was lost. It had just had a new $7,000 motor installed. The captain of the *Suyapa* took his boat up the coast and on to Nicaragua to get away from the bad weather. It reminded me of Columbus. The story is told that on his fourth voyage he was caught in a storm and fled along the coast until he found shelter in Trujillo Bay, naming it *Cabo Gracias a Dios*. In English this means Cape Thanks to God. He also gave Honduras its name—depths. -*Qué honduras,*- he said. "What depths!"

In January we held our first Bible School in Trujillo, with an average attendance of 95. George had 22 in his sixth grade class, I had 21 in fourth, Jean 19 in second, Lorraine 23 in first, and Grace 21 in kindergarten. The missionaries in Tocoa told us on our radio that they had 96 pupils in their Bible School.

Bible School in Trujillo.

The evening before Bible School started we had a delivery at the clinic, and that mother stayed with us for five days. I was called from my class one afternoon to go to the home of two of our students to deliver another baby. That same evening a woman came to the clinic and had her first child the following morning.

**The Miller family.
Ruthie, Miriam, J. Mark, George, Grace with baby Rachel, and two helpers.**

Just when Ruthie Miller was to leave for school in Siguatepeque the MAF plane was crippled when a wave caught and tipped it as Paul Weir was landing on a beach at Cocobilo. Instead of ferrying missionary children to school, Paul and Don Ackerman showed up in Trujillo with the damaged wings one morning on their way to La Ceiba for repairs.

Dr. Rivera left in mid-February for a three-year course in x-ray at Boston City Hospital. He was replaced with two student doctors—Wolfgang Auerbach for Trujillo, the other man for outlying areas.

♔

The morning after I met the new doctor I packed my folding cot, mosquito bar, clothing, and teaching supplies, and, with a blackboard borrowed from the church, was ready when Don Emilio Gonzalez's cayuco arrived at six to take me to Santa Fe for two weeks of Bible School. I set up my cot in the one room of the Gonzalez home between the hammocks of the mother and a daughter. Two other daughters had cots in the other small room, and Don Emilio had his hammock in the kitchen. The hammocks were suspended from hooks in the walls, but tied into knots during the day to be up out of the way.

The floors of the house were hard-packed ground, which was swept twice a day with a bunch of palm fronds tied into a bundle for a handleless broom. Each time, the floor was sprinkled with a mixture of water and creolin.

The kitchen was the typical clay or mud building with double thickness walls of tree trunks and poles plastered together with mud. On the rafters under the high pitched thatched roof, a piece of zinc served as a cupboard for sugar and other perishables. The boat sail was stored there and the rafters were also used as a place to cure new lumber.

A fish was drying on a forked stick by the kitchen stove, which was a small wooden frame elevated on posts with a strip of metal across the top. A hen and her chicks were behind the post at one end of the stove, and another hen was setting a clutch of eggs behind the post at the other end. The dishes were on a wooden stand, but the kettles, mostly iron, were on the floor under it. That end of the kitchen had some low benches, and two wooden rice mills with their pestles hung from the rafters. They were hollowed-out sections of logs a couple feet long. The rice was hulled by stumping it with a wooden pestle. A double door was at one end of the kitchen, and at the opposite end, a door made of thatch tied to bamboo and secured with a rope slung over the rafters.

A sewing machine and two wooden tables were at one end of the kitchen. The larger table where we ate our meals had a neatly ironed tablecloth, and the smaller one held a tin tub with a wooden lid containing drinking water which was brought from the river about a mile away. Solita, the pup, was always under and around the table when we ate, ready for any bones or pieces of food offered to her.

Solita also went with Don Emilio each morning to his *monte* (garden) in the mountain where he raised bananas, plantains, and corn. Don Emilio also had a place where he raised rice for his family. Any surplus was sold for cash to buy things like salt and sugar. While I was in Santa Fe he spent part of each day working on a tree trunk to make a cover for his boat.

His wife and daughters worked hard in their own garden plots using hoes with thick, four-foot handles. Each one had perhaps an acre where they were raising yucca in all stages of maturity.

The walls of the main house were a single thickness of wood, and with its tin roof it got very hot when the sun shone. At night the wind came through cracks and holes, and I slept in all my clothes plus a pajama top and sweater. My sheet was folded to four thicknesses and my bedspread double, and I was still cold and spent part of each night sleeping and part of it wishing for morning and the warming comfort of the hot sun. The others, sleeping in their deep denim hammocks, didn't seem to mind the cold.

I had expected the food would be mostly rice and fish, which we did have, but the women made an amazing variety of good soups from beans and yucca, and even tomato soup made with coconut milk. They also served boiled green bananas, a variety of other native dishes, eggs, and tortillas. I told them I could drink only boiled water, so they always made tea for me. The river provided water for drinking, cooking, and to wash the dishes, as well as for bathing and washing clothes.

The women worked hard in their gardens and in preparing food. To make casave, their bread, Eloina, one of the daughters, dug up about a half bushel of yucca. She peeled and washed it and then grated it on a board about four feet tall by 18 inches wide that had sharp stones hammered into it. Since the board stood in a pan on the floor, Eloina got a lot of bending exercise. Women in groups sang or chanted to the rhythm of their grating.

After the yucca was grated, Eloina packed it into a six-foot-long tube about four inches in diameter called a *culebra* (snake). The tube was diagonally woven of reeds so that when suspended from the rafters and weighted at the bottom with small rocks, it stretched and squeezed the liquid from the yucca. The dried yucca was rubbed through a sieve to make a rather coarse flour. The next morning a fire was built on the floor beside the stove and Eloina baked the casave on a 30-inch round piece of iron. The iron was placed on three spikes driven into the floor, and when it was hot, she put a handful of flour on it and smoothed it out with her hand. More layers of flour were added and smoothed out until it was about as thick as a cracker. When the bottom was nicely browned, the cake was turned and browned on the other side. The finishing touch was to trim the edges and cut the rather tough cake into quarters. We ate some, and Eloina sold some to neighbors.

For baths the girls and I went up the mountain side to a beautiful spot in the forest along the river with a pool big enough to take a little swim, although I enjoyed swimming in the ocean better. I knew the water had been the bath water for many people and animals up river and I never felt quite clean. It was upstream from where they got the drinking water and when I mentioned this they said, "Yes, because up here there are bushes around and where we get the drinking water is closer to home and not so far to carry it,"—very logical! The other part of the bathroom was the beach. As we walked through the forest on our way to the bathing place we saw many birds including hawks and large birds with short tails that looked like handles. Their bodies were about ten inches long and their tails four or five inches. The heads were black with some white feathers, their backs and breasts were chestnut colored, and the rumps were green. They had a gentle song and softly said, "Hoo-hoo, hoo-hoo."

On certain days Eloina filled the wash tub with the family clothes and a wooden washboard, put it on her head, and went to the river to

Wash day at the Rio David.

do the laundry. I took my clothes down a little later and found her standing in the river in the sun, scrubbing away. The clothes were rinsed in the running river water and spread beside the river to dry.

Other women were also washing clothes and children. I watched as one little boy was scrubbed from head to toe, screaming all the while because of the cold water.

The children's Bible School class started before seven in the morning so they could go to regular school at eight o'clock. They were lovable and enjoyed hearing Bible stories—stories they had never heard before. We built the town of Nazareth in Gonzalezes' wash tub with a landscape of sand finished off with grass and flowers the children brought. The houses, a school, and a synagogue were constructed out of paper. We started with 19 students and ended with 23.

The young ladies came in the afternoon, but attendance was scattered because of work in their gardens and doing laundry in the river. I prayed much over these women and rejoiced to see the intent interest of one who sat quietly and drank in every word. She often attended the adult class in the evening also.

The adult class in the evening was the largest and most regularly attended. Attendance varied from 20 to 26, but for some reason a few women didn't want their names on the enrollment sheet.

We were studying the teachings of Jesus, and we could feel the Holy Spirit's presence.

The Holy Spirit was working, too, with two believers who were estranged. Each refused to go to the other's house, which was an insult.

Santa Fe believers.

This had been going on for some weeks; it was a great concern to all of us in the mission. Many, including my parents and our home churches, were praying. I was hoping I could help to get it settled while I was in Santa Fe and was much in prayer before I went and while I was there.

I visited both men separately, and after a lot of talking and counseling, both agreed to meet with the rest of the believers in the home of Jorge, a trusted brother in the church. By evening, however, the one man's anger returned; he said he was not going to the meeting the next day.

I was greatly burdened. A weight, almost an agony, was on me. I couldn't eat, and I felt I had to get alone to pray. I went down along the beach and poured out my heart to God. The question heavy on my heart was, *Would this thing come out right?*

The following day we met in Jorge's house, and both men were there. Before long the one who had been so angry the day before lashed out, and in spite of Jorge's good peacemaker efforts, that man walked out of the meeting. The rest of us discussed the situation, and I admired the love and the absence of anger as Jorge gave some good advice. The second man in the conflict was quiet but not repentant.

After supper I walked, heavyhearted, down the path to pray. The urgency was not on me like the night before, but my heart was very sad. The situation was physically taxing, but at the same time there was joy in knowing the Lord had used me. Although reconciliation was not effected at our meeting, a sweet assurance came as I walked the dusty path and contemplated the palms against the still-light sky in the west. I told the Lord I didn't mind the mosquitoes, the cold of the night, the heat of the day, the food, or lack of conveniences as long as He was using me.

At the close of the two weeks I figured our average attendance for the Bible School was 56. Many of the people asked how soon I could return for another school. "No one ever came and taught us such things before," they said. Though they worked hard for their food and were often hungry, the people showered me with gifts: four eggs; a hand of small, very good bananas; a pan of sweet potatoes; a piece of casave; and more.

♔

And I did enjoy the conveniences of home when I returned to Trujillo. To take a bath in a bathroom and feel really clean was a luxury. Milk and even water tasted wonderful, and fresh fruit was deliciously refreshing.

Jean had been busy with several deliveries while I was gone—one a stillborn after a difficult birth. He was delivered with a fractured skull. Dr. Auerbach brought in a Paya Indian woman from Jerico and said he would return for the delivery. The woman couldn't speak Spanish which made communication difficult, but didn't hinder the arrival of the baby that was born before the doctor returned. Relatives

The Paya baby ready to start home.

were to bring a horse for her when she was discharged, but they came without a horse, so she walked off toward home carrying her child.

Jean had a letter from her parents while I was gone stating they were planning a visit. I wrote to my parents and suggested that if they ever wanted to come to visit me and see the mission work firsthand, this was an opportunity to come with someone younger who could help them in their travels. When I wrote, "This could be the chance of a lifetime," little did I realize how true it would turn out to be.

Letters continued back and forth, and soon I began to believe that a visit would really become a reality. I passed on all kinds of advice in my letters and suggested that they get birth certificates so they could apply for passports. I also warned Mother not to bring her fountain pen because the air pressure while flying would probably force the ink out of the cartridge and make things a mess.

I started ordering things from mail-order catalogs and having them sent to Mother for her to bring. The list started with typewriter ribbons, onion skin paper, wax to polish my homemade desk, and pressure cooker escape valves to replace the one that was blown out when the cooker overheated on the wood stove. I added an order from a drug company for scissors, bandages, catheters, and hemostats for our clinic and Grace Hockman's clinic in Tocoa. Diapers for the clinic would also be appreciated if a church group wanted to send something, and a jar or two of peanut butter would be most welcome.

The price of peanut butter in the stores was beyond our limited budgets, and it seemed all of us got hungry for it. I tried to make some, but it didn't taste right. In 1960 when Dorothy Showalter returned from a trip to La Ceiba with several pounds of peanuts, she had better success. After roasting them she ground them and added some cooking oil. The results were wonderful.

The Catholics held Good Friday celebrations, and most of the town folks as well as many from the surrounding areas joined the processions carrying the sacred images and accompanying little girl angels. It didn't rain that day, so I wondered where the priests would get the holy water that was handed out each year. I got my answer later in the day as I walked past the Catholic church after visiting a patient. First I noticed a boy carrying a white garment and a tapestry scarf to a priest in black robes. The priest slipped on the garment, hung the scarf around his neck, and got out his black book. About a hundred Carib children were gathered in front of the church with cans, kettles, and bottles for their holy water. That year, at least, the priest blessed the water that came out of a hose attached to a faucet.

I watched the processions pass our house and heard the music from the dance in the hotel across the street. Our cook arrived in the morning dressed in a beautiful blue nylon dress so she wouldn't have to go home to dress up for the dance that evening. We missionaries had communion services for baptized believers that afternoon.

Saturday evening we had about 30 high-school-age young people in for a social. Prizes were awarded for the most beautifully decorated Easter egg, and to the winners of various games. Jean played her accordion as we sang hymns and choruses, and then Cuta, a Plymouth Brethren believer, had a message about the rich young ruler.

Our Easter service was well attended, and one of the believers gave a Spirit-directed message in Spanish. He pointed out that although people fear the atomic bomb, they don't fear the judgment of God, which is far more certain to occur.

I wrote to Mother that our Easter *ham* that year was a baked fish, and not too good a one at that. We also had rice and beans and patastillas, a vegetable somewhat like a squash but almost flavorless. In the midst of typing that letter, I heard something fall with a thud on the desk beside me. I figured it was a piece of plaster from the ceiling, but when I glanced over, nothing was there. I checked over the edge and looked down on one of those four-inch, monkey-faced, hairy-legged spiders—a tarantula. I called Jean and Lorraine to help me pull out the heavy mahogany desk so I could kill the spider and add it to my specimen bottle. I recalled it was Easter the year before that I was stung by a scorpion. Already that week I had killed two scorpions.

I was grieved in my spirit when a Catholic bishop visited the church across the plaza from our house and preached over the loudspeakers against the *fanaticos* that come with their medicines and false teachings. He preached about the future's holding a dark problem and admonished his people to be good Catholics and go to their priests, who could forgive their sins. George's message that same evening was about the One who *can* forgive sins.

I guess some of the mosquitoes in Santa Fe had gotten to me even though I had used my netting to sleep and wrapped my legs with my bedspread during the evening adult classes, because I wasn't home long until I spent a day in bed with malaria and dosed myself with Aralen and Camoquin. Dr. Auerbach was on vacation, and Jean and I had a lot of malaria patients.

I considered the natives blessed to be immune to the red bugs, sand flies, and ticks that made my trip to Tarros so memorable. Flavia, the girl who helped in our house at that time was from Tarros. She had told us her father wanted us to come to his village and have clinic sometime. Jean had gone twice for clinic, and George had held a short service each time.

My first trip was in April with George, J. Mark, Julian, and Flavia. The village was 30 miles from Trujillo by road but not nearly so far "as the crow flies." The dense jungle, however, made us use the road. For the first 25 miles we used the only road that headed in that general direction—the same road we used to go to Tocoa, then turned onto a road called the Camino Real. It was very dense jungle, and there were ruts in the road so deep it looked as though a bushel basket could be hidden in them. We bumped and bounced along with tree branches and vines reaching out to scrape both sides of the truck, while overhead the branches met, giving the illusion of a long green tunnel. Just as we were about to drive onto a bridge, a passenger we were taking to Tarros banged on the back window and informed George that the bridge was not safe. He slowly made a detour through the woods and found a place to ford the stream.

All three messages Flavia had sent telling the day we would come had gone astray. Nobody was prepared for our visit and quite upset they couldn't provide the usual hospitality. Flavia's father was away

Flavia's sister preparing *café* on her *fogón* (clay stove).

working in his fields, but his cook gave each of us a peeled orange. One of Flavia's sisters served us black coffee with sugar, and another one served us hot milk with sugar and apologized for not having any food prepared for a meal. She said if we could wait she would fix an *iguana* (lizard) for dinner. We regretted we couldn't wait that long because we were to meet the Hamiltons at the Aguan River and take them back to Trujillo with us.

I had no patients since nobody knew we were coming, but about 40 school children and over a dozen adults attended the little service we held. There was great interest in the flannelgraph story I told of the resurrection and in Julian's testimony. Julian was known in the village because he had fathered a child to one of Flavia's sisters. The child and Flavia's mother had been killed in a jeep accident the year before.

The Hamiltons brought us welcome gifts from Tocoa of plantains, beans, cabbage, and tomatoes and stayed over night with us. Next day they went to San Pedro Sula to get their passports and then on to vacation in Siguatepeque.

When I saw them off, I had no idea I would soon be joining them. A few days after they left, however, I felt the effects of malaria again—just the ordinary kind, but it was the sixth time in six months with each time worse than the last. The MAF plane was taking an accident victim to La Ceiba and returning empty to Siguatepeque, and although we were anticipating three deliveries, Jean insisted I go to the mission hospital in Siguatepeque for a checkup. I was taking Camoquin but figured it was only keeping the malaria at bay most of the time, so I submitted to Jean's advice.

Dr. McKinney put me on Daraprim for ten weeks to kill the organisms that stay in the tissues. I noticed slow but steady improvement and continued to take Camoquin about every twelve days. I thought of the poor people in Santa Fe who suffered from chronic malaria and couldn't afford proper medication.

After a short time of bed rest, I moved to a guest room and enjoyed the cool, pine-scented mountain breezes and long visits with Jessie Hamilton. The Millers had sent a package and a letter for Ruthie, and I was invited to have supper at the school with her one evening.

The day before I returned from Siguatepeque the governor's wife had a son in our clinic, and another woman came in a few days later. So we had patients to feed and care for again.

Jean with the governor, Don Moisés Lopez, and his wife, Doña María Ester, as they leave the clinic with the baby.

An interesting break from our regular work was a visit to an 84-foot-long yacht anchored in the bay about a mile out from Trujillo. It was owned by a German millionaire and had been built in Norfolk, Virginia, at a cost of two and a quarter million dollars. The owner was not aboard, but the Captain sent an invitation to the missionaries, the governor and his wife, and several others to visit. An inboard motor launch picked us up one morning and took us out. We climbed up a rope ladder to be greeted by the Captain and crew of 18 men and were given a royal tour. The yacht had luxuries some of us had seldom seen and that were certainly never seen in Trujillo—beautiful bedrooms, dining room, living room, bar, kitchen, pantry, and a laundry with all the equipment normally found in a well-furnished home. We were entertained on deck for an hour or so and served ice-cold drinks—root beer or beer. Trujillo looked like a lovely picture from the deck, and before long we were taken back across the bay.

One morning our cook came and said that the pipe to the stove had fallen out of the chimney. On closer inspection we discovered the area where the pipe elbow came out of the stove had rusted through and that the stove itself had rust holes eaten through because of the salt in the air. Since many Hondurans had their kitchens in a separate shelter, our cook didn't mind going over to use Hesses' stove.

Ten days later we were back to normal. A man from Cristales

came with his son and cemented in a new piece of metal, cleaned the whole stove, put up new pipe, and cemented a crack in the oven. He was even able to rivet together one of the stove lids that had split into two pieces.

It wasn't only stoves that rusted. The screens at our windows also deteriorated in the salt air and needed to be replaced. I had suggested patching them, but George said if one place gave out it wouldn't be long until more holes appeared.

In May, as I was reading in my Bible about Jesus sending out 70 of his followers as witnesses, I felt Him prompting me to return to Santa Fe. I did, for three days, and held flannelgraph-illustrated meetings in the evenings, and during the day I tried to get at least a portion of Scripture into each home. Because of the haphazard layout of the village, I wasn't sure if I visited every home or if I might have been in some twice. Not everyone could read, so where there was little interest or where the people were too poor to afford a Bible, I handed out penny Scripture Gift Mission Gospels free. One old lady was sucking on a peppermint and said she couldn't afford a Gospel because she had spent her last penny for the candy. At the end of my stay I had actually taken in more money from patients for medicine I had taken along than I had for sale of Scriptures.

The two village schools were crowded and had only a few benches and no desks. I noticed many children took their own little stools with them to school, carrying them on their heads. The teacher of the older students was one of the few who purchased a Bible. Heriberta, who had worked in our clinic during Tilda's absence, was teaching 40 of the younger children.

That May and June we had plenty of rain and we didn't have to water the garden; the tomatoes grew into a wilderness of vines with fruit that had a watered-down taste. The days were hot and heavy with temperatures that climbed into the high 90's. Afternoon showers almost every day dropped it back into the low 80's. One afternoon it rained so hard it came in under my bedroom door, across to and through my closet, and on under the partition into Hesses' bedroom. The following day another heavy rain started the water flowing in under my door, but I armed myself with mop and bucket and mopped as fast as I could. I didn't dare open the top half of the door during the storm so I worked in semidarkness and filled almost two buckets before the flood abated. That was only once of many times I rushed into battle with bucket and mop.

Jean, with Lorraine for company, went to Tocoa to take charge of Grace Hockman's clinic for six weeks while the Hockmans went on vacation. We were especially glad for the radio which kept us in contact twice a day. Jean said the clinic was very nice and reported as high as 24 patients one day, including a few suturing cases.

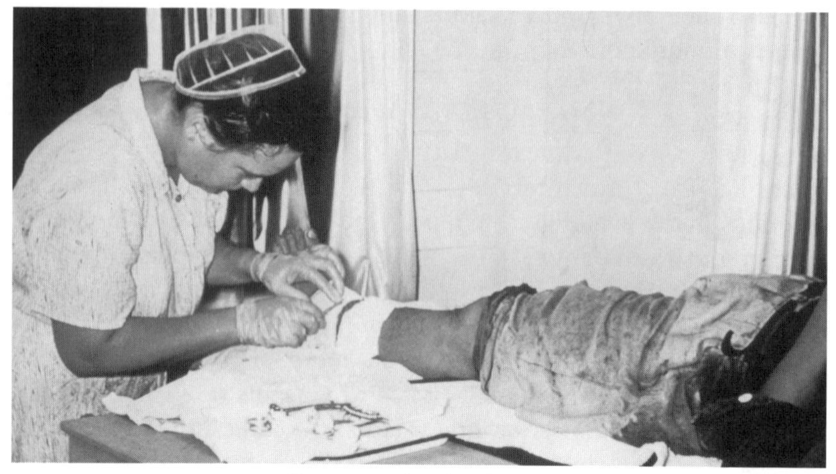

Jean suturing in Tocoa.

I forgot to mail a Father's Day card in June but wrote in a letter, *"Father, let me tell you that I do appreciate what a good father you have been and all you have done for me. May God bless your declining days with much joy as you yield yourself to follow His will."*

I couldn't forget John the Baptist's birthday, however. The celebrations began early in the morning of June 24, and the band played *Happy Birthday* eight times without stopping.

Before clinic the next morning, I hurried to the home of an 82-year-old woman from one of the wealthiest families in town. I had been giving her injections each day, and she never failed to send a gift home with me—a bag of fresh rolls, some cookies, or a cupcake. She was friendly and courteous but wanted nothing to do with the Gospel message. I reminded myself that I was ready to defend my faith and the way I had been taught since childhood. She was also being faithful to the teachings she had received, but how I wished she could be set free from the bondage of traditions into trust in my Jesus.

A woman from another important Trujillo family met me on the road one day. She owned a Bible and had been reading it. Although somewhat more open-minded about the teaching at the mission church, she was not ready to attend. When we met she said, "Pray for us who don't go, perhaps we are in the wrong way and don't realize it."

The beginning of July brought a radiogram stating that my parents and the Garbers were having difficulty getting visas to enter Honduras. News in *Time* magazine and on the radio told of student uprisings in Guatemala City and other places. In Tegucigalpa students had littered the streets with tacks during a protest—a hazard to bare feet. I told Mother, "These countries are HOT in more ways than one."

But the greatly-anticipated visit of Father and Mother and Jean's parents finally began on July 19, after a five-day wait for visas. In fact, I wasn't sure they would get visas and didn't know they had continued on their way until we got a radio message from Easy Harold that they had been in San Pedro the day before and were ready to come on to Trujillo. I believe the wait was God-directed because the MAF plane which brought them to Trujillo from San Pedro had hit a dog somewhere on a runway and was being repaired during those five days.

It was an exciting time for all of us. The governor and his wife and a number of other people came to welcome our guests. Some brought flowers, one person brought a cake, and one woman presented us with a highly-spiced roasted chicken.

Our parents arriving in Trujillo.
I am on the left by my father, Jean is between her parents, and my mother is on the right.

Almost immediately Clarence Garber and Father found things to do around the house. Clarence fixed several doors that were so loose the wind sometimes blew them open, and Father worked on wobbly and broken chairs. Together they changed washers on leaky spigots and did many things we had *just-put-up-with* because we were too busy with our work to *get-around-to-it*.

Jean, Verna Taylor, Dora, Edgar Taylor, and Clarence Garber. Vera Garber took this picture in the dining room of our house. Maruquita, our cook, is standing by the refrigerator.

Jean buying oranges from a woman who carried them to our door in a pan on her head.

Our parents were introduced to a new method of grocery shopping.

On Wednesday evening Mother spoke at the English Bible Study about "Why I became a Christian." Mrs. Garber gave a testimony on "Why I remained a Christian," and Father spoke on "How to have victory in the Christian life." Father had sat on the porch most of the afternoon studying his Bible, and his message was about faith and unbelief and how the Israelites failed to enter the promised land, not because of disobedience but because of unbelief.

Jean and I took turns working in the clinic so that each day one of us could go with our parents. They accompanied Jean on a trip to Tarros, and then we planned a trip to Santa Fe for July 26. The Garbers, Father and Mother, George, J. Mark, Mr. Colon the captain, and I left Trujillo in the *Caridad* on a beautiful, calm sea and ate our breakfast of oranges and honey-cinnamon buns as we went along. After passing the mouth of the Mojaguay, we soon saw the smoke of Santa Fe cooking fires ahead of us.

Without warning the boat tipped to the left and then turned completely over. I found myself under the capsized boat and only one thought entered my mind, "This is serious!" It seemed to take me a long time to swim to the surface and then the boat righted itself and I saw Mother was in it. Before I had time to rejoice that she was safe, the boat overturned once more, but again Mother managed to remain with it and soon climbed inside.

Mrs. Garber was the farthest away; I called to her to stay on her back. Father was on the opposite side of the boat from me swimming, but then he called out for help. I grabbed two life-preservers and swam to him, but just as I reached him he stopped struggling and his head went under the water. I got him to the boat and George and I, with Mother inside, managed to get him out of the water.

There was so much water in the boat we couldn't lay him face down, but I tried to give him artificial respiration. The paddles had stayed with the boat and Mr. Colon was in it paddling while George bailed. Mr. Garber and J. Mark clung to the sides of the boat as we headed for shore. Just when Mrs. Garber, who had stayed floating on her back, was about exhausted, a Carib man on the beach grabbed a cayuco which was there and rescued her and took her to shore.

When we reached the shore, we carried Father up on dry sand and started artificial respiration. We got a lot of water out of his lungs, but there was no other response to our efforts although we kept it up for almost an hour.

Mrs. Garber was totally exhausted and lay down on the sand. Mother was sick from the gasoline she had swallowed in the water but sat on the shore and cried aloud to God that His will be done. By the time the *Comandante* from Santa Fe arrived, we realized our efforts to save Father's life were to no avail. Mother's prayers then changed to rejoicing that Father, her husband of 46 years, was safe with the Lord.

People began arriving from Santa Fe and showed kindness in many ways. Men with their machetes made a palm-branch shelter from the sun over Father's body. The two men were there that had been counseled by Jorge and the believers from the Santa Fe church when I was there for Bible School in February. I brought them together, one on one side of Father's body and the other on the other side, and asked each if he was willing to forgive the other. With tears in his eyes, the man who had walked out of our meeting angry, said yes, for God had forgiven him much. The other man also expressed forgiveness. Then Mother spoke to them and told them how she had been praying every day for them to forgive and that God would use whatever means it took to bring it about. Her prayer was answered, but it took the death of her husband to do it.

I asked a boy in a cayuco if he could locate our belongings, and before long two more boys joined him in another cayuco. Soon I saw them diving repeatedly, and as far as I could tell, every single item we had in the boat was located—even the arch supports that had been in Mother's shoes and the spoon we had used to put honey on our cinnamon buns. The water was 40 feet deep but so clear the articles were visible.

A judge and his clerk came and filled out reports of the accident, and then we were free to return home. A large motorboat, sent from Trujillo, appeared shortly after we started back in two cayucos and we transferred into it. We arrived at the pier shortly before noon and found a large crowd of people, including the governor, waiting to express condolences. Mother was deeply touched when she saw several women waiting with a cot and clean white sheets to receive Father's body. A truck was also waiting to provide transport to the house.

Jean and several women used my bedroom to prepare Father's body, and then brought it to the living room for viewing. All day the house was full of people who came to express their sympathy and many brought beautiful live flowers or wreaths of paper flowers. Several persons stayed all night according to the local custom. Two men went to the cemetery to dig the grave.

Mother told me that only a few weeks before, Father had reminisced about the coffins of his grandparents that were made to fit the body and mentioned that when he died he didn't want a fancy coffin. I am sure Father would have approved of the plain, neat coffin the carpenter, Mr. Arch, made and that Pearl lined.

Burial within 24 hours of death is the law in Honduras, and Helen and Maynard Headings and Norman Hockman traveled all night from Tocoa to arrive the next morning for the 7:30 funeral service at the church. Twelve soldiers from the *Cuartel* came with the bugler and another officer. The soldiers acted as pallbearers from the house to the church. Norman read from II Corinthians 15 and led in prayer. Cuta brought a good message from Psalm 23.

To the amazement of most present, Mother spoke a few words at the service. The Lord gave us both strength and a great peace so that we did not give way to tears during the service. In fact, through the sorrow there surged a joy and the joy was greater than the sorrow. We sang, "Shall We Gather at the River," and George spoke briefly. The body was taken in the mission truck to the old cemetery outside the town. At the grave there were prayers in both Spanish and English and we sang the hymn "I Love to Think of My Home Above."

The outpouring of kindness from people she had never met touched Mother and helped her greatly. Some of the people who came to visit had resisted the friendship of the missionaries, and I was so glad to welcome them to our home in spite of the sad occasion that moved them to come. One woman said it was the first time she had seen a smile on the face of a dead person. A few weeks later I heard that a wooden cross has been erected on the beach where Father died. I hoped it would be a reminder of the uncertainty of life and a question-raiser that would provide many opportunities to witness to the local people.

According to plans the Garbers and Mother left Honduras on August 4, and went on to Guatemala for a few days before heading back to the United States. The only change was that instead of Father, I was Mother's traveling companion. We decided that I would use vacation time to accompany Mother home and spend a short time helping to sort out family and business matters. Jean also went as far as Guatemala for a short vacation with her parents.

From Guatemala City we went to Casa Contenta, Panajachel, on a Sandoval Tour, a private tour by car, with a stop in Antigua to see the ruins of several old colonial churches destroyed by an earthquake in 1773. Until that time Antigua had been the capital city of Guatemala, but after the earthquake the capital was moved to the next valley. We also stopped to go through a textile plant where a dozen Indians were weaving tablecloths on foot looms, and at a pottery factory where we saw clay being ground. The potter's wheels, however, were not in use that day. At Patzun we went through a very beautiful 300-year-old church. Its ceiling, pillars, and 11 altars were of hand-carved wood.

The road was up and down and turn upon turn as we climbed to 8,500 feet, with air cool enough for us to appreciate sweaters and jackets. We skirted ravines so deep that from our seats we couldn't see the bottoms, and the peaks around us were so high that we were constantly craning our necks to get glimpses of the tops.

Everywhere we saw Indians—65 percent of the population is Indian, 20 percent mixed Indian and Spanish, and the rest Spanish. These people had never accepted the wheel and many Indians we passed on the road were on their way to market carrying loads on their heads. The men wore straps over their foreheads attached to big racks on their backs loaded with pottery or bundles of blankets, clothing, and other items for sale or barter. The people were short and most of the women and children were of chubby build.

In Chichicastenango we visited the Church of San Tomás built on the site of an earlier Indian temple and, therefore, up a lot of steps. The church, built in 1543 and rebuilt several times since, was filled with the scent of burning candles and incense. Indians squatted on the floor with candles they were burning for the dead or for personal requests. The stone floor was coated with wax from dripping candles and the silver altar was black from the smoke. White and red rose pedals were scattered to signify purity and the guilt of sin.

Our guide told us these were pagan rites combined with Catholic influences. One of the three priests from Spain had a clinic and provided some medical help to the Indians, but they had never been able to convert them. When the church was full, the priest went through to collect pennies and to sprinkle the people with holy water from a bucket.

The Indians didn't have faith that their prayers in the church would be answered, so after they left the church they went up the hill to pray to their spirit gods. We were told they have three types of witch doctors. One is the priest who helps them in their worship, the second is the medicine man who does incantations and gives them herbs, and the third is one they don't have much to do with. He is supposed to be in league with the devil and will put the evil-eye on their enemies.

When we left the church, we encountered men selling souvenir knives and women selling caps, beads, and hand-loomed napkins. One man came up and asked if we were Evangelicals. He said he was Pentecostal and told us his testimony.

We also had a trip across Lake Atitlán to visit San Pedro's market and church. The streets were cobbled, and one interesting thing we saw was an Indian woman weaving on a hand loom. When we returned we left Jean with the Central American missionaries and went on to Guatemala City. It was time for the Garbers and Mother and me to fly to New Orleans and pick up the Garbers' car. We arrived at Morgantown on August 15.

To welcome us, my sister Joyce had a family meal with only Melvin and a few grandchildren missing. Of course, Father was missed most of all. The shock of Father's sudden death had affected every one of us in his own individual way, and in the midst of a few silent tears we all felt closer than ever before.

A memorial service was held at the Frazer Mennonite Church, and Mother and I gave our testimonies. The service brought a sense of closure to friends and family members and gave them an opportunity to show their love and express their loss and grief.

In profound sorrow
we announce the death of

Edgar H. Taylor
Husband of Verna Martin Taylor

Died July 26, 1956, at Trujillo, Honduras

Memorial services will be held
Saturday, August 18, 1956, at 2:00 P.M.
From the Frazer Mennonite Church, Malvern, Pa.

Burial was made July 27, 1956, at Trujillo, Honduras

Memorial card.

It was so nice to be home. There were many things to do, but in less than a month Honduras was calling me back. Mother would have loved my company, but she was quite able and willing to stay alone, and we both felt I should return to my work. Family members promised frequent visits to her, and Glenn took over a lot of the work around the house and yard.

During my stay Lois's husband, Wilbur, had part of a lung removed, and I spent a short time after his surgery helping with his care in a hospital in Philadelphia. I also showed slides of the Honduras mission work at the Frazer church, and attended a Spanish worship service at Landisville, Pennsylvania, with over 1,000 Puerto Ricans present.

Although I had bought a bus ticket from Lancaster to Washington, Mother, Glenn, Catherine, and their daughter, Mary Jane, took me down. I got my visa at the embassy at 5405 Sixteenth Street, N.W. and around noontime we ate lunch in a nearby woods. Then as Mary Jane read the map we saw Mount Vernon, the Capitol, the beautiful Lincoln Memorial, and Glenn, Mary Jane, and I walked the steps of the Washington Monument. When we were down, I recalled that I had walked those steps in 1933 and now again in 1956. I said, "If I get back in another 23 years I might do it again."

At 7:00 p.m. I was in the air, and at 11:30 the plane landed in Miami. We took off again at 7:00 a.m.; five and a half hours later I was in San Pedro Sula after stops at Havana and Belize. An afternoon plane took me to La Ceiba, and it was cheering to see Betty Brown there in the red United Brethren Mission truck. That was where things slowed down. I had forgotten September 15 was a holiday similar to the United States' Fourth of July, and I didn't get a plane to Trujillo until Monday. I did get in touch by radio and heard that Jean was up all of one night with a stabbing case and the following night with a delivery.

When I got there, I was soon busy enough to forget the slight homesickness that always accompanied leaving home—wherever home was, Trujillo or Pennsylvania.

Dr. Armando Pavón, who replaced Dr. Auerbach, started sending patients to our clinic for nursing care and bed rest—one a rheumatic fever patient. We charged our usual small fee to the patients and were glad for the contacts and opportunities to witness. After visiting Grace Hockman's clinic in Tocoa, Dr. Pavón told me he was quite impressed and hoped to set up similar clinics around the district.

He also told us the government was planning to build and improve roads and bridges in our district of Colón and make various improvements in Trujillo, including a water and a sewer system and a hydroelectric plant that would provide 24-hour service. The new operator of the electric plant at that time was doing a good job. During the hours we did have electricity the lights were bright, and the chore of ironing was quickly finished with an iron that heated up properly on a good supply of current.

Dr. Pavón also had great plans to turn our clinic into a hospital with a laboratory, a dispensary, an x-ray machine, and a home for nurses to live in while nursing and getting additional training under him. He also wanted to add a second story to the building for patient wards. I didn't know what the Mission Board would think of all his plans, but if the town developed as he expected, we would certainly need better and bigger facilities.

Even without the extra facilities we were already running a hospital. Early in October we had four women and three babies in our maternity ward at one time. As fast as one left, another one arrived. Sometimes the doctor sent or brought a patient, and sometimes a woman walked in. One night, four Carib men and five or six women carried in a patient. She had already delivered a baby boy that forenoon, but the second twin wasn't eager to arrive. I sent the men to get the doctor, When he arrived, Jean gave the ether, I acted as scrub and circulating nurse, and Lorraine held the patient's hands. After some hard work the doctor delivered a 5 lb. 10 oz. girl, who was ready to go home a few days later.

One mother-to-be arrived at our door every evening for about two weeks and spent the night with us so she wouldn't have to come alone in the dark if she went into labor during the night. The doctor had told her the baby would probably arrive between November 28 and December 7. When both those dates passed with no action, she decided the baby would arrive with the change of the moon. Finally, when nothing happened on that date either, she got discouraged and said it wasn't worth coming any more. I told her it was even more important because she was certainly going to have the baby sometime, and every day was one closer than the day before.

All our beds were full, so we had a carpenter build us a cot which was soon occupied by a young Spanish woman George brought in the truck. Bed sheets were wearing out, and with so many patients at one time, we sometimes had our only spare ones drying on the wash line.

When the Hesses returned the end of November, they brought along a barrel of things Mother had accumulated for us, which included PEANUT BUTTER, but more importantly bed sheets and pillow cases from Frazer Mennonite Church. Before they arrived, however, I spent one whole day sewing drape sheets, mosquito nets for the bassinets, and a canvas mattress cover for one bed.

On October 28, Jean delivered a seven-pound girl while Lorraine and I had breakfast. While Jean and Lorraine had lunch, I delivered another seven-pound girl, and we teased Lorraine that if a third seven-pound girl arrived during supper, it would be her turn even though her profession was school teacher.

One day we had two babies named after *Suyapa,* a very popular virgin who was supposed to have performed many miracles in Honduras. The first girl was born in the clinic and named Vilma Suyapa. The second baby was born on the boat *Suyapa* and was brought to the clinic with her mother on a mattress on the back of a truck after the boat docked at Trujillo. That baby was named Suyapa Marina.

It wasn't only maternity cases that used our facilities. A young man with pneumonia spent some time with us, and occasionally we had a stabbing victim. A mother and her son came with influenza, and a woman with amebic colitis. The doctor sometimes brought in someone who needed to be kept under observation, like the boy who had fallen from a horse and had internal injuries. Once he brought a two-month-old girl suffering from diarrhea and malnutrition. She weighted only 5 lbs. 6 ozs.

One evening a man with meningitis, who had been carried 35 miles in a hammock, was brought to the clinic. The doctor did everything that could be done, even a spinal puncture to inject penicillin, but to no avail. He had been sick too long and hadn't been able to talk for 15 days. Even the priest brought in a patient one evening, an old woman who needed medical care for a few days. Some of the people stayed with us for several days after they were well enough to be discharged because they had no one to care for them at home.

We noticed that in the rainy seasons we usually had only serious cases because the people didn't go out in the rain for minor illnesses. They had no protective rain wear, so they stayed at home to avoid getting wet.

I prayed often for the patients in our care. I prayed for their physical healing and for spiritual awakening, but a constant prayer was for their safety. Scorpions were a very real danger, and one day while working in the clinic I saw the big, furry legs of a tarantula in a corner. It was at least six inches across. Maruquita, our cook, said, "It's a bad spider, kill it! It could kill a horse." I got the fly swatter and that was the end of that one, but I knew where one was another could come. I learned later they aren't quite as deadly as Maruquita had said, but for a baby or someone in a weakened condition their bite could be fatal.

October brought two traumatic situations: one in our house and one in the country of Honduras. The one in our house was caused when Jean discovered she had head lice. She said, "I never thought I'd stoop this low."

I told her, "You haven't stooped low unless you choose to keep them."

She got to work on them while Lorraine and I kept close watch on our own heads, hoping we wouldn't get them from her or whoever gave them to her.

The traumatic situation in Honduras was political unrest. Elections were held with only Reform or Blue party names on the ballot. Many Liberals or Reds were thrown into jail even before the elections. Several of our friends from various villages were picked up during that time. With Red supporters in jail and unable to vote, and with none of their candidates even listed on the ballot, the results were a sure thing. I heard that in the past, members of the controlling party often had a cayuco ready and waiting for their escape to Belize or some other nearby country in case they lost elections. One year I noticed that as soon as a person voted he had to stick one finger in a bottle of red ink so the officials could be sure he didn't vote twice.

It wasn't more than a few days after the election, however, that the military took over and the president was asked to resign. *Time* magazine called it a polite revolution and reported it was not only Honduras's 135th revolution but also their first bloodless one. Governor Don Moisés Lopez, who was so kind to us when Father died, was replaced by a new one and moved to his farm.

On June 28 of the following year, two horses arrived with a *mozo* or hired boy from the former governor's farm. Next morning, after being up all night with a sick baby and a woman in labor, I mounted one horse and Margarita, the governor's sister, the other, and we set out for a visit at the farm. The *mozo* had ridden a horse in but walked with us back to the farm and then back again to Trujillo when we returned, to take the horses back to the farm. He said he considered it a holiday away from his usual work.

We started out by going down the steep cobblestone hill to Cristales and along the beach. Margarita's horse, named *Conejo* or Rabbit, kept checking if the sea was really salt water. My horse insisted on being first in line, but as soon as he got ahead he slowed down. About half way to Santa Fe we turned left and headed up the mountain. I was surprised to find the path, although only five or six feet wide, was paved with foot-square cobble stones like the streets of Trujillo. Don Moisés told me later that it had been built by the Spaniards several hundred years before at the time Trujillo was an important seaport. The horses picked their way carefully through broken-up areas, and in some places the road was so steep there were switchbacks to ease the climb. Birds sang joyously, and sometimes trees and vines crowded so closely on both sides that I could pick a flower or fern as I rode by. For awhile we followed a river that rushed and tumbled among rocks as big as houses. The banks were covered with beautiful, white, starlike flowers; the forest was so thick beyond the banks that it looked like a green-black wall.

We rode the three leagues or nine miles in three hours. The last 20 minutes were off the main trail and climbing to reach the elevation of the farm—about 2,000 feet above sea level. Just beyond was a peak that rumbled at times. From the mountain we could see the Trujillo Bay, Cristales, and the Bay Islands in one direction and in the other direction, the Aguan Valley and four more mountains—one behind the other.

At the entrance to the property was a sign with the name of the farm, *La Confianza* (Trust), and beneath in Spanish were the words, "In God We Trust."

The house was large and comfortable, constructed of adobe with thatched roof and earthen floor. Don Moisés' wife, María Ester, was from San José, Costa Rica, and I marveled at how contented she was living in a home with no modern conveniences. Each morning she took all the children to a mountain stream below the house and bathed them under a little waterfall. Laundry was also done in the stream, and all the water for cooking and drinking was carried up the mountain to the house. María Ester with two girls to help her cooked all the meals for the family and about a dozen *mozos* who worked on the farm.

Don Moisés said he carried the little Testament Mother had given him because it was convenient to take out and read when he rested from his work. He was a devout Catholic, and in their living room near their Catholic Bible a candle burned before a little altar and statues of several saints.

Mango, guava, orange, grapefruit, and banana trees grew on the farm, and they raised corn, rice, and hogs, but their main business was raising cane and making *dulce* or coarse brown sugar blocks. Two oxen provided power for the grinder to press the juice out of the cane, which was then boiled down and ladled into molds to form one-pound blocks.

♛

STICA, the same government organization that conducted the grasshopper patrols, started giving classes in Trujillo on the preservation of food. About 30 women attended the first session, and we missionary women were pleased to be invited, although one woman said, "I don't know what you will learn that you don't already know."

The kitchen was a room with a ground floor in the high school. The two stoves were made from a drum cut in half. The open ends were set on the ground and half filled with stones. The upper eight inches had a door to stick in wood for the fire, and our kettles sat in a hole cut out of the top. The natural consequence was that the bottoms of the kettles were smoked up and so were we. When we went home, we took the smell of smoke with us in our clothing and hair.

Our first lesson was on how to can grapefruit and orange juice. Each woman was told to bring fruit, sugar, a knife, an apron, and one lempira to help pay for the jar and use of the stove. The teacher brought a pressure cooker and jars. The classes were interesting with everyone talking at the same time telling what they were doing and how they were doing it. All the ladies joined in the discussion about how to divide the class into groups until I wondered who was listening. Once one woman who was talking loud and fast turned around and said, -*¡Qué bulla!*- (What a noise) and went right back to her previous volume.

One day we made guava jelly. When the women skimmed off the frothy scum, they just flung it over the floor. We also canned chicken and made candied papaya. At our house, we were already getting papayas from the 18 trees we had planted after the Hesses left on furlough the year before. One weighed over nine pounds; another one weighed ten pounds and five ounces. They had a flowery smell and were *sabrosas!* (delicious).

The cooking classes came to an abrupt end one evening when the women had a squabble. I was glad none of us from the mission was there when it occurred, because we had enjoyed making new friends and wouldn't have wanted to take sides in the disagreement.

I visited Father's grave on his birthday, November 18, and left one of the paper wreaths that had been given at the time of his death. Vines with little yellow flowers and other wild plants had almost covered the mound that marked his grave. When I received the deed for the burial plot, and after the rainy season, I hired a man to make a three and a half by seven and a half foot raised concrete grave cover. He mixed lime in the cement to make it white and left an opening at the head end for a plant. At the foot end he placed the engraved metal plaque made by my Uncle Noah Steffy in the United States.

Mother donated money to purchase a pulpit Bible for our church. When it arrived the next year, I had a man inscribe the following:

Father's grave in the Trujillo cemetery.

Obsequio a la
Iglesia Evangélica Menonita
Trujillo, Honduras
por Verna, viuda de Taylor
en memoria de su esposo,
Edgar H. Taylor
26 de julio de 1957
Primer aniversarie
de su entrada
en la presencia de Cristo:

which translated into English reads: Presented to the Mennonite Church, Trujillo, Honduras by Verna Taylor in memory of her husband, Edgar H. Taylor, 26th of July, 1957, first anniversary of his entrance into the presence of Christ.

♔

We were all looking forward to the return of James and Beaty Hess. We had done our best but could barely wait for James with his command of Spanish to take over services in the villages and baptize several believers who seemed spiritually ready for that step. The man who did much of our carpenter work and repairs said he was ready for baptism. The woman he was living with had decided she was also ready, and if she was, then they would be married and baptized when

James returned. A short time later, though, Luís said he thought his woman was deceiving him in that and various other things. If so, he would leave her so he could be baptized. They had a child and he seemed willing to support it even if he left her. In 1963 when I was getting ready to leave Honduras, they had four children but were still not married.

The people we were working with had many such situations that needed to be dealt with before they could become workers in the church. Christian standards had been unknown before the missionaries arrived, and it was hard to change and go against the previously-accepted immorality, deceit, and sin.

The Hesses returned the end of November, and we threw a big welcome-back party, inviting about 40 people. Only 20 came—some people were sick and some probably didn't come because we had invited people from all social levels. I was actually glad everyone didn't come because the first batch of ice cream took far more time to harden than it should have (I was too stingy with the salt in the ice.), and there wasn't time to turn the second batch. We were also glad we didn't have any patients because we pushed back the beds and used the clinic for the party.

The day we opened the barrels the Hesses brought was like Christmas. Besides the sheets and pillow cases from Frazer Mennonite Church, there were bed gowns, a quilt, dried corn, and canned vegetables and fruit. The New Danville Sewing Circle had made lovely little dresses and kimonos for our new babies. We had peanut butter for supper that evening and canned strawberries from Canada the next day. Jean graciously shared a box of chocolates with everyone, but she kept us waiting until Christmas day to taste her gift of a fruit cake. It was wonderful to have all those gifts and think of all the kindness and love that had prepared and sent them.

One of the things we had in common with North American Christmas celebrations was poinsettias. Back home our families went to greenhouses and bought plants with one, two, or three blossoms. We stepped outside and cut flowers from bushes up to 15 feet high and covered with 70 or 80 blooms. The only snow we had was cotton snow, but the Jesus we worshipped was the same wherever we were.

We had a youth meeting one evening during the holidays and about 25 young people came. George showed a film strip depicting the life of Christ while James explained it in Spanish. Jean showed slides she had taken in Guatemala and Trujillo. Then we put to use the popcorn popper Jean's parents had sent. Did our guests eat! I wouldn't have been at all surprised if some had come to the clinic in the middle of the night, but nobody did.

The year ended the same as any other evening—the lights dimmed and then blinked into darkness.

1957

Forty persons enjoyed cocoa, cookies, games, and a talk by James Hess at our Watch Night service at the Millers. I had only one patient so was able to go over for part of the evening. I took another vacation from work the following day—in bed with amebas, a parasitic intestinal disease, with the usual symptoms—pain, diarrhea, and fever. I took Wintodon, and by the time Paul Kraybill and Raymond Charles arrived on January 5, I was ready for the annual conference to plan the future of the mission work in Honduras.

It was wonderful to sit down with those Godly men and share the concerns and expectations of our work. We had an opportunity to air any differences or problems, but I was blessed by the harmony and agreement that was evident as major decisions were reached.

One item on the agenda was which nurse would take charge of the clinic in Tocoa. At first I thought Alma Longenecker, who was due to arrive shortly, would go. But when I discovered she had only high school Spanish, I thought I might be the one transferred because the nurse at the Tocoa clinic would need a good command of the language. When it was decided that Lorraine would start her school for the children of believers in Tocoa instead of Trujillo, the decision was made to send Jean to the clinic because the two women were closer in age, and companionship was a consideration for placement in an isolated location.

The results of that decision caused Jean to say, "Oh, I feel as if we got a divorce," as we divided the jars and cans of food on our pantry shelves—one can of oatmeal for me, two for Lorraine and Jean, etc. It was a good decision, however, because Jean left in August to get her B.S. in nursing. By that time Alma was more proficient in Spanish and could move over to take her place.

One thing we couldn't divide was the gift of two scrapbooks a friend had made for Jean. Almost as soon as she had packed and sent them ahead on the plane, we had a young patient in the clinic and had nothing to entertain him. I immediately wrote home and asked Mother if she could possibly find some friends willing to make a scrapbook. I suggested that no poems be included because very few of the people could read English, but everyone enjoyed colorful pictures, even the adults.

MAF pilot Don Berry flew in to take Paul and Raymond to San Esteban, but the weather in that direction delayed their trip, so he started flying things to Tocoa for Lorraine and Jean. Large items such as beds, however, went to La Ceiba by the *Suyapa*, to Masicales by train, across the river by cayuco, and to Tocoa by oxcart!

Before Jean left we hired a new helper in the clinic, Ruth Ruben. She was Seventh Day Adventist and therefore wanted off work on Saturdays, which allowed me to have off for Sunday services if patients were in no immediate crisis. Ruth spoke English and was taking a correspondence course in nursing. Before she had worked very long, she liked her work so well that she visited us on her days off.

One of the first days Ruth was with us, I took her along to Santa Fe to give her a broader view of our mission work in Honduras. That was the first trip James was making in the new molded fiberglass boat he had brought from Tampa as a gift from Worldwide Gospel Fellowship in Lancaster, Pennsylvania. The boat had a windshield, but even better, a canvas sunshade. It was a vast improvement over the *Caridad*. The boat was wide enough to seat three people across and rode high in the water with little roll from side to side. I had not been to Santa Fe since the accident in July, but I enjoyed the trip and especially the four porpoises that played around in the water near us. We made the trip down in 20 minutes, but because of wind and rough seas, our return trip took 35 minutes.

We went to Guadalupe first to visit a believer and then returned to Santa Fe to visit Don Emilio's family and the homes of several other friends. When we held a service in Don Emilio's house, I was happy to see the two men who had been reconciled on the beach following Father's death worshipping together.

The new boat made it possible for James to begin early Sunday morning services in Santa Fe and still get back to Trujillo for the 9:30 service. Forty persons attended his first Sunday service there.

James also started a chorus for the young people in Trujillo, but with the first session he discovered he had to start with the very basics. After saying he wanted everyone to hum the first note before starting to sing, he blew on his pitch pipe and everyone obediently hummed—but they hadn't realized he meant them all to hum the same note he had given—Amazing Disharmony! About the same time that occurred we heard that a rumor was going around in Tocoa that Eldon Hamilton sucked something out of a little thing every time before he started singing, and shortly after that we discovered that some people had

Jessie with David, Elsie, Alice, James, and Eldon Hamilton in Tocoa.

decided the reason Jean, Lorraine, and I sang so well as a trio in church Sunday evenings was because one of us put a little thing like a bit into her mouth before starting!

Evaristo went with James one week to teach a Sunday School class in Santa Fe. He was a new believer whose mother was totally opposed to his decision to attend our church and be baptized. I knew he was quite concerned about the spiritual welfare of both his mother and sister, and since he enjoyed coming to our house to listen to Spanish gospel records, I told him he could borrow the records and player to take home occasionally. The second or third time he did so he told us that his mother seemed to enjoy listening to the music, and before long he said she had softened in her attitude towards him and his commitment to Christ. His sister, Dora, later worked in our clinic.

Evaristo was taking a correspondence course in mechanics and hoped to learn how to repair motors and trucks. His plans included buying his own truck, getting some Spanish gospel records, a player, maybe a projector and gospel films and then make Sunday trips into some of the villages to teach the people what he had learned about Jesus. The music on the records would attract the people and the films would give the message better than he could. He wasn't waiting until he could fulfill all his plans before beginning to witness, because when I talked to two young men from Cristales I had as patients they already knew quite a bit about the gospel story from Evaristo.

The new nurse, Alma Longenecker, arrived the end of January and moved into Jean's room and right into clinic work. Her blue eyes were quite a subject of conversation in a country of dark-eyed people. We scheduled her in the clinic for two days a week and put her to work the rest of her time learning Spanish. Without a grasp of the language, she couldn't run the clinic or see patients alone. I taught her the grammar, and Estela, a school teacher friend, taught her the phonetics.

Dora holding twins.

The changes in our lives didn't change the clinic work in any way. A woman in a coma was brought in following a heart attack, but when the doctor said nothing could be done for her, the family took her home to die. Babies continued to arrive on time, ahead of time, behind time, and sometimes two at a time.

A man from Cristales came in and said he was bringing his señora. She arrived in George's truck, and it took a half hour to get her out of the truck and onto a cot in our clinic. She weighed at least 350 pounds, and I was afraid the cot could break, but it stood the strain. George said he had to make three tries before he got the truck up the hill from Cristales with the heavy load. Ruth, our new helper, said the woman had been her mother's midwife when she was born.

After we had her in bed with six pillows propping her up so she could breathe, the woman didn't move all night. The doctor said she had dropsy and prescribed for her, but her heart was very weak and her pulse was 120. The next morning we inserted a catheter because it was impossible to put her on a bedpan. It was also impossible to change her sheets, so we prepared another cot; it was almost more than George, Alma, Ruth, and I could do to get her moved over. We made sure she was lying on the opposite side from the night before. She looked much more comfortable, but all of a sudden she stopped breathing! I ran for an injection of Coramine and sent Ruth for the doctor, but she was gone. We notified her family, and then George and several others placed her body, still on the cot, back on the truck and took her home.

We all fell in love with a dear little old Carib woman who came with amebic dysentery. She was our only patient for several days and we enjoyed her company. The year-old grandchild of friends was brought in close to death and died before we even diagnosed his illness. His death was closely followed by the birth of a baby girl only 15 minutes after the arrival of her mother at the clinic.

In February a nine-year-old girl was brought to the clinic with possible polio. Her father came the following morning to take her to the hospital in La Ceiba, but the girl died before arriving there.

That Sunday evening I was called out of church to attend to a nine-year-old boy with a sore throat. Since people had been warned of the early signs of polio, the boy's father wanted to be sure he was given prompt and proper attention. Neither Dr. Pavón nor I was sure it was polio, but we kept him in bed. He had a bit more fever in the morning, so the doctor changed his medicine, and he was soon well enough to be discharged.

Dr. Pavón ordered polio vaccine which arrived along with Dr. Zúniga from Tegucigalpa. We had quite a yelling and screaming time as we inoculated 200 school children under the age of ten one day, and 500 pre-schoolers the next day. Dr. Pavón and some teachers filled out forms on each child, two of Dr. Pavón's workers filled syringes and sterilized needles, a soldier and four school girls brought the children in and held them, and Dr. Zúniga and I administered the vaccinations.

Dr. Pavón had moved his family to Trujillo and was living in the house just beyond Miller's. When one of his five children had a birthday, I helped his wife make a birthday cake and enjoyed getting to know the family.

We had to be inventive and use our ingenuity at times, as when a 20-month-old boy was brought in scarcely able to breathe. His trachea was almost closed, so we rigged up a steam tent and kept him in it for 30 hours. His mother stayed with him the whole time and even slept with him because we had no cribs; she needed to watch that he didn't roll off the cot. Before he left we admitted a six-year-old boy with an abscess in the groin area that needed to be lanced by the doctor, and also a woman with severe anemia.

Word from Tocoa was that Lorraine had 12 students in her school and was kept busy. Jean was adjusting to work in the clinic, and she and Grace Hockman had started holding meetings for the women believers.

In March the Hamiltons flew home for Mission Board Meeting at the Weaverland Mennonite Church near Blue Ball, Pennsylvania.

Jessie was in need of surgery, and it was decided they would not return to Honduras immediately. I was pleased to learn that someone had initiated plans for a baby shower for her because I knew she would probably be in need of just about everything.

In late March a Bible conference was held in Tocoa with James Hess and Oliver Perry, a Baptist missionary from Olanchito, as speakers. Perry came part way by train and was met at Masicales by a man from Tocoa with horses. The roads were too muddy to drive the whole way, so our group—Alma, Ruth, and James and Beaty and their children—started off in the Trujillo pickup. After crossing the river they had to leave the truck and walk several miles through mud to where Norman Hockman could meet them in the Tocoa Jeep. The loads they were carrying—Dicky and Gerald, the suitcases, and everything they needed for a two-week stay—got heavier every step of the way. When the MAF plane made a flight to Trujillo several days later, Beaty returned home with the boys. She admitted the trip over had been more strenuous than she had expected.

I had stayed at the clinic with a woman with endometritis, a typhoid fever patient, another woman who had had a heart attack, a sick baby, and a woman with some ailment we hadn't been able to diagnose. Four babies were also due. A young girl filled our sixth bed, and with all of them full, I was glad for Claudia who came to help and for Carlota, a Carib girl who had asked us to teach her nursing. She was a pleasant person, quick to learn, and worked well with all of us.

Ruth returned with Beaty; by then I had delivered two of the babies, and the other two had arrived before the mothers got to the clinic. My in-clinic patients had gone home, and I was free to accept a ride back to Tocoa on the plane to attend the end of the conference. Maruquita went with me to help cook and even made bread twice for Jean and Lorraine.

The chapel had been enlarged and had lovely mahogany benches and pulpit. Jean and Lorraine had a comfortable home in part of the chapel building, and the clinic was very nice. When I visited Lorraine's school with its 12 students, I found everything quiet and orderly—not a typical Honduran school.

One man and three children accepted the Lord during the evangelistic meetings, but a horseback trip to a distant town by the evangelist and several of the men was less productive. On their return they reported three things—an evening meeting in a school house with 40 present, a hot trip, and a wicked town.

We left Tocoa by Jeep—Norman driving, Alma and I as passengers in the front seat, and Danny, Larry, Filemena, another woman, and two men and all the baggage in the back. James rode on one front fender and Luís on the other. We got stuck in the mud once—in a muddy stream—but with all the passengers to help, it didn't take long to throw in some logs and planks and get out.

We crossed the first of the 13 high bridges, but the rest appeared too unstable to trust, so we all piled out, said good-bye to Norman and started to walk to where the Trujillo pickup had been left. It wasn't until after Norman had turned the Jeep around on the high, narrow road with swamp down either side that I learned the Jeep's brakes weren't working. Norman was as good a driver as he was a missionary.

The road from Durango had been scraped since the rain, and for one short distance we sped along at 40 miles per hour!

The rainy season ended in March and the temperature reached 97°. Alma said, "It isn't getting any cooler, is it?" It would get hotter, as she found out.

The climate, diseases, primitive living conditions, and nursing responsibilities were things I accepted. However, even trips such as the one to Tocoa, with spiritual input and adventures, were wearing on mind and body.

I had discovered that mission workers need time to be rebuilt physically, mentally, and spiritually, and because they are often so busy just getting through their normal duties, they need an opportunity to stand back and view their work from a distance. I chose to begin my vacation at the Reformed Mission's girls' boarding school in San Pedro Sula, the second-largest city in Honduras after Tegucigalpa, which provided Christian companionship as well as refreshing rest and quiet times. My accommodations were comfortable and my meals at the teachers' table were of highly spiced native food. I was introduced to other missionaries and met Miss Kroeler, one of two nurses from the Reformed clinic up in the mountains. She said they had as high as 1,500 patients a month.

Instead of teaching a Sunday School class, I was able to sit in a class of 46 unmarried women over the age of 17. More than 300 persons attended that Sunday School.

I spent the next weekend in La Lima and went with Louise Filger when she held an afternoon service in the park for children. Because it rained, only about 70 children came.

While there, I met missionaries Paul and Sara Heckert. They were from Pennsylvania; Paul from Lewistown, and Sara from Lancaster.

They had just arrived from language school, and Paul was hoping to visit the more than 70 banana camps in that area. Sara was in the hospital with hepatitis, and it was suspected that Paul was starting with it also.

My next stop was at the Central American Mission church in Santa Rose de Copán, an old town with cobblestone streets and houses with tile roofs and floors, and then it was on to the evangelical youth convention in Dulce Nombre. The days were packed with prayer meetings, teaching sessions, round-table discussions, consecration services, a communion service, and lots of music. The meetings were attended by over 200 young people from all parts of the country, and 200 or 300 people from the town and places nearby. Mariano González from Tegucigalpa brought good, Spirit-filled messages that resulted in many decisions for Christ and filled the platform the last evening with young people ready to consecrate themselves to God.

Accommodations were simple—beds with strips of cowhide for springs and a piece of matting for a mattress. The food was fried beans, fried eggs, tortillas, and black coffee for breakfast; soup, rice, potatoes, and cabbage/tomato salad for lunch; and for supper fried beans, fried eggs, tortillas, fried green bananas, and black sweet coffee. Everything tasted good, but with all the fried foods being served I was glad I didn't have gall bladder trouble. When I tasted my first tortillas soon after arriving in Honduras, I thought they tasted like cardboard and wondered why people ate them, but I soon learned to enjoy them with the greasy, salty beans and highly seasoned soups and meat.

Dulce Nombre had only two wells, which often dried up in summer and many of the people carried their water in buckets or clay pots from as far as a mile away. There was a bathing place a couple of kilometers away in a stream so shallow that a basin was needed to collect enough water to bathe, which was done in full view of passersby so it was inappropriate to take off all one's clothes. The road was so dusty I felt I would be dirtier by the time I got back than if I didn't go at all.

The people were so kind, loving, and unselfish that as I left I realized that in spite of a few inconveniences I had enjoyed my stay in Dulce Nombre more than in some places where accommodations were much better.

Following the last meeting, I left in the morning with a group of 90 persons in an old bus, a truck, and a pickup. We forded a couple dozen rivers, or maybe only a few meandering rivers over and over again, where the drivers often stopped to fill the radiators with water.

Once we broke a spring on the bus which was patched together somehow. When a tire went flat, however, the drivers decided that since it was only one of two wheels it could wait until we arrived at our destination. The trip across valleys and into mountains was hot and dusty but very scenic.

There was a lot of fun on the bus and once when the driver stopped to fill the radiator a girl got out and drank from the stream. After she was back in the bus, she was told that somebody with athletes' foot was probably taking a bath upstream. The next time we stopped, another girl got a drink, and the teasing went on. It reached its zenith when just a little later we rounded a bend and there, sure enough, an old man and several boys were in the water bathing.

I spent Easter Sunday in Santa Rosa de Copán at the home and church of Pedro Pineda, the pastor of the Central American Church. After lunch and a siesta a group of us went to a lookout on the edge of a cliff north of town. Immediately below us was a little village, and off in the hazy distance was a mass of high mountains.

Don Juan Ayala Velásquez, an inventor, was also visiting the pastor's family. He mentioned he had 54 inventions to his credit and had received medals and been honored in the United States, Mexico, and Central American countries. The remarkable thing was his humility and testimony. When toasted at receptions, he said he accepted the glass out of courtesy, but then quietly set it down untouched. That often brought questions and gave him an opportunity to say he was *Evangelico* (Christian) which usually resulted in further questions about the gospel. Sometimes those conversations with scientists and people who moved in the upper levels of society lasted an hour or more.

His Spanish was rapid and accompanied with many hand motions, but I was able to understand most of what he said as he explained some of his inventions. He showed us a fountain pen with a light, which he invented the day after his aunt insisted he turn off the lights one evening when he wanted to write a letter. After eight years, the light was still bright.

He concocted an insecticide after he noticed ants died when they came in contact with a certain plant, and he invented a machine that could make 3,600 tortillas an hour, but he couldn't sell it because it would have put a lot of people out of work. He was able to sell the invention that did the work of 20 men—a seed planter that was pulled by a tractor and dug a hole and dropped the desired number of seeds in each hole.

Don Juan was also a piano tuner and had made an instrument with earphones that allowed him to tune a piano in half an hour. He said he had earned his way to a convention by tuning pianos.

Monday I took a plane from Santa Rosa de Copán to San Marcos to visit Virginia Miller. She didn't know I was coming, but I had met her at language school in 1955 and knew how much I would appreciate a visit from her in Trujillo. Virginia was the only missionary on the Friends' mission station, which had a native pastor. She was principal of a school of 84 students in six grades and had four teachers under her.

Her teachers helped entertain me and took me to see the sights. They said it was rumored that there is an ancient Maya village buried under the airport and pointed out a hill in the shape of a pyramid. The area around San Marcos has never been excavated, but the village itself is not very old. I visited just at the time the people were holding the annual celebration of their patron saint and was awakened by firecrackers between three and four in the morning after just falling asleep to the sounds of all-night marimba band music.

The teachers, the pastor and his family, Virginia, and some of the students went to the airport to see me off, and I wrote in my journal, *These people just can't be beat for friendliness, and when they are believers one feels it means more.*

Two of the boarding students gave me a letter to deliver to their parents in Copán near the Maya ruins Jean and I planned to visit, and Virginia cabled to say we were coming. Jean joined me back in Santa Rosa where our accommodations were rather unusual. The family got their water from a deep well with a bucket. The *inodoro* or toilet was a close second to one I remembered in the Italian Alps. Above the door, written in chalk were the words, *-Por favor no orinen en el suelo ni echen papeles afuera de la capa. Gracias.-* or "Please don't urinate on the floor or throw papers outside of the container. Thank you." The concrete seat was high and deep and always wet.

Another memory was waking up the first morning to a strange sound I was unable to connect to anything I knew. The windows were closed, but the murmuring noise seemed nearby—almost in the room. I discovered what it was when some pigeons walked out from under my bed. The second morning I knew what to expect.

The best memories of that visit, however, were the lovely, intelligent children. There were six with the oldest 13 and the youngest ten months. I heard the baby cry only once, and there was no fighting or fussing from any of them. I couldn't help wondering why some families have so much trouble training their children to behave and get along with each other and other families live in such harmony.

When Jean and I flew into Copán Ruinas, the pastor of the Friends church, the father of Virginia's students, met us to pick up the letter his daughters had sent. He told us his wife was preparing dinner, and we walked to his home about a mile from the airport. Dinner was chicken soup, chicken cooked to perfection, rice, cabbage salad, tortillas, and fruit. Earlier the man had arranged for a boy with a horse to take our suitcases from the airport to the *pensión* where we had a room for the night.

The Maya ruins were all and more than I was led to believe. I had read *The Ancient Maya* by Sylvanus G. Morley, which stated the community at Copán had once been home to 60,000 or more able-bodied men and was the scientific center of The Old Empire. The city spread over 75 acres with the central ceremonial complex consisting of pyramids, terraces, and temples covering 12 acres and rising to 125 feet at its highest point. One of the temples was dedicated in the year 756.

Our guide had worked in the excavations since 1934, and had, in fact, worked with Mr. Morley. He told us many interesting details of his work, the discoveries, and what was believed to be the history of the Maya civilization. He showed us around and would have allowed us to climb some of the high places, but Jean wasn't too thrilled about venturing that high and I didn't have the energy. One altar showed the 16 months of their year. Everywhere there were hieroglyphics and interesting figures of people, turtles, plumed serpents, jaguars, tigers, and many unexcavated areas.

Hot and thirsty, we headed back to the *pensión*, and on the way we saw a man unloading twin nets of watermelons off a horse. We walked right over and bought one for 20 cents, and the man cut it in pieces so we could eat it. It wasn't cold, but it was sweet and juicy.

Next day after taking our suitcases to the airport and making arrangements to fly to San Pedro, we walked back to the ruins. Forests surround the excavated areas, and while Jean cooled off in the shade I went exploring down a path which ended in a thicket. Although pretty well obscured by the trees, there were more mounds and lots of carved stones lying about. Suddenly, I heard a plane which started to circle for landing. I scrambled back up the hill, and Jean and I hurried to the airport. It wasn't our plane, however, because when they finished loading tobacco, they shut the doors and took off at once and we had another hour to wait.

Jean returned to Tocoa by way of Tegucigalpa, and I continued home by way of La Ceiba. There was only one patient in the clinic, a man with typhoid fever, and I was able to lead him to the Lord the first time I met him. The second night when I went to get him ready to sleep, he asked me to help him pray. He had spent quite a bit of time that day reading a Bible.

While I was on my vacation, Daniel Ray Miller arrived, but not in Trujillo. Grace had complications in March and went to the hospital in Siguatepeque where her son was born on April 6. She brought him home in May when he weighed 5 lbs. 13 ozs.

Nicaragua and Honduras were threatening war—once again over their boundary lines. Everyone in Trujillo was urged to gather in the town plaza for speeches, which were loud and full of emotion—"Defend Honduras," "defend our rights," "to die defending one's country is glory," etc. etc. High school students rode through the town in a Jeep waving homemade signs saying, *-Viva Honduras, Viva Honduras Libre-* (free). Radios played full blast shouting out patriotic speeches, martial music, and reports of how many Nicaraguans had been killed.

Added to all that, the temperatures soared to over 100° day after day, and one night I stepped on and killed a scorpion when going to check on a patient around midnight. Another night Beaty found a scorpion under the netting in Gerald's bed only a foot away from him. Later I went to the bathroom to wash my hands; when I turned to reach for the towel, there was a big one not three feet away. A hearty swing of the fly swatter ended its life, and an hour later I killed another one at almost the same spot.

Good news about Tilda drifted back from the hospital in La Ceiba. She was working well and the patients said she was *different from the other nurses—more kind*. We knew Alma would transfer to Tocoa when Jean left for school so George contacted Tilda and asked if she was ready to return to work in the clinic in Trujillo again. Her classes had stopped, so she returned in May and we decided to alternate 24-hour shifts so that neither of us worked every night and both of us could attend church at least once every two weeks.

Grace Hockman was then spending some time in the hospital in Siguatepeque because of amebas and Jean needed help. Alma, still learning Spanish, moved to Tocoa so Jean could train her in their clinic procedures before leaving. Since no English was spoken there,

Alma quickly picked up the conversational Spanish necessary for the job.

Dr. Pavón wanted to be prepared if the war brought us casualties, so he started giving instructions on hospital procedures to Tilda, Ruth, Carlota, and three women he was training to work with him. One day in the middle of a demonstration on operating room techniques such as how to scrub up and handle instruments, Tilda broke out laughing and said, "That woman who was making fine speeches on the plaza about being willing to die defending Honduras is not so brave. She started taking the doctor's classes but fainted at the sight of blood!"

Nightly blackouts ended when war was averted, but the training of the nurses was not wasted. They had gone through scrubbing and imaginary operations for several days, and I hoped it had helped strengthen my teaching of sterile techniques. I had once caught Carlota rinsing a sterile syringe under the spigot before she planned to give an injection.

One Sunday when Tilda was on duty, I went with James for his early service in Santa Fe. More than 30 children were in the audience, and I noticed the parents were distracted by the children's restlessness. I suggested we start a class for the children. The following week Tilda, who was already preparing for a Sunday School class in Trujillo each week, accompanied James. Her class in a separate house greatly improved the learning atmosphere for both children and adults.

Kerah and Calford.
Gladys, Jimmie, Tilda, and Lannes.

Tilda Imbott and her two boys, Lannes and Jimmie, and Calford McCoy, an older boy, lived with Tilda's aunt, Kerah Edwards. Later they took in a girl named Gladys. Kerah and Tilda were among the first members of the Trujillo church.

The temperature continued to break the

records I had been keeping since my arrival in Honduras in 1951. We had one stretch of nine days with temperatures of over 100°, and after a brief respite it started climbing again in June—100°, 104°, 105°, and 107°. The nights were warmer than normal also. Fortunately for me, I always minded cold weather more than hot weather. Unfortunately for all of us, rain followed the heat and mosquitoes followed the rain and mosquito bars surrounded our beds just when we wanted as much air circulating as possible.

In mid-June we held a Missionary Council Meeting with the workers from Tocoa. It was decided that when Hamiltons returned from furlough they would open mission work in Gualaco, a town with

Puente hamaca **or hammock bridge over the Gualaco River.**

Coffee drying on an animal hide on the plaza.

no water supply except the river, no paved streets or roads, and mud houses with tile roofs and tile or earthen floors. The people raised coffee, seemed intelligent, and had heard the gospel from a team that visited once a year. Gualaco was about 55 miles from Trujillo and took 45 minutes flying time. By trail it was a horseback ride of several days. SAHSA provided plane service twice a week, so in one way it was not as isolated as we were.

Another decision reached during our meetings was that we would wear black veils instead of our North American style white prayer coverings. The black veil was more in tune with the Central American culture and certainly served the same purpose and was far more practical than white. We cut one yard of material in half to make two veils which when hemmed were about shoulder length.

Right after our meetings, I got a new patient. A 17-year-old boy was brought in with a deep gash that bled profusely. He had fallen on a spiny tree and although able to get to his home three miles from where the accident occurred, he had been brought to us in a hammock from La Brea, 24 miles over the mountain. They had left his home at 6:00 p.m. Saturday and arrived at the clinic at 1:00 a.m. Sunday. Dr. Pavón called his nurse and sutured him while we gave the boy ether. He recovered without problems as did a little three-year-old Carib boy from Guadalupe. When we were ready to discharge the three-year-old, no one was there to take him home. I asked Tilda what we were going to do with him. She laughed and said, "When he gets a little bigger, you can use him to run errands for us." A little later, however, someone came for him, and I had no cute little future errand boy.

The doctor sent in a school teacher with on-again-off-again labor pains. She didn't trust to go back to her village so stayed with us until two weeks later when her baby arrived, making her the mother of seven. Only a few weeks after she went home her husband had a bad case of malaria and was in our clinic. By then the mother and baby, Aristides Lempira, were both doing fine and looking healthy.

Three other men also spent some time with us in June, but all needed hospitalization in La Ceiba and were sent off one by one on the plane or the *Suyapa*. There were, in fact, only three days in June that we didn't have any inpatients.

The next boarder to arrive was a big parrot. His owner went on vacation and entrusted him to James, who built him a perch outside the chicken house. He was mostly red but had bright yellow and blue feathers in his wings. His tail alone was about two feet long. I enjoyed watching as he crept along the spouting and hung upside down squawking what might have been words.

The Hamiltons also stayed with me when they returned in late August until things were arranged so they could begin the new work in Gualaco.

I was glad for the several July deliveries, which went well. I had both Ruth and Carlota observe as part of their training, but I was also glad they went well because the doctor was in Tegucigalpa. While he was gone his son fell off the swings at school and broke his collarbone. I fixed him up with a sling, and a telegram brought his father by plane to take him back to Tegucigalpa for x-rays.

Since my nurses were not trained to take complete charge, I often had to work on my nights off duty if difficult cases came in. This resulted in losing my cook, Maruquita, for a short time. She and her half-sister, Elena, who worked for Beaty, were good friends and often visited by shouting across the dividers that separated the rooms in our apartments. When I was on day duty, their chatter didn't bother me, but when I had worked a full day and all night as well as additional nights when emergencies arose, I needed my *siesta*. Time after time I asked Maruquita to keep the house quiet, only to be jolted awake by shouts and giggles. We talked about the problem, but her only reply was, "I forgot."

Getting rest was important to me, so I decided I needed to help her remember. "If it happens again," I finally said, "I will deduct something from your pay to help you remember in the future."

In the past if she didn't like my instructions she would walk around for several days with her head held high, but that time she walked off without finishing her work and went home. With several patients staying in the clinic, I needed help and asked Claudia if she would return to work for me until I found a permanent replacement. The news traveled fast and it wasn't long before Maruquita's mother came and asked if I would take her daughter back.

She did return and we had a long discussion about how there would be no problem if she followed instructions. We also talked about how Satan tempts us to do wrong. Since she seldom talked about such things, I used the occasion to probe her knowledge of the things she had been hearing for the past year. She quietly told me, "I know all people are sinners and only Christ has salvation."

"What then?" I asked.

"Someday I will accept Christ," she answered.

"And what will that mean?" I continued.

"To ask to be forgiven for sin," was her reply, and I knew she understood.

She didn't understand, however, the recipe I gave her for cookies. I told her not to put the balls of dough too close together on the cookie sheet because they would spread out while baking, but when they came out of the oven they were still little round balls. When I tried to eat one I discovered they were hard. We went over the recipe together, and I saw I had used ditto marks to indicate one cup of sugar under the written-out one cup of flour. She said that in the bread recipe the ditto marks meant one tablespoon, so she thought I always meant tablespoon when I used those marks. The little balls had been on the trays for our patients also, and all were returned to the kitchen uneaten! Another try at the recipe the following day resulted in edible cookies and restored Maruquita's confidence that she could make good cookies. Later Maruquita, then called María, worked in the clinic and became a good helper.

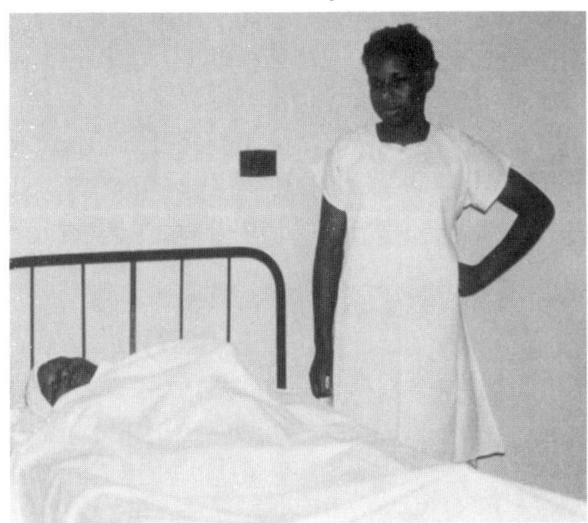

Maruquita (María) with a patient.

Although I was committed to providing the best medical care possible, I was even more concerned about the spiritual well-being of the patients and their families, the other missionaries, the villagers, and the local officials. I prayed constantly and solicited the prayers of my family and home church for all the people I met. To strengthen spiritual ties with neighbors and clients, I started teaching a Sunday School class for women. I usually had from two to five women and occasionally a husband came, too.

Sometimes I failed to help someone because of misunderstandings such as the time a poor, uneducated, young woman came to the clinic for a prenatal examination but failed to return for delivery. When she didn't come, I thought she was overdue. I met her mother-in-law on the street one day and she told me her daughter-in-law had heard we put our patients to bed and left them all alone. Afraid to deliver alone, she had delivered at home but the baby had lived less than three days. From the details I got, the baby had had a lot of mucus, and I wondered if perhaps we could have saved its life because we always aspirated the babies at birth. That was the fifth child she had lost either at birth or shortly thereafter.

Many suturing cases came our way because of machetes. A neighbor rushed in one day with the tip of her finger cut through the bone, and one day two men arrived with blood streaming. One was drunk and had threatened the other with his machete. In the scuffle over the machete, both were cut. The drunken man had a cut on his thumb, and the other man's knee was cut into the bone.

The toughest suturing job, however, was on the heel of a man who probably never wore shoes. He was Carlota's brother and he had a deep cut from a stone. Tilda keep telling me, "Go easy or you will break the needle."

I said, "I am going easy, but I have to push as hard as I can to get through the skin." His skin was like leather and before I got the wound closed I had broken one of our biggest and strongest suturing needles.

I never got a chance to witness or give medical care to a man who fell while repairing one of the bridges on the way to Tocoa. He had a broken jaw and broken neck. His companions had picked him up, loaded him on a truck, and were bringing him to the clinic, but just before they arrived he breathed his last. His was the most distressing case either Ruth or Carlota had ever seen and both were quite upset. Ruth, in fact, didn't like to be left alone on night duty for quite some time after that.

Easier to handle were the many sick babies that arrived after an outbreak of Asian flu. One day we had 17, but then the count dropped to three or four, with only a few who needed to be admitted. I also made home visits to give injections. The flu continued for several months and many patients also had malaria.

Saturdays were always busy. People from other villages came to shop in Trujillo and many Caribs came to our clinic sales room to purchase Vaseline for their hair and magnesia powder for purges. Before the magnesia fad they had used castor oil but the magnesia was not as messy. Purges were considered important for good health.

When Don Emilio was bitten by a Tommy Goff, he didn't come to me or Dr. Pavón. Although the Tommy Goff is extremely poisonous, the people had their own cures for snakebite; someone in Santa Fe took care of him at home and he recovered.

In mid-August Dr. Frank Cline, a medical doctor from Nebraska came to Trujillo on vacation. He had worked in a hospital where many La Junta Mennonite Hospital nurses had worked, and he recognized me as a graduate from there by my nurse's cap. He was interested in plants and wildlife, and after one hike up the mountain he gave me three kinds of orchids he had found. Maruquita and I tied them in our trees so they could attach themselves and grow.

The former governor Don Moisés's sister, Rosita, and I took Dr. Cline up to *La Confianza*. We decided to walk up and ride horses back, but when we were halfway up, it started to rain and continued all day. The clouds came right down over the house and it was very cool and damp. When it was time to return, Don Moisés said it was too dangerous to ride horses, especially when we would get to the cobblestone road down the mountain side. He expected the rivers would be too swift and deep to cross safely. I was willing to stay even though I was not prepared, but Dr. Cline felt he might be getting flu or amebas and wanted to get back where medical attention was available. I stayed, but he walked back to Trujillo and said the one river was up to his waist. He was sick in bed the next day.

After Dr. Cline left the house to walk home, Don Moisés and Doña María Ester and I had an opportunity to talk about their spiritual lives. I discovered they listened faithfully to Christian radio programs over *Voice of the Andes*. At the supper table they prayed a table prayer, a Hail Mary, part of the Lord's prayer, and Don Moisés finished with a personal prayer. When Doña María Ester put the children to bed, she took each one, starting with the youngest, into another room and I heard her saying prayers, which were repeated by the child. The child then came to kiss his father good-night, and to each one he said in Spanish, "Good night and God bless you."

After the children were all in bed, we adults also retired and I went to sleep to the sound of the others repeating Hail Marys and other prayers. I had no doubt the peace and contentment in that household came from a true faith in God even though not all their beliefs were the same as mine. By morning it was safe to use horses on the trail, and the following day I was neither sore nor stiff from the nine-mile walk up or the ride back.

Only two weeks later I went up again. Doña María Ester went into labor early and her mother wasn't due to arrive for another week. Don Moisés sent a *mozo* with horses for his mother and me, and we urged them on so that we arrived in slightly over two hours. Doña

María Ester met us at the door when we arrived, and I knew my prayer was answered that she wouldn't have to deliver without any help. Her labor stopped and we decided the grandmother would stay to care for the children while Doña María Ester returned to Trujillo with me, because I wasn't sure I could return in time later if I had other patients at the clinic. It was also the rainy season and it might not be possible for anyone to cross the rivers. Don Moisés accompanied us over the roughest part of the trail and we arrived at his mother's house without incident. Doña María Ester's mother arrived from Costa Rica ten days later and since Doña María Ester was feeling well, they decided to return up the mountain. About a week later I received a letter announcing the birth of a healthy eight and a half pound girl.

I had another mother arrive in labor, but when her pains stopped, she didn't leave. She said, "If I go home now, my three little children won't want me to come back when I need to."

A nine-year-old boy was carried 20 miles to the clinic by his father. He had been hit with a piece of flying wood. In addition to cuts and bruises he was also suffering from malaria. Someone was driving in the general direction of his home when he was discharged, so he and his father were able to ride most of the way.

One afternoon, after a brisk shower, I stepped out on the patio to an unusual sight. A swarm of some kind of insects was flying around, and in our sour orange tree were about 20 king birds, two brilliant yellow Dicha Fes, a blue-gray bird, and a big grackle. At least a dozen of these birds were in the air all the time snapping up insects. The only sound was from their wings and the snapping of beaks.

September 15 arrived with all the usual celebrations. I didn't really mind the firecrackers, but I never could understand why all the noise had to start at four o'clock in the morning. During the day I could barely hear myself think when a lively soccer game was played on the lot next to the house with dozens of enthusiastic spectators, and a marimba band was stationed six feet outside the clinic window facing the town square. With lots of skill and utter abandon, the band swung into lively, loud tunes and finished with grand flourishes. There was a large marimba played by two men, two saxophones, a bass viol taller than the tall Carib who thumped it, and a set of five drums with plate and bell, all manned by another Carib. The one saxophonist also beat two sticks together at times and shook two *maracas* (rattles).

As I watched the men, I prayed they would someday come to know the Lord. A young man in the Instituto Bíblico in Puerto Rico was

Trujillo from the air.
The black-roofed building was ours.
The clinic was in the right-hand end, the home I shared with various missionaries over the years was in the left end, and Hesses' lived in the "L" partly hidden behind the mango tree.
The building to the right is the *Cabíldo* or town hall.
To the left of our house is the *Cuartel*,
and in front of our house is the *parque* or park.
The Catholic church is in the upper right corner of the picture.

once a marimba player in Tocoa before he became a Christian, but as I thought of the multitudes of unsaved in Trujillo, in Honduras, and in Central America I knew what I was doing barely scratched the surface of what needed to be done to reach the lost. I prayed for an outpouring of the Holy Spirit to bring convicting power to pierce the terrible indifference and self-righteousness around me.

I, too, needed to repent because I realized when things were going well in the church and clinic, I neglected to pray as I should for the unsaved around me. Satan also used busyness and tiredness to push away prayer time, and although I was refreshed by listening to the *Luz Y Verdad* radio program from Puerto Rico Sunday mornings, I was grateful the Holy Spirit used the noisy marimba music to remind me to pray for a revival in Honduras.

Only one child showed up for Sunday School that day because all school children had to be at the park for a patriotic program or pay a fine of five lempiras—two and a half U. S. dollars.

That afternoon, in the midst of the celebrations, I watched a three-month-old baby die from a heart defect he had from birth. He was brought in only a few hours before death and there was nothing to do except pray with the parents who had lost their only other child six months before. The young mother told me she was resigned to whatever was God's will, and when the last struggling breath was taken, she shed quiet tears unlike many women who cry out and wail hysterically when a death occurs.

♔

September was baby month—eight! One of the mothers, Enid, came from Hog Island several weeks early and stayed with Tilda. Some of us were having bouts with amebas, and when Enid started feeling sick, Tilda brought her to the clinic and said she had what the rest of us had. We all thought Tilda's diagnosis was a good joke when Enid delivered a five and a half pound baby girl an hour later.

Dora Soliz joined Tilda, Carlota, and Ruth in the clinic and, of course, needed to be trained and supervised. After her hospital training in La Ceiba, Tilda wore a uniform, which consisted of a blue Indian Head cotton material dress and a white apron. When I saw some blue crinkle crepe in one of the stores, I bought enough so Ruth, Carlota, and Dora could make their own uniform-type dresses. I wanted people to recognize the nurses held their positions because of special training; a uniform would increase their status in the eyes of our patients.

With four women to trade shifts, I released myself from regular night duty although I was still available for any nighttime crisis. My daily work schedule included working out the menus and schedules, doing reports, keeping all records, and placing orders for drugs and supplies, as well as a daytime shift in the clinic.

The Asian flu was still going around in October and I was glad it was the time of year for sweet, juicy oranges. I bought them by the hundreds—50 for 50 cents—and the patients had an abundance of juice and vitamin-packed desserts.

I was called out one night to attend to a woman with a temperature of 104°. I gave injections of Conmel and Ascorbic Acid and left Sulfadiazine, and the next morning her fever had broken, but there were many others still very ill. In the clinic were two very sick babies, and one afternoon when I was on duty alone, the one died. At the same time I had an eight-year-old boy and an older man with typhoid fever and malaria. The same night another man was brought in with typhoid fever and he too had malaria. It was a week before he was strong enough even to sit up in bed.

A welcome break in our routine was the wedding of Victoriano, a believer in Santa Fe. We were all hoping the weather would allow us to take the boat so more of us could attend, but I decided if we couldn't, I would walk with James and J. Mark. The wedding was announced for 7:30 in the morning and we planned to start at six. When I woke up, I could hear the breakers on the shore, but soon James announced the sea was calming down and we would use the boat. We packed our good clothing, and it was good we did because it started to rain before we got there. We went to the home of a friend to change and she gave us some delicious papaya. The mayor of San Antonio, who married the couple, didn't arrive until eleven o'clock because of the rain. When he read the marriage laws, I learned the legal age for a man to marry is 14 and for a woman 12. The couple married that day was older.

The bride had a long white dress and veil which had been used by several other brides. The groom wore shoes, miss-matched trousers and coat, and a necktie. Their two little daughters proudly wore new white shoes, but their dresses were not new. The cost of getting married in an acceptable style kept many couples from going through the ceremony, but this groom wanted to join the church and was asked to marry the woman he was living with before being baptized. The bride was not a believer, but we were all praying for her.

For the meal which followed the ceremony I sat at a small table with J. Mark and the bride. The other guests were served wherever they were standing. We started with chicken and rice and ended with cake and something to drink.

I invited Victoriano and his bride and some friends to come for a meal the week he was baptized. He was so happy and was trusting the Lord for everything. Heavy clouds on the mountain threatened rain when it was time for them to return to Santa Fe, and I told him that since he had just recently been in the hospital with TB he really should not get wet in a storm. With new-found faith he declared, "The Lord will keep the rain back until we get home because He knows it would not be good for me to get wet."

Sure enough, it didn't rain that night. He told me later that when they passed through Cristales, a storekeeper told them they were going to get wet because it was going to rain hard. Victoriano's reply was, "No, our Lord Jesus Christ that I have accepted for my only Savior is not going to let it rain till we get there."

The storekeeper laughed at him, but I was blessed by the witness Victoriano had given. Even though he could not read, he was growing in his Christian life. He told me his wife was softening; he knew she would come to the Lord but was afraid to do so because of her family.

When the rains came, I again mopped puddles. A new roof for the entire building was on a budget list, but that didn't keep the rain out nor did the screens on some windows or the canvas curtains on others. Before the storm started, the sea was rough and we had quite a fireworks-like show as the phosphorescence on the waves broke in showers of glistening lights.

Hurrying down the street one day, I met a very nice, polite young man from Tocoa. He had been one of my father's pallbearers the year before, so I was pleased to greet him. My pleasure turned to dismay as we walked along and he asked me if I had never been married and if I wouldn't like someone to take care of me. He went on to tell me he had never been married either—not even once—that he would like to get married and admired me very much. I hastened to explain I thought marriage should last a lifetime and was not a decision to be made quickly. -*Magnífico*-—he was delighted! That was exactly how he felt, and he wanted even more to marry me and then went on to explain he was only 25 and had only a third grade education. When I said education shouldn't matter but people should love each other, he broke in to say, "Then what is to stop us? I think we could marry with about 400 lempiras."

I next tried to tell him it was impossible because I was much older, but he swept that excuse aside by telling me that after marriage our ages would balance out. I told him that a Christian should marry only another Christian and he had to admit he had never *entered* but was reading the New Testament and liked it very much. I told him to continue and that he should accept Christ and ask God to lead him to a good Christian girl. "There are many fine Christian girls in Honduras," I said.

"Yes," he answered. "There may be 50, but what if you just love one?"

He was a most persistent suitor, and it was with difficulty I finally got away on my errand after making sure he understood he was without hope of finding a wife in me. Whenever I met him on the streets after that, he always flashed me a big smile, and I was glad my rejection of his proposal had not caused him to feel rejected as a person.

My forty-seventh birthday was celebrated three weeks later by opening packages that had been sent by family members with returning mission workers and saved for that special day. A can of cranberry sauce was put aside for Christmas. A box of candy was shared immediately, and Jell-O® appeared on the table for dessert one evening and junket the next, but once again peanut butter got the most attention. I'm not sure why I craved it so much, but in my thank-you letter to Mother I told her I was already planning to eat a lot of peanut butter when I was on furlough the next time.

♔

Ever since I had heard about the road over the mountain to Tocoa I had wanted to try it. My opportunity came in early November. There were no patients in the clinic, my file cards showed no deliveries expected until December, and a woman who had been visiting her daughter in Trujillo was ready to go home to Tocoa.

She had ridden over the mountain with a *mozo* to care for her horse but was planning to walk most of the way back, at least until she was over the mountain. I knew she was a strong woman, but since she was 64 years old and quite stout, I figured I could keep up with her, so I asked if I could walk with her.

We planned to leave at three on a Saturday morning, but since I heard it raining hard, I didn't get up until the usual time. At ten the sun came out and Doña Zoila telegraphed to Tocoa to check on the weather there. They replied that the weather was good and would she please bring back the mule the *sub-comandante* had ridden to Trujillo.

We started off along the beach at one in the afternoon. I was on Doña Zoila's white horse, she rode the larger mule, and Santiago, the *mozo*, walked. When we reached *La Culebrina* (culebra means snake), the ancient cobblestone trail over the mountain, Doña Zoila was afraid her white horse would slip on the wet stones and break a leg so we dismounted and began walking. Santiago rode ahead of us on the mule leading the horse.

Doña Zoila took off her shoes and on bare feet plunged straight ahead through the mud. My feet were too tender to do that, so I had to hunt for spots where the mud wouldn't go over the tops of my galoshes. She may have been a slow walker but her steady pace covered ground, and when I would have gladly called a halt to rest, she wasn't even breathing hard. We did stop for a breather at the spot where I had earlier turned off the road to go to *La Confianza*, the farm of the former governor, Don Moisés.

The road from there was steeper with more areas where the cobblestones were broken out and where erosion had cut the trail into a deep ditch. I was riding again when the trail went between rocks so high I couldn't see over the top and at times so narrow my feet were knocked out of the stirrups unless I tucked them together under the horse. If a flash flood ever caught someone there, it would surely drown both horse and rider. Vines, ferns, and all kinds of greenery constantly drew my eyes down, up, and from side to side, and the air was filled with the songs and chatter of birds and of water rushing through the rapids in the many streams. A change of scenery occurred when we rounded a bend and entered a completely barren gorge with red, sandy soil.

Because of our late start, Doña Zoila planned to sleep at La Brea or, if darkness caught up with us before getting that far, at Higuerito. We were still walking down the mountain, however, when night closed in on us. At places the descent was so steep Doña Zoila had to use her hands to climb down, but I found a good stout walking stick and it was quite an adventure to walk along like that in the forest at night by flashlight.

At the foot of the mountain we mounted our animals again, and Doña Zoila said we would spend the rest of the night at Higuerito even if we had to sit up. I had been imagining how good it would feel to stretch out and sleep and when she said that, I thought, *Oh, I hope I can lie down even if it's on somebody's ground floor.*

Forty-five minutes later we reached the house Doña Zoila was aiming for and even though it was probably after eleven o'clock, we heard greetings and "Where did you come from, where are you going, and come in." Soon we were in a large kitchen dimly lit by glowing embers on the earthen stove in one corner. A large bake oven shared that end of the room, and the other end had a small table and benches and stools. I discovered I knew the woman from visits to the clinic and had twice delivered babies for her daughter. Doña María quickly spread the table with a tablecloth and served us coffee as we got out our food. By cutting up my three apples I was able to share with everyone.

Doña María left the room and returned a short time later to announce our beds were ready. The bedroom was quite large and had five native beds which are not quite as wide as a double bed. The *springs* of the beds were inch-wide poles laid against each other and bound to a frame of larger poles resting on forked sticks stuck in the ground at the corners. The *mattress* was a piece of canvas folded and laid over the *springs*. There was a pillow but no sheets or covers. Doña Zoila and I shared a bed, Santiago slept on a piece of canvas on the ground floor, and the seven family members shared the other four beds. I put my raincoat down over my legs, covered my face with one of my father's large hankies, and went straight to sleep in spite of mosquitoes buzzing all around me.

Some time during the night I woke up and had to remind myself how much I had longed to lie down while back on the trail. The bed seemed to get harder and harder and before I was able to doze off again I surely wished I was back on my horse. However, when Doña Zoila said, *-Nos levantemos,-* "Let's get up," I wasn't really ready to wake up.

Doña María again served coffee to go with the food we had with us, and probably around five o'clock we mounted our horse and mule and struck out once more for Tocoa. The jungle had been cut back so that the trail there was about 30 feet wide and straight. The dense growth consisted of vines flowing down in 50-foot falls of shimmering green heart-shaped leaves from massive, tall, straight trees. Fruit and brightly colored flowers including gorgeous bird-of-paradise blooms dazzled us at every turn. Colorful birds flew in and out among the vines and thick corozo palms, whose graceful arching branches almost hid clusters of brown nuts. One squirrel was the only animal I saw, and no snake appeared to startle us or our mounts. We crossed seven rivers or large streams, but only two were so high that we had to take our feet out of the stirrups to keep them dry. At one we crossed in sight of a waterfall and I marveled at the beauty all around us and in my heart just worshipped God, who created it all.

Two hours on the trail brought us to La Brea, a small village of thatch-roofed mud houses. Next we went through savannas, open green plains with patches of forest, and following that, the countryside changed again to pine trees on low rolling hills of gravelly soil. Another three leagues or nine miles brought us to Ilanga. This was a detour because of washed-out bridges; the four or five miles from there to the Aguan River were pure mud—four to twelve inches deep. It was there I gave the most thanks for the horse and mule. There was no way to get around the mud and it would have pulled my galoshes off at the first step. Santiago went right through it barefooted.

At the Aguan River Santiago unsaddled the horses while we fought off mosquitoes and waited for a boy with a long dugout to come from the other side. Another woman on a horse arrived while we waited, and we three women and the saddles went across first with the two horses swimming along side with us holding their ropes. Santiago said the mule would kick too much to swim with the horses and so he came on a second trip with it. According to the pole used to steer the dugout, the swiftly-running river was probably about 12 feet deep at that spot. The cost of the trip was a nickel for each person and animal.

From the river we had about an hour of gentle rain as we rode the league to Tocoa—mud all the way. Perhaps the anticipation of surprising the mission folks kept me from feeling too tired, and after a brief stop at Doña Zoila's daughter's house for coffee and cake, I went on to the mission station around one o'clock in the afternoon and was not disappointed. No one answered my knock, so I opened the door and walked in. It was *siesta* time and Alma was just sitting up in bed and wondering who would walk into her house like that. Alma, Lorraine, and I had a good visit, and when Norman Hockman came over with a message, he was certainly surprised to find me there.

Alma was getting along fine in the clinic and still working on Spanish. The girl who helped her in the clinic told me that one day as Alma got ready to pull a patient's tooth she heard her say, *-Abre la vaca para sacar la mula,-* which is "Open your cow to take out the mule." She meant *-Abre la boca para sacar la muela,-* which means "Open your mouth to pull the molar." Only a couple letters' difference!

During the night Alma was called out to deliver a baby and she asked me to go along. The mother-to-be was young and terribly frightened. After checking her, Alma said we would be back later, but she practically went wild when she was alone with her mother-in-law and grandmother. I stayed about three hours and went back again after breakfast and again had quite a time getting her calm. She didn't deliver until mid-afternoon, and I felt the Lord had directed my trip at that specific time to relieve Alma, who had to be in the clinic part of the day.

Before four the next morning Santiago was at the door with a plump, white mule which I soon discovered was strong and sure-footed. We reached the river before daylight and then again had to fight off mosquitoes while waiting for the boy with the dugout, apparently asleep on the other side.

After the crossing we made much better time than before and soon passed Ilanga and reached the pines. I asked Santiago to find me a small pine tree that I could plant in the church yard, and then we continued through La Brea, crossed all those seven beautiful rivers again and reached Higuerito by maybe eleven in the morning. Doña María again served coffee as Santiago and I ate the lunch Grace Hockman had packed for us.

Before long we came to the animal gate installed at the foot of the mountain to keep domestic animals from straying up the steep trail.

Santiago said, "Grab hold of the mane hard," so I clung to the mule who seemed to know what he was doing. Some places the descent was so steep the mule had to jump. It was a thrilling ride! I had to walk only once for a short distance, and in the muddiest places and the deepest streams Santiago rode on the mule behind me so we could get through faster.

When we reached the beach the mule suddenly lurched sideways throwing me off balance. In desperation I wrapped my arms around his neck but almost before I knew what was happening my head hit the ground. A dog had run out and bit the heel of the mule and I could only be thankful it had happened in soft sand instead of on the cobblestone road. As it was, I was dirty from the wet sand and couldn't see much out of one eye the rest of the way home. I was also slightly dizzy.

I left Santiago and the mule at Cristales about 4:15 and walked home. Beaty's invitation to use their bathroom for a hot shower was indeed welcome. My muscles were sore the next morning and I felt a little shaky, probably from the fall, but by afternoon all that was left were the memories, scratches, mosquito bites, and the thrill of having been able to do what I long wanted to do.

After our first trip to Tocoa in 1952 Elias Kulp had declared, "I wouldn't have missed it for a good bit, but I wouldn't give five cents to do it again." That is a little the way I felt about this trip and I was glad I didn't have to do it every week as the mailman did. The more I thought about it the more I realized the Lord had certainly looked out for me in my ignorance and had even provided a mule so that I didn't drop by the wayside or end up stuck in the mud.

Tilda had covered in the clinic for my weekend vacation, and so I had several days of work to make up to her. A ten-year-old boy was brought in, who had fallen on a knife and cut his neck. It took eight sutures to close the gash. We also had a young man for several days with acute arthritis in his left foot, and another man injured on the side of his head from being struck by a heavy log. He was brought from a distance—to one of the unsafe bridges, where George met him with the mission truck. He had no open wounds, so I put him to bed with medication for pain and made arrangements to send him to La Ceiba for x-rays.

The doctor was out doing a survey on malaria and parasites for the World Health Organization, and how I wished for his help when a Carib woman who owned one of the village stores was brought in with a dagger wound. A drunken man had entered her store to kill a customer. Because she didn't want her store to get a bad reputation, she placed herself between the two men and ended up with a cut in the thick part of her hand between the thumb and first finger. If ever I needed three hands, it was then. I could stop the steady stream of blood by applying pressure on her wrist, but then I couldn't take care of the wound. The woman who brought her in just couldn't get the knack of applying pressure and finally I had to send her to get James Hess and sent the husband to get Ruth. Even with their help it was still some time before I had anesthetized her hand, found the bleeder, and got the wound closed. She had lost a lot of blood, so I put her to bed and gave her half a liter of intravenous solution.

Our December Bible School had up to 115 students in six classes. Four of the classes were held in the church, and the children were used to talking and reading out loud in school so we had few quiet times. I learned that one of the requirements for a school teacher in Honduras was to have a strong voice.

Christmas brought visitors—James and Jean Gingerich and Rebecca Herr from Costa Rica, and the Hamiltons from La Ceiba, but even with their help our Christmas caroling was a washout. Just as we were ready to start out it began raining. We waited awhile and finally went out in the rain, but it rained so hard we doubted the people could hear us, so we sloshed home in the mud and went to bed.

Jean and James Gingerich holding their twin daughters, Trula and Twila.

The year ended with the news that Maynard and Helen Headings had a baby, Steven Dean, born December 30.

1958

Another Watch Night Service—this time the Hesses invited about 35 Honduran brothers and sisters to watch some gospel films and sing and pray together and, of course, have refreshments. I wasn't there. In spite of taking Camoquin twice before Christmas, it was malaria again. During daytime hours I was well enough to work, but when evening came my temperature went up and I experienced shortness of breath. A couple injections of Aralen and some early-to-bed evenings soon had me feeling well again.

The clinic was busy and on January 4, I delivered the second baby of the new year. One was the most contented newborn I ever saw, but the other one was lively; his noisy cries sounded like a crow cawing! There were house calls too—to Rio Negro for a rheumatism patient and in Trujillo to see an old woman with a cold and sore throat and to dress the infected leg of a man.

A man vomiting blood was brought in from a nearby village. I made arrangements to send him to Tegucigalpa for tests, but he seemed better even before he left. The people of his village believed he was vomiting his liver as a punishment for not having a feast at the time his mother died 50 years before. They told him his mother's spirit was demanding liver, her favorite food, and that he should make a feast with enough chicken and liver to treat all his friends and relatives.

The man was educated and no longer believed in that superstition, but superstitious beliefs and fear of spirits controlled many people. From among the books I had in the clinic I gave the man a *Jungle Doctor* book about witchcraft to read and hoped it gave him a better understanding of why Christians didn't need to fear such things.

Another example of how frightened people are of spirits occurred one day when I left the clinic to go to the home of a patient to give him an injection. I was barely outside when I realized I had forgotten something and went back in through another door. My three nurses had seen me leave but didn't know I had returned. When Carlota heard the medicine closet door open in a room she thought was empty, she shrieked and ran out of the house. When I hurried to find out why she was screaming, she told me she was so frightened because she thought it was spirits making the noise and she didn't want to be in the house with them.

Don Enrique and Meca Carvajal. Florinda and Lillian.

♛

Dr. Pavón left and the rumor that Dr. Auerbach would return proved true. Another rumor was also true. Meca Hode, my Christian Arab friend, was engaged to Don Enrique Carvajal, one of the soldiers who heard the gospel at Father's funeral and later accepted Christ. They married and in the next few years I delivered two daughters for them.

A small boat heading for Panama stopped in Cristales because it had sprung a leak, and when the occupants could produce no passports, the *Comandante* there became suspicious. After some checking he discovered the one man was a gangster from the United States and the woman and other man were escaping from the law in Mexico. He sent to Trujillo for soldiers who arrested the three and jailed them in Trujillo until they could be sent to Tegucigalpa to await deportation. They were returned to Trujillo by government plane the end of June to be transferred to a Mexican Coast Guard vessel waiting in the bay. Because some of our Arab friends were leaving on a SAHSA airplane, a group of us was at the airport to say good-bye. Seconds after the SAHSA plane landed, the government plane started coming in but suddenly veered straight for the spot where Beaty Hess and I were standing beside the mission pickup.

My first thought was that the prisoners aboard had somehow caused the pilot to lose control, but later it was said the braking mechanism on the one side didn't function, causing the plane to veer in the other direction. As I ran a few feet and threw myself flat on my face, my second thought was that unless a doctor was on one of those

The Chahin family just before the airplane accident.

planes I would have to take care of the accident victims. I heard and felt things falling around me and in seconds was back on my feet.

All around me were living people—no one was killed, but Hessie Chahin, sister-in-law of those planning to leave, had blood streaming over her head and face so fast I couldn't even tell where or how serious her injuries were. Her husband was almost hysterical but as frightened as she must have been she was trying to calm him. Within seconds we were in a car being driven to the clinic. I was so busy trying to stop Hessie's bleeding and calm George that I never even noticed who drove the car. It took about 25 stitches to close her wounds: one a long cut from above the hairline down across the forehead and about one inch along the nose. Another two-inch cut was in her hair, and there were several puncture wounds on the back of her head.

Several other people arrived at the clinic with minor cuts and bruises from flying debris or from falling as they fled from the path of the plane. The government sent a Taxi Aereo, or small plane, the following day to take everyone who was injured to Tegucigalpa for examinations. When Hessie's stitches came out and I checked the amount of scarring, I wrote in my journal, *Not bad for an amateur.*

The Lord was very gracious to us! Most of the people were able to run out of the path of the plane, but the wing smashed in the roof of the mission pickup's cap where Dicky and Gerald Hess were watching the events. When their mother, who had watched helplessly, asked the boys if they had crouched down when they saw the plane coming, Dicky replied, "No, I'm a big boy."

Six or seven others were standing behind the truck, which had its wooden top ripped off. If the plane's wing had dipped just inches lower, the results would have been quite different, but as it was, most of the injuries were from pieces torn from the wing as it struck the truck. If the truck hadn't been there, the plane might have continued on into a small house.

The accident also broke the one side of the pickup's windshield, and thereafter the truck had a wooden windshield on the right side.

♔

Dr. Auerbach returned to work in Trujillo and then left on some business. I was beginning to think he had left us permanently, when finally he returned after 16 days instead of the two he had told us he would be gone. The first patient he sent to the clinic was an eight-month-old baby with amebic dysentery who weighed only 11 pounds. I kept close watch all night and thought she seemed slightly better, but at 7:30 in the morning she got worse, and although the doctor did all he could she died an hour later.

I had witnessed to the parents, and after the baby's death they started attending church and finally during a visit to their home they both accepted the Lord. That same week, on pay day, former drinking friends urged the father to join them. He agreed to have a soft drink with them, but they kept after him until he gave in and was soon drunk. James heard about it and went looking for him. He was repentant, but the next day it happened again and that time he had a machete, a gun, and his hunting knife and got into trouble with the police and ended up in jail. After that both he and his wife stopped attending services altogether. I visited them and the mother said she wanted to come but their daughter had a bad chest cold.

Next I heard they left town to cook for a road crew some distance away. Shortly after that all their children caught whooping cough and were brought to Trujillo to the grandmother's home. The three-year-old girl, after coughing for more than two weeks, was brought to the clinic with a high fever and vomiting, and passing worms. I wasn't sure if the worms were the cause of the fever or not, but in spite of all I did, she slipped away to join her little sister in heaven. Many children had bad cases of worms, mainly Ascaris or round worms. In May we lost a little boy to a worm attack.

The last day of January I delivered the fifth baby of the year in the clinic. Other patients were a young woman with a temperature of 106° from malaria and a pelvic infection, a young boy with a rheumatic heart, and a woman with a threatened miscarriage.

The scrapbook Mother sent for the clinic was enjoyed so much by our young patients and adults who couldn't read that it became a loose-leaf book. Mother helped me repair the book by including gummed hole-reinforcements in several of her letters. She also got a Sunday School class to make a new one.

Don Alfredo Melhado was eighty years old on February 10. I was one of three persons, other than family members, invited to his birthday party. The Melhado family was perhaps the wealthiest family in Trujillo. They had permanent hotel accommodations in both Tegucigalpa and New Orleans. The first half hour of the birthday party was spent visiting, drinking cocktails and other drinks, and eating hors d'oeuvres—enchiladas, chicharrones, caviar, hot peppers, cheese, crackers, etc. Dinner was buffet style—fried chicken, rice, little sandwiches, potato salad, pickles, dates, peanuts, a birthday cake, iced cookies, and coffee. Ada, the niece who delivered my invitation, told me that cocktails would be served but that they understood I would not drink any.

All at once everyone seemed to be sick. Tilda was down with malaria and unable to attend church on Sunday or work for a few days. Carlota missed two nights of work with malaria, and Ruth said she didn't feel well either. Even the doctor did not show up for several days. Grace Miller heard that some workers building a dam were bathing and washing their clothes in the reservoir that supplied water to Trujillo. I am sure they didn't see anything wrong with that because the people usually used the same river or stream to bathe and wash clothes as they did for drinking water. I had once noticed someone washing her dishes in the same hand basin the family used for bathing.

Ira Buckwalter and Donald Lauver arrived in mid-February with greetings from the churches in the United States and held services at the various mission stations. Their visit to Trujillo was cut short when a Central American Mission worker in the western part of Honduras died, possibly from a brain tumor caused by amebas. Don Berry of MAF had to fly Buckwalter and Lauver to San Pedro Sula and then go to Siguatepeque for the body.

While the two men were visiting us, they had a meeting with a citizens' committee about a new hospital in Trujillo's plans. The Mission Board needed to know the expectations of the local officials and tell them we would close our clinic when the hospital opened. The citizens' committee informed us they would like us to run the hospital, buy supplies, hire workers, etc., but all that was in the future.

♛

I had been giving piano lessons to a young Arab girl for several years. When she reached high school age, the family decided to move to the United States and offered me first chance to buy their piano. I had enjoyed spending free time in their home playing and knew I would miss it when they were gone, so after prayer and advice, I purchased it. James brought it in the truck and how we enjoyed the music! When the young people met in my house, we played and sang. James also enjoyed slipping over in spare moments to play it, so I decided it was a worthwhile purchase, even though a bit expensive for a missionary's budget.

♛

A 12-year-old boy was brought in one day in March with about half of a five-and-a-half-inch harpoon in his foot. One of the four imbedded hooks was around a tendon, and the doctor worked a long time to free it without causing more damage. The boy had never been to school and enjoyed coloring pictures and looking at the scrapbooks.

An English-speaking man from one of the islands had jaundice for which the doctor ordered complete bed rest. Many times, however, I found him sitting on a chair. He said his eyes bothered him if he tried to read, so that left him with nothing to do for most of a month.

At the same time those two patients were sharing our facilities, a Carib man was brought in quite dizzy but without a diagnosis, two old women were brought from Santa Fe, and a judge with possible diphtheria spent three days in the clinic before a special plane came and took him to Tegucigalpa.

Don Alfredo, whose birthday party I had attended, had a light stroke and although the family hired a Carib boy to care for him, they offered me a free trip when they took him by chartered plane to Tegucigalpa. His niece Ada said she wanted me to go as a companion for her, but mostly they wanted to give me the gift of an all-paid vacation. I wasn't due any vacation time just then, but to refuse such a gracious gift might have jeopardized our relationship and shut off opportunities to witness to the family. After prayer and talking with the other missionaries, it was decided I should go and allow the Holy Spirit to use me in whatever way offered.

Tegucigalpa was dry and dusty. We stayed in the Viera Hospital just as one would stay in a hotel, and I received invitations to visit several people who had once lived in Trujillo. Before we returned, I met Dorothy Showalter, a secretary, who had just arrived after getting her residence visa in El Salvador. She returned to Trujillo with us, and Don then flew her on to Tocoa in the MAF plane when he came to pick up Phyllis Taylor, a nurse from Massachusetts working at the Siguatepeque hospital who was sent to the Hesses to convalesce from hepatitis.

A letter from Mother was waiting for me that told all about the big snow of 1958 in Morgantown, and I wrote back telling her of temperatures close to 100° and wondering how I would survive the cold on my furlough the following year.

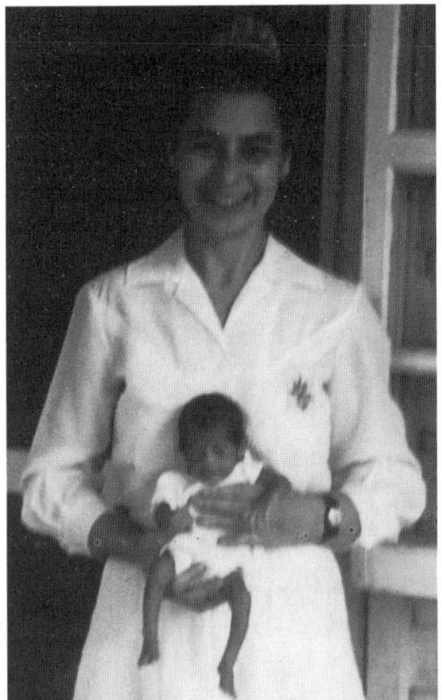

Olguita's first picture.

At the clinic the man with hepatitis was still enduring bed rest, and a new patient with a stab wound in his chest had the next bed. I gave him a book about salvation. Later when I passed the door, I heard him reading it to the other man.

Within 15 minutes of admission a 19-year-old girl delivered twin girls. She had no idea she was having twins and hadn't expected to deliver that soon. The one baby was three pounds and the other three pounds, two ounces. The firstborn died the next day after having a number of *blue spells.* I think her lungs weren't fully developed. The mother didn't mind the death at all and had told Tilda she could have one of the babies because she couldn't raise two at a time. Olga Lidia, the smaller baby did well but was too weak to breast-feed and since we didn't have a breast pump, the mother used hot compresses and milked her breasts. We knew the baby wouldn't survive if sent home, so

Tilda and Olguita.

Olga and Olguita.

we had interrupted nights for the next few months. Since all our other babies went home with their mothers *Olguita* (Little Olga) gave my nurses practice in caring for a baby. When her mother went home, we put Olguita on SMA, a liquid formula.

Olga visited in early May and could hardly believe Olguita was the same baby. We had been feeding her with a medicine dropper, then graduated to a Breck feeder, and finally to a regular bottle. By May she was slightly over five pounds, but she still slept most of the time. The next step was to wean her from the formula to cow's milk, which we did by decreasing the percentage of SMA each day and increasing the cow's milk. Within two weeks she was totally on cow's milk with no adverse affects.

The nurses all enjoyed caring for Olguita and dressing her up with a ribbon in her hair, and pretty dresses. Most of the dresses we had were much too large for her, but Tilda made tiny clothes out of sewing circle flannel diapers. When her mother took her home late in May, she weighed almost six pounds. On her first visit back she looked well and had gained three more pounds.

Dicky Hess also provided us with an emergency. He caught a finger of his left hand in a door and tore the end almost off. I took one look and sent James for the doctor. I held Dicky's arms, James held his feet, and Tilda and Ruth helped the doctor as he sutured. Dicky didn't like what was being done to him and used all his strength and all his lung power in an effort to get away. He wore everyone out including himself, because he fell asleep as the last suture was put in place.

The next suturing case was a two-year-old girl who was bitten in the head by a dog. The dog's teeth had apparently slid on the bone leaving three long slits. I had to shave the whole back of her head so the doctor could do his work. We had her stay for a day or two, and although she spent most of her waking hours crying, she found some comfort playing with a doll included with some toys sent from friends back home.

April ended with a week of hot, dry, strong winds—the kind that unlocked and opened doors, blew pictures off the walls, and stopped the cuckoo clock by blowing the pendulum off rhythm. It also blew out matches, and after I finally managed to get a lamp lit, quite often blew it out. We couldn't close the windows because they were just screens. The benefit from the winds was that it blew the mosquitoes away and for a little while we slept without nets.

With May came the beginning of fresh fruit. Papayas ripened every day. Before the mangoes were ripe James had to trim branches where they touched the electric wires and Beaty and I harvested the green fruit and made mango sauce. I used the jars the Frazer Mennonite Church had sent full of fruit and vegetables. I didn't have any new lids so reused the old ones and most of them sealed. By the end of June I had ten different kinds of fruit in the refrigerator at one time, but almost no vegetables. Most of the fruit was yellow so we were getting plenty of vitamin A. Green bananas were five for one cent, and María, as we now called Maruquita, boiled three for her lunch each day. I wasn't very fond of green bananas even when she sliced them and fried them like potato chips.

María wanted to know how to make mango/orange jam, so we made one batch together and gave some to her mother. She also wanted to learn how to use the sewing machine. I helped her cut out a dress and then gave her instructions. At first she had trouble keeping the treadle going steadily enough to make the machine go the right direction and kept moving her chair back until she was so far away she could barely reach the machine. Finally she conquered the technique and enjoyed it from then on.

Grace, Beaty, and I had started a sewing-circle-type meeting for any women interested in attending. Twelve women attended our May meeting, where we worked on little kimonos to give to mothers when

Women's Sewing Circle.

they left the clinic with their new babies. It was a novel experience for most of the women to sit and visit and work together.

James Hess and a young man named Merrill Wood, who had accepted the Lord in the clinic, went on a trip down the coast. At Rio Esteban, a Moreno village, James set up his loudspeaker and before he preached in Spanish, he played some Moreno records, which drew 200 people to their first meeting. The next day the two of them went on to Cayos Cochinos for another meeting.

Merrill Wood

Merrill also started teaching the children's Sunday School class in Santa Fe. They were soon meeting outside under a tree because there were sometimes 75 or more pupils. Adults who didn't go to the service James had in a house often stood around to listen to the Bible stories Merrill taught. Beaty, thinking about the noisy village schools, asked him how he managed to keep that many children quiet. He said, "They are always quiet so they can hear the story, but when I hand out cards, they all clamber and reach." A few years ago I heard that Merrill was a minister in Gran Cayman.

The World Health Organization had a malaria-eradicating plan for Central America and sent teams of men around to spray houses with DDT. They did the Millers' house first and after I saw all the cleaning Grace had to do afterward María and I moved the furniture to the center of each room and covered it with sheets. We took the medicines off the shelves and clothing out of closets, but just covered up the jars on the kitchen shelves. Instead of washing each item, we only needed to do a quick housecleaning after the men left, but it was still a big job to do it all in one day. Patients were moved out on the porch during the invasion of the sprayers and for quite some time we saw no ants or scorpions and only a few mosquitoes in our houses.

When the sprayers came in 1963, they told us that was the last year of the program. Eighty percent of the people in the country had malaria before they started, and although the goal was to eradicate malaria completely, we were told that 20 percent still had it. We were definitely seeing far fewer malaria patients than in earlier years.

I often wondered how missionaries ever did without the MAF

(Missionary Aviation Fellowship) planes. They transported the sick and dying, the incoming and outgoing missionaries, the missionary children to and from boarding schools, took missionaries to remote villages, and hauled supplies. What a blessing those pilots, Donald Berry, Paul Weir, Arthur Snider, and others, were to us. When we had our June meetings in Tocoa, it took three flights to get us all there—14 minutes each way instead of hours on the road.

While there I spent one day in the clinic with Alma, who had several children with gastroenteritis, a patient with swollen glands, one with an infected hand, and several with malaria.

Soon after I got back to Trujillo I had my own variety of patients. A very sick Carib boy was brought in with a possible case of worms. His eyes were open, but he didn't respond to anything. The parents took him home, thinking he would die anyway, and I felt the same. A threatened miscarriage interrupted my siesta after I was up most of the night with the boy, and then a man came in who had been bitten by a pig 24 hours earlier on a distant farm. A second maternity case arrived before evening, and next morning Ruth felt sick with what I suspected might be appendicitis. I made plans to send her to La Ceiba that evening by boat, and about that time Dora said she felt as though she had the grippe.

Two days later at two in the morning, the night nurse woke me up to care for a man from Colonia who had been *machetado* (cut with a machete) by a man who wanted to kill him. It had happened about seven the evening before, and friends took him as far as the bridges in a car and then carried him the rest of the way on a cot. Eight men and a nurse arrived with him. The nurse told me all the fingers of one hand were cut off, and since we were sending him on to La Ceiba I didn't disturb that bandage, just reinforced it. I did clean the deep wound on his right shoulder where the machete had cut through the collar bone. I placed the edges of the bone together and bandaged his arm to hold it in place until he got to the hospital, gave him saline solution, penicillin, liver, vitamin K, and Commel, and put him to bed. A few hours later I gave him Amigen, an intravenous fluid containing proteins, and that helped him quite a bit because he had lost a lot of blood. I heard later he had operations in La Ceiba and was doing well. When he was with us he seemed no more concerned about the loss of his fingers than I would of a paper cut.

Berta, the girl who took Carlota's place when she left, was getting lots of experience in the clinic. In less than a week following the *machetado* patient, we had a stillborn birth, a heart patient, the birth of a healthy baby, and a 17-year-old boy with his thumb almost cut off. The tendon was not cut, but the doctor had to remove bone splinters before sewing the thumb back in place.

I wished for my camera the day an old Carib woman was released from the clinic. Three men brought a rocking chair to take her home. After getting her comfortably seated, two of the men lifted the chair, one on either side, and the third walked behind holding the rockers. I wasn't sure how he was helping. Jean suggested he might be pushing.

After the Melhado clan returned from a month in New Orleans, I gave Don Alfredo injections twice a week at his home. On one visit Carlos started telling stories about the Paya people. There is a village of them called El Carbon a few days' journey from the Melhado farm. Although Carlos had once seen a building that looked like a church, the people have never accepted the Catholic religion except to baptize babies. Instead, they worship the devil called Maiserá. Carlos saw altars at El Carbon and a place he thought was used to execute people or perhaps to hold human sacrifices.

Those people still use blow guns with poison darts. Carlos once heard that eight men were buried alive with only their heads sticking out of the ground. He had seen the bodies after the villagers had finished killing the men. He also saw the bodies of men who had been hung by their heels with their heads cut off. Carlos said the whole village banded together to take vengeance and kill offenders when a crime occurred.

Once Carlos came upon a place in the forest with a stone column carved with faces. Some of the Paya people were there and asked him to leave because he was trespassing on their sacred place. A bit farther on he noticed a hole in a high inaccessible place in the mountain where a river emerged and a rock that resembled a monkey was visible. The village people worship the rock monkey and at a certain time of year take the last-born child of the village and place him on an altar, perform some rites, and leave the child there for the devil Maiserá. They say the child is always gone the next morning.

On a trip out to the farm one day Carlos planned to spend the night in a certain clearing. When he and his *mozo* got there, they found a little shelter and a man and a woman. The woman was in labor and would probably deliver during the night. The couple said they had not eaten because the people in the last town wouldn't sell them tortillas, and the man had no bullets to hunt meat.

Carlos managed to kill a deer and the couple immediately started roasting it. The woman had her baby later that night. When Carlos left in the early morning hours, he asked them where they were going. They were headed for a village 44 kilometers away. He offered to take their two heavy bags to the next village on his horse and they took out whatever they needed before he left. His farm was 32 kilometers from the place the baby was born, and only 48 hours later he saw the couple walking past. The mother carried her baby, and the father had the two bags plus the remains of the deer slung over his shoulders.

Eighty-year-old Doña Victoria joined in the conversation at that point to tell me that when a Paya woman is close to having a child she makes a simple roofed shelter by a river. When she is in labor she goes into the river to have the baby and uses a hot machete to cut the cord after tying it two and four inches from the navel. It seemed almost impossible that these things were occurring only a couple days' ride away through the forest or less than an hour's flight by plane. They sounded like stories from long ago and somewhere far away. However, they made me realize that there were many, many people right on my doorstep who had never heard the Gospel.

A government inspector and a lawyer arrived unannounced from Tegucigalpa in August, and a big shake-up occurred in Trujillo with almost everyone from the governor on down being fired for graft. The investigation revealed that although the police payroll was for nine persons only four persons were on the force. The prison books disclosed a similar situation. They also found irregularities in the post office, which possibly explained why so many letters were lost or arrived late.

Deadlines for mailing letters changed according to airplane schedules out of Trujillo. Letters were not dropped into a slot at the post office, but rather presented personally to the clerk at the window after waiting in line. The clerk checked if the envelope was properly addressed and if the correct amount of postage was affixed. I never heard any complaints about where the stamps were pasted, even if on the back, but I did hear mention about dirty envelopes.

Don Alfredo had another stroke, and I made several visits to the home one Saturday and stayed until midnight. When I went home, I found a maternity patient in labor. I got about an hour of sleep before helping in the delivery of an eight and a quarter pound boy who arrived at 5:03 in the morning. At 6:00 I went back to the Melhado home and found Don Alfredo had slipped into a coma. When the doctor arrived, I helped get an intravenous started, gave some injections, and used my homemade aspirator to clear mucus from his throat. I was there most of the day until he died Sunday evening, August 10, at 10:05.

Even though I was very tired, because I had been accepted as a friend of the whole family I stayed all that night and most of the time until the funeral was over. Doña Victoria gave me Don Alfredo's magnifying glass and postal scales as gifts of remembrance. Since she would be wearing mourning for several years, she also gave me a couple new dresses of hers, which I was able to alter and use.

The Millers left on furlough, and even though they had Sunday supper at my house I wasn't there to enjoy their company. I did manage to get home for Monday breakfast with them but was too busy to go to the airport to wave good-bye.

The following Sunday evening a delirious nine-year-old girl was brought in with high fever and obstruction of the bowels from worms. The doctor and I immediately started her on two liters of intravenous fluid.

A man was brought in with machete wounds, and the doctor returned again. Before the doctor could begin suturing, we had to clean the wounds of the dried leaves that had been put on to stop the bleeding; it was after midnight before he finished. There were three wounds: one across the forehead, a deep one on the shoulder, but the worst was a thumb almost cut off. All the bones were smashed and it had to be amputated. With the amount of blood that man was losing, I thought he would die before the doctor was finished, but he didn't. We got him to bed on intravenous fluids as soon as the surgery was finished, but just then another man was brought in with a deep shoulder wound. The doctor patched that man up temporarily and told him to come back the following day.

♔

Leroy Mellinger was sent by the mission board the beginning of August to do maintenance work. I walked into my room one day to find the sun pouring in and Leroy standing amidst wood shavings with sweat dripping off his hands onto the floor and his shirt and trousers completely soaked. A few days later my room had a lovely window installed above a new concrete window seat, and the baby ward had an extremely handy shelf above the Bathinette. I also suggested he tear down a partition, which caused us to lose a spare bedroom but enlarged the living room so we could hold our young people's meetings there.

Jean and Lorraine returned the end of August and I invited some 40 people to a welcome-back party. I wasn't there much, however, because just as the party began, I was called out to help the doctor suture an old Carib woman's leg—an accidental machete cut.

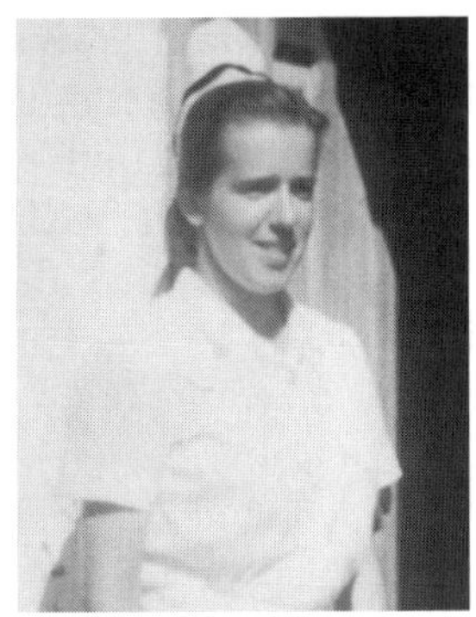
Rebecca Herr

Because I would be leaving on furlough in a few months, Jean started that term in Trujillo, but Lorraine returned to Tocoa. In September Rebecca (Becky) Herr arrived from language school in Costa Rica to observe and help at our clinic before going on to open a clinic in Gualaco, the new mission station. I was glad for her help because we had three or four patients most of the time, besides emergencies and deliveries. When Becky left, Jean went along and spent three weeks with her to help open the clinic and help her with the diagnosis and treatment of common tropical diseases.

Ernest and Barbara Garber also arrived in September, and in October Amzie Yoder came to start an agriculture program in Tocoa. They all stayed in Trujillo until housing in Gualaco was ready for the Garbers. The latest change in government had also changed the rules and regulations about getting baggage for missionaries into the country duty-free. October and November passed before Jean and Lorraine got theirs and the supplies Jean and Becky had brought for our clinic and to set up the new clinic in Gualaco. Leroy was waiting for his carpentry tools, the Garbers for their housekeeping equipment, and the Hesses for some things they had ordered. I was waiting for a new kitchen stove and whatever my family had sent for birthday and Christmas.

Barbara and Ernest Garber

Our September evangelistic services with World Gospel Mission evangelist Don Enrique Peñalva from Tegucigalpa were a spiritual feast and over too soon. Leroy and I helped Jean make posters, and James set up his loudspeaker system and record player. He played hymns before the services began, which attracted as many as a hundred people to fill up the plank benches set up on the porch and on the grass between the porch and the park. Many people hung around in the park and heard the messages over the loudspeaker system; some

Don Enrique and Leroy Mellinger

told us they could hear everything quite plainly in their homes. On Sunday Don Enrique went with James to Santa Fe, and after six days with us he went on to hold meetings in Tocoa and La Ceiba.

Although Don Enrique thought at least 40 persons had raised hands when he invited people to receive Jesus as their Savior, only eight attended the instruction classes James held for new believers interested in baptism and church membership.

Our adult church attendance slowly increased after the evangelistic services even though the priest denounced us in his church.

Mr. July, who occasionally did odd jobs for us, was one who came for instruction. He gave his testimony at church one evening and told us how he used to drink a lot. After his conversion, four friends (or enemies with Satan as their leader) came to invite him to join them at the tavern. When he turned down the invitation, his friends insisted that his blood was so used to alcohol he would certainly die if it didn't get any more.

He and the woman he lived with for many years were both sincere about their decision to join the church and immediately indicated they wanted to marry. They were already grandparents but had never been able to accumulate the money necessary to marry, and until they became Christians it had not seemed important. There is even a word, *marido,* that is used instead of husband in a common-law marriage. In one of my letters home, I mentioned their situation, and Mother sent a small check to help them pay the fees. Beaty told them she would make the wedding cake and I promised the drink.

Mr. July was born in Jamaica and his woman in Belize. Neither had birth certificates, but since they had lived in Honduras so long, they hoped they wouldn't need any. Banns needed to be posted for three weeks before the wedding. James and I were asked to be witnesses of their marriage, which finally took place in January.

I finished lunch one Saturday and settled down to write letters home, but the doctor arrived with a critically wounded patient. It turned out there were three men who had been in a fight—with machetes, of course. The first one had a six-inch cut on his head that had cut the skull open. We cleaned him up, dressed the wound, and put him to bed to wait until a plane could take him to Tegucigalpa for surgery.

The second man had five not-too-bad cuts. By the time we were finished with him, it was five o'clock, and we had to stop and sterilize everything before we could go on to the third man. Before we got started on him, an 18-year-old man was brought in with an artery cut on his right hand, and it was eleven o'clock at night before we finished.

While Jean was in Gualaco helping Becky set up her clinic, I had my hands full with an epidemic of vomiting and diarrhea. Several children died in their homes and one baby at the clinic. He had a temperature of 107.6° and even with cold enemas and alcohol spongings I couldn't get it below 104°. The same day a woman died with what the doctor thought might have been meningitis.

A man came to buy medicine one day for his wife. When I asked what was wrong, he not only told me but gave demonstrations of how she breathed. A literal translation is, "She has a system of snoring like this. . . . It's nothing but air that she expels. It seems as though she has a storm that is coming out of her stomach!"

♔

The rainy season started in mid-October with so much rain the planes couldn't land at Trujillo for almost a week. When one finally came in, it brought Jean and me a lot of mail. After I delivered a baby at supper time and we had a youth meeting in our enlarged living room in the evening, I stayed up until midnight reading all my letters and birthday greetings.

Jean made me a birthday cake over in Beaty's kitchen, but it wasn't a surprise because Danny and Dicky came over to visit after supper, and Danny said, "Let's go now and eat ice cream and cake." He followed that statement with, "I know a secret." Then turning to Jean, he asked, "Is it still a secret?"

Beaty and Leroy made the ice cream, and after Bible study that evening some friends stayed to help celebrate, and the Hess boys got their share.

Jean said Gualaco, which lies in a valley with mountains on all sides, was so cool she slept under blankets and a quilt at night. I had just started using a top sheet in Trujillo and Gualaco's weather sounded wonderful. Water was brought from the river or bought for 50 cents a donkey load. The village priest tried to discourage people from attending the meetings James Hess and Eldon Hamilton held on the patio at the Hamilton home, but at least 70, mostly adults, attended, with others outside the fence listening.

Jean and Becky had unpacked their medicines and used the boxes as cupboards. Their first suturing case was the mayor, who had cut his leg with his machete. A bench served as their examination table and a trunk as a utility tray to spread out the sterile equipment.

♛

I answered a knock on the door one day to find Ernesto, a smiling little Carib boy, with a small turkey in his arms. As he held it out and put it in my arms, he explained it was from Kerah, Tilda's aged aunt, who lived on a small plot of land outside town. Ernesto lived with them and helped with the farm work. There had been a dispute about ownership of their property; for awhile it seemed certain they would have to give it up even though they had a deed of ownership. I had told Kerah and Tilda I would pray for them, and just when they were certain they had to move, a lawyer took their case and their deed was declared valid. The turkey was a thank-you for my prayers. I fed him grated coconut and cornmeal and wondered if my four-pound gift would put on enough weight to make a Christmas dinner for me and some guests. He didn't, so a big rooster joined him in the oven.

I spent one of my free days on Kerah's farm. We had a delicious chicken dinner cooked on their mud stove, but best of all was the good fellowship. With her old wrinkled face beaming, Kerah told me that although she couldn't bring herself to pray in public, she did pray when alone. In fact, she told me that after Ernesto went to his bed in the loft one night and she was late getting ready for bed, he had called down and asked her if she wasn't going to pray that night. Both Kerah and Tilda had had many trials and privations, but they were refined rather than embittered by them, and I knew they both witnessed to friends and neighbors about their faith.

On December 7 a Paya woman in labor for two days arrived on horseback. It was her first child and Ruth and I got her prepared immediately, but after doing everything I could with no results, I sent for the doctor. He worked for more than an hour, but after realizing the baby was already dead decided to send her to La Ceiba rather than do a cesarean in our clinic. Knowing a poor Paya woman didn't have money for a plane trip, a dentist from Tegucigalpa, working in Trujillo as part of his training, cared enough to ask people in the town to contribute toward her ticket.

An 11-day-old baby was brought in with tetanus. The doctor tried to save its life, but it remained stiff in spite of penicillin, tetanus antitoxin, subcutaneous fluids, and milk by a tube to the stomach. When we told the parents there was nothing more we could do, they took it home to die.

Our next patient was a half-starved old woman. She was retarded and had dysentery for an extended period of time. Unable to communicate with her normally, we were almost at our wits' end by the time she was well enough to go home.

Only nine days before Christmas I watched a casket, under a protective piece of plastic, brought out of the Catholic church across the street. A procession of big, black umbrellas followed it to the cemetery in a pouring rain. The woman had been bitten by a Barba Amarilla when she stepped out her back door to get water. The family called in the *curandero* or herb doctor, but after treating her for two days, he said he could do no more. Then they called in someone else. Finally four days after being bitten, she was brought to us unconscious. We thought it was probably too late but gave her a double dose of anti-venom and several other injections. Her heart did improve, but she never regained consciousness and died about eight hours after being admitted. The family cleared the vegetation from their yard and found and killed three more Barba Amarillas.

When I bought a load of wood in 1962, it gave George Miller an opportunity to meet his first Barba Amarilla. As he and Carlos were loading the wood on the truck, they found the snake. Almost before George could register the danger, Carlos had pulled out a small pistol he always carried and shot the snake.

James put me in charge of the Christmas program and we started rehearsals the end of November. As Christmas drew near, the Sunday School children all knew their parts, but with all the giggling and laughing at each other and themselves, I wondered if they would do the same thing the day of the program. It went off without a hitch, however, and I was well pleased. The first part was about the prophecies, the second was about the birth of Jesus, and the third part was our response to God's gift. Berta, Mr. July, and Esteban gave their testimonies for the last part, and two young women sang Spanish Christmas carols.

Our caroling that year wasn't washed out like the previous year, and nobody in the town seemed to go to bed that night. The Catholic church was still bright with lights when 14 of us returned from caroling about two in the morning. We served coffee and tamales to our guests and after they left, Jean and I decided to open our gifts. One of mine was a cookie cookbook from the Hess boys.

Just after Christmas five young men—Daniel Hess, James Lapp, Linford Gehman, John Rutt, and Edwin Martin—visited from EMC, now Eastern Mennonite University. They had the English service Sunday morning and the Spanish service in the evening with James Hess interpreting. In the afternoon we had a memorable trip through heavy rain to Castillo where they gave a program in English. Leroy, Jean, James Hess, the five men, and I went in the truck.

At the lagoon we walked across the bridge with rain running down our faces and dripping off our noses, but the truck had to go on a homemade raft. Leroy and Danny rode with it, and for a short time it looked as though they might be swept out to sea. The person handling the raft lost control, and we had some exciting moments before several of the fellows managed to grab the attached rope and haul it back.

The service was almost drowned out by the rain on the tin roof of the house where we met, but when we sang the closing song, "Beneath the Cross of Jesus," even the rain was drowned out by the singing of a woman sitting behind me.

Jean and I finished the year with a move to the Millers' empty house. We moved everything connected with the clinic, but as little of the other furniture as possible, and Leroy with two helpers started tearing out the partitions and termite-eaten back wall of our house. All the lovely poinsettias and the big pink double hibiscus with several orchids on it had to go. The following February Clyde Horst came to help Leroy with the carpentry projects, and Ben Stoltzfus joined Amzie Yoder in the Pax agriculture program in Tocoa. In 1960 when Amzie left, Sam Lapp replaced him.

Jean became head nurse in the clinic, Dorothy Showalter moved over from Tocoa to help her, and after that I was able to get ready to go on furlough.

Dorothy Showalter

1959

The MAF plane brought a carpenter to Trujillo to help Leroy with the house repairs and renovations, and I took advantage of his stop in Trujillo to fly with Becky to Gualaco—my first visit to the new mission station. The property consisted of about four acres in a nice location. The elevation was 2,200 feet and the nights were cool. Morning temperatures were as low as 60°, and we wore sweaters morning and evening. The sun, however, made things hot during the day unless there was a breeze.

Becky invited me to stay with her and Ernest and Barbara Garber in their new mud house with tile roof and concrete floor. So that hospitality didn't all fall on one family, I had breakfast and supper with the Garbers and Becky and dinners with Eldon and Jessie Hamilton.

The village had slightly over 100 houses and 800 residents, and I think there were at least 800 animals in the village also—burros, horses, oxen, pigs, dogs, etc. Work had already begun on a garage/workshop for the mission, and two houses, a clinic and a chapel were in the planning stages.

I visited Becky's clinic and attended the Sunday morning service held in a small house the missionaries rented. Twenty-seven persons attended that service. In the afternoon we had a service in a village three miles away. In the evening another service was held in Gualaco with about 50 persons present—mostly young men plus a few women and children. That service was held before our supper at 5:30 because there was an eight o'clock curfew in the town.

James radioed I should go on to Tegucigalpa and get my passport renewed before returning. While waiting there for several days until the new one was ready, I visited some people I had met first in Trujillo. One woman had her chauffeur take us for rides to places of interest outside the city.

Saturday, the day the Julys planned to marry, I was in the airport in Tegucigalpa ready to go back when just before boarding time the passengers for La Ceiba and Trujillo were called to the office and informed the plane would go no further than Tela because of bad weather along the coast. I decided to go at least that far and was glad to find the Vernon Macys at home. Vernon found out by radio that the

MAF plane was stranded in Tocoa and could stop for me when the weather cleared. He also discovered the July wedding was postponed because of the heavy rain in Trujillo.

The sky cleared so the plane could fly Sunday morning and I got home for the wedding. It stopped raining just long enough for the people to get to the church, which was decorated with ferns and flowers. The bride wore a nicely fitted white dress she had made and Mr. July wore a suit. James had a short sermon and performed the ceremony, and Jean, Dorothy, Beaty, and I sang three songs. Dorothy was a good soprano who used to sing in *The Mennonite Hour* chorus. All the guests went with Mr. and Mrs. July to their home for refreshments. As promised, Beaty had made the wedding cake and I provided punch. I noticed the living room had new curtains and a small linoleum rug on the floor bought especially for the wedding.

The July family.

The evening after the wedding the Julys and three others were baptized. Someone once said, *Revenge is sweet*, but what I found sweet was the joy of belonging to the Lord and occasions like this.

Bro. Garber came and preached the preparatory sermon two weeks before their first communion, and the newly-baptized converts gave testimonies. As always, Mr. July expressed himself in an interesting way. "When I was baptized," he said, "I asked the Lord to forgive my sins, and a 100-pound weight rolled off my back. After sailing wild seas all those years, at last I found a harbor and have anchored there."

Bible School was our next big event, with attendance as high as 110. My class of 29 first-graders was separated by only a muslin curtain from Beaty's class of 30 kindergartners. At times the noise level in our room made us both wish for a room of our own. Several pupils were sent home for misbehavior each day, but they always came back the following day. We could only entrust them to the Lord and pray we were planting living seeds of truth and that the Holy Spirit would bring them to Christ some day.

The MAF plane came to take Danny Hess back to school in Siguatepeque and dropped off Jacob Linkermann and Saul Gómez Díaz who were working with the American Bible Society. Don Saul talked to the Bible School children, and Mr. Linkermann spoke at the workers' prayer meeting before sailing off into the blue sky on the next SAHSA flight.

The doctor brought in a grumbling, groaning, dissatisfied-with-life heart patient who tried our patience. Heavy drinking had caused several health problems, and although he was only 46, he looked like an old man. We told him the *Good News* of life in Jesus and he eagerly received Jesus into his cold, hard heart. When discharged from the clinic, he went home a changed man.

Meantime I was trying to accomplish all the tasks I had assigned myself before leaving on furlough. I handed out Scripture portions to all the homes in Rio Negro and spent a few days in Tocoa to bid my friends farewell. Some mothers brought their babies to visit and say good-bye and show me how much they had grown.

Just as I was trying to finalize plans on how to get out of the country, rumors started about another revolution; almost all pilots and planes were used to send troops to Santa Barbara. I dashed around the house packing as quickly as possible so I could go to La Ceiba on the *Suyapa*, but an hour before the boat left, word came over the radio that things had been settled peacefully and plane service would resume. Two days later, on February 12, I left Trujillo for San Pedro Sula, the first stop. I stayed there with friends until the fourteenth and then joined up with James, Beaty, and the two boys for a flight to Miami.

From Miami I flew to Tampa and spent three days with friends from my mission-work days there. Mother, Lois and Wilbur, and Joyce and Melvin met me in Tampa, and the drive home was like a big family reunion. *If you want to appreciate family, just stay away from them for four years!*

Part of every missionary's furlough is spent talking about the work he or she left behind, and I put a lot of miles on the '51 Oldsmobile I had asked relatives to purchase for me. I traveled to speaking engagements, visited family and friends, and went to La Junta, Colorado, for a visit to my nursing school, and to Mission Board Meeting at Hesston, Kansas. I also took four courses at Eastern Mennonite College in summer school. My roommate at EMC was Agnes Shaffer of Uniontown, Pennsylvania, who had spent 12 years in Nigeria and was taking home economics so she could teach it on her return.

In between everything else, I did a lot of sewing for myself and family members and went shopping. After four years of writing home and asking people to buy everything from pens to hair nets, and not even knowing what was available, it was great fun to walk through stores and see the wide variety of items on display. Instead of two or three letters back and forth with requests and comparing prices I was able to choose my own purchases knowing exactly where and how I could use them and know immediately if they fit into my budget. A dutch oven caught my eye and I knew it would be a much used item on our wood-burning stove. A utility cart would be invaluable in either the clinic or our dining room. A venetian blind for my new bedroom window was the perfect solution to give privacy and light while blocking out the hot sun.

In the fall Lois, Mother, and I drove to Canada where I was invited to visit Lorraine Roth's parents, the Sidney Roths, and speak at her church.

All too soon and yet with eager anticipation, I boarded a plane in Philadelphia on December 30, and flew to Miami. While waiting for my next flight, I struck up a conversation with two women—one from Buenos Aires, Argentina, the other from Lima, Peru. I left Miami at six Thursday morning and returned twenty minutes later to the amazement of my two new friends still waiting for their flight. Strange sounds from somewhere in the plane had sent us hurrying back for repairs. Two hours later we took off again and arrived safely in San Pedro Sula in time for me to make my connecting flight to La Ceiba, and by Saturday I was back in Trujillo. My total airfare for the whole trip was slightly over $113.00.

1960

I reached San Pedro Sula Thursday at one-thirty in the afternoon and La Ceiba at five and took a nap before supper. By seven-thirty I was back in bed to catch up on the sleep I had missed the night before. The New Year's firecrackers disturbed me no more than a mosquito's buzzing might—I knew they were there, but I was too sleepy to care.

I had forgotten how curious the people were—at least four stopped me on the street and asked the three polite questions—where I came from, where I was going, and how long I would stay. As I walked the dusty, hot streets on my way to visit with friends at the United Brethren Mission while awaiting the Saturday flight to Trujillo, I remembered how the people in Pennsylvania had complained of the summer heat, which I hadn't considered really hot.

Trujillo was home—the *cabildo* or town hall picturesquely painted deep rose and trimmed in green with red roof tiles, the guards on duty and their plaintive whistling back and forth at night, and even the mosquitoes that seemed to have increased in number. The welcoming bouquets and good nature of the people lifted my spirits, but the indifference of many to spiritual things grieved me as it had before. How small the Carib people were after seeing the tall, husky citizens of the United States. Ruth's and Elena's jokes brought many smiles to my lips as did Dicky's so seriously-asked question, "Are you going to give injections to people in the clinic?"

Yes, I was home and what a joy it was to greet old friends. Even greater was the joy of attending services and seeing those who had remained faithful and hearing how the children were learning good lessons in Sunday School from teachers who were also growing in faith and knowledge.

Soon I was checking the renovations to the house. How convenient Leroy and his helpers had made everything! Part of the front porch was screened in according to my request for a place to dry laundry on rainy days, but before long we were using it almost every day. With the old kitchen table, several chairs, some benches, and a few plants it became a comfortable, bright, airy place to entertain visitors, write letters, and have the women's sewing circle meetings.

Leroy had also divided the clinic space into two patient rooms, a maternity ward, and a small office. We still used old boxes as bedside tables until my sister Joyce's Sunday School class sent money in August that paid for stands to be built, with casters and hinged doors. To stretch the money as far as possible, I bought varnish and finished them myself.

The sales room, with new counters and built-in cupboards, was much more convenient than it had been. The kitchen had a double window over the sink that could be opened and shut, and the dining room had one also, which meant daylight could enter during storms. The rooms had always been dreary and dark when the old window shutters had to be closed to keep out rain, wind, or dust. Those two rooms were divided by a table-like counter extending from one wall with hanging cupboards above. New counter tops with cupboards above and below extended out on either side of the kitchen sink. The dining room was pale green, and the kitchen yellow with dark green linoleum on the counters. The bathroom was divided; one part was turned into a wash house with a door to the outside. The enlarged living room was being used every week for youth meetings with 20 or more persons attending.

My baggage didn't arrive until mid-February, but I still had a great deal of unpacking to do. Jean packed her things to go back to Tocoa. As she cleared shelves of her dishes and pots and pans, I unpacked mine from the barrels they were stored in, washed them, and refilled the shelves.

Before I was completely settled in, I started work in the clinic—during my first eight weeks back, I delivered eight babies. By that time I was delivering a second or third baby for mothers I got to know during prior deliveries.

Once again the government doctor had left and the only one in the area was doing private practice. He sent patients to us and we were thankful for his expertise. Later the government health department sent an Arab doctor.

I had the same grade-level in Bible School as I did the year before and had Mrs. July to help me with my class of 24. Merrill Wood returned to Trujillo to help also. He was working as a carpenter and supporting his mother, his invalid father, and three younger sisters in Gran Cayman. He jokingly told me that sisters take a lot of money, and that he had taken some young men around to the house but nothing happened. His faithfulness to the Lord was a blessing, and my heart was stirred when I heard him give his testimony at the youth meeting Saturday night and when he preached on Sunday morning.

So many people who expressed interest in accepting Jesus as their

Savior found the commitment to live for Him too demanding. Several stated openly that it cost too much, and they never went beyond the stage of raising a hand in a meeting. Others were eager to come for instruction for baptism but dropped out before it occurred. Some were baptized and received into the church but then returned to sinful living. Of those, a few repented over and over and showed real remorse but never seemed to gain total victory over long-established sinful habits. Those dear people were an illustration of the parable of the sower and the seeds that fell on different types of soil. Some sprang up eagerly but soon withered away. Others were choked by the attractions of the world, and some were simply so untaught they didn't understand; they never got their roots deep enough to hold fast and prosper in their Christian walk. It was the ones who grew and were faithful, however, that caused us to rejoice.

Another way used to discourage new believers was that many were told they would go crazy if they accepted a new religion. Some became so nervous and upset that it was easy for them to believe it was happening. One young man told me that on the way home from church one night, something, which he believed was an evil spirit, grabbed him and forced him backward two steps and told him he must give up the Lord. He said out loud that he would not turn back and was soon able to go on. I did not doubt his word because I knew he had served the devil before his decision to serve the Lord, and, of course, the devil would do his best to win or scare him into returning to his evil actions.

The man who was reconciled with another on the beach when Father died was one who had a soft heart and desired to live for Jesus but was frequently the victim of temptations. During his fallen times, his face and manner betrayed his guilt and unhappiness. The times he knocked on my door with beaming face I knew he had once again repented. Time and again he made the rounds of church members to confess his sins and ask their forgiveness and was filled with joy at knowing God also forgave and accepted him back. He was one I felt needed to be forgiven the *seventy times seven.*

His home life was difficult and his past filled with superstitions that seemed to hold him captive. His wife also gave in to what I considered unreasonable fears and at times made life difficult for both of them. Once she left him because she insisted she was pregnant to a man she had lived with five years earlier. I tried to convince the husband that it was impossible, but he repeated old-wives tales of its happening before, and I finally told him time would prove it an impossibility. Satan had many such inroads into the lives of the people because of witchcraft, curses, and generations of other evil practices.

In 1962 his sad life ended. He had been drinking heavily for some time and was found near death on the beach near his house. Those who found him took him home, but he soon died. James Hess went and held a short service in his home with the believers in Santa Fe. His life was a commentary of desiring to live a righteous life but of giving in to the power of sin and evil.

Another example of superstition was the words of a friend who brought me a piece of beef. She said it was small because they had butchered in the waning moon. If they had waited until the moon was on the increase, the animal would have weighed more.

In 1958 James had started going on preaching trips by boat, and in a village 20 miles down the coast a woman, Doña Chon, and Pablo, her 18-year-old son, accepted the Lord. Years before she had bought a Bible, which was practically worn out from reading, so the seed had been sown even before she heard James' messages. She and her son made occasional trips to Trujillo for James to instruct and prepare them for baptism and church membership.

Doña Chon and her 18-year-old son, Pablo, and another boy.

One Saturday in January 1960, the two of them left their home at eight in the morning and walked to Trujillo, arriving at six in the evening so they could be baptized the following day. The water in the three rivers they had to cross was up to the woman's waist because we had had over 32 inches of rain during December and more than 16 inches already in January. By the middle of June we had over 60 inches of rain for that year.

When it rained, it poured, and that applied to patients as well as real rain. A two-day-old baby was brought in hemorrhaging from the navel. The parents had waited too long to come, and although I got the bleeding stopped, the baby died. They said the midwife was old and probably couldn't see what she was doing. Next, a teacher from a neighboring town was brought in with a graze wound to the forehead. The father of a pupil shot him because he disciplined his son. When the shooting occurred, the student's mother fell over in a faint; that frightened the father enough that he didn't finish his intent to kill the teacher. Before I was finished bandaging that wound, a six-year-old boy was brought in with blood on his forehead from a stone thrown by another boy. Next, a boat brought a woman and two-week-old baby to the wharf and the mission truck went down to bring them to the clinic. The woman had no one at home to care for the baby, so while we nursed her for typhoid fever, worms, a malaria fever of 105.2°, and a hemoglobin count so low it didn't show on our scale, I often had the baby with me as I did paper work and worked in my room.

The following morning another baby, sick for 15 days, was brought in with malaria and worms. The mother said she hadn't brought him sooner because she thought he might get better. I treated him and sent her home, but she soon returned with him in her arms and said he died.

"Your baby is not dead," I said.

"He just came back to himself," she answered, and I realized she meant he had fainted. He recovered with proper medical care.

When questioning patients, I always got answers, but some of them left me wondering if I had really asked the question I thought I had. A mother brought her child to the clinic with a classic case of worms. She declared she had given him worm medicine, but he didn't *botar* (throw out) any.

I asked when she had given the medicine.

She replied, "Five months ago."

Certain the medicine would have had the desired effect, I asked, "And he didn't *botar* any?"

"No," she replied, then added, "only three."

I asked a store clerk, "Is the SAHSA agent coming today?" and got an answer that certainly didn't tell me what I needed to know.

-Siempre viene aveces,- he said, meaning, "She always comes sometimes (usually)."

I asked an old woman how old she was and she said she was 78. I knew I had her as a patient several years before but couldn't remember when, so asked her, "How old were you when you came to the clinic?"

I guess she couldn't remember either because her answer was, "I was younger."

María set me straight one day when I asked if she or Elena, both 16, was the older of the two. Her reply was, "Elena is older and she always has been! She's my sister on my father's side, but not on my mother's side." María also told me the big pink roses on my lovely new curtains looked like the purple things that come in cans. I finally figured out she meant the red beets I had brought from Pennsylvania.

♛

In February the barrels I had packed in Pennsylvania arrived. I could hardly wait to get my venetian blind installed in my bedroom, but I hadn't counted on the hardness of the mahogany window frame. I had to reach up high and worked and worked to get the screws started. When my arms gave out, Dorothy took over and did all she could, and then a young man happened to stop by and finished the job.

It looked wonderful, but when I went outside to see how it looked from there I discovered I had hung it one inch too high leaving a gap at the bottom. It wasn't nearly as hard work to remove the screws, and James came over at just the right time and offered to reinstall the brackets. Many were the times I was thankful for the way the missionaries demonstrated harmony as we worked together and helped each other.

Another young child was brought in close to death with worms. We did all the medical things we could for her, but I truly believe it was an answer to our prayers that pulled her through. She was so sick the carpenter was already making a box for her burial when she started to recover.

♛

All over Honduras the churches were praying for a revival. We held prayer meetings once a week starting in February and ending on Maundy Thursday. It was wonderful to hear the prayers of our new Christians. Mr. July's prayers were an encouragement to me in my clinic work, for he usually prayed that even as I injected medicine into the veins of my patients, so I would also inject the Word of God into their souls.

♛

After James and Beaty with Dicky and Gerald spent a few days in Guanaja, one of the Bay Islands, James insisted Dorothy, Grace Hockman, and I should also spend a weekend there. The mother with malaria and typhoid had just died after confessing her sins and asking forgiveness of God, her baby was taken home, and someone came for the remaining patient, so there was nothing to keep me at the clinic. The boat trip was rough and we slid around all night in our bunks. Dorothy got seasick, I got a terrible headache, and we all lost sleep. With our feet once again on solid ground, however, we were prepared to relax and enjoy our break.

Guanaja was built on two keys off the east end of Bonacca. When we visited the Hog Key, it was perhaps 30 times larger than it was a hundred years earlier. People built walls of broken coral about 18 inches higher than the water level, probably on top of coral reefs, extending out into open water. Then they carried mud from the island to fill the walled-in area and built their homes on the new land thus formed. In another area, houses were built on pilings right over the water (sewage disposal conveniently provided) and connected with boardwalks. Water could be seen through the cracks in the flooring of the houses. The post office, a church, and a two-story school house were also built on pilings, and I suppose the boardwalk was the school playground.

The people were Scotch, English, Jamaican, Negro, and a few mixed Spanish. English was the main language. I met an old man who told interesting stories of the early days when he was a child. When his family moved from the islands to the key because of malaria, there were so many alligators that his mother tied him by one leg so he couldn't wander off and be eaten.

I felt as though we had two Sundays that week. We attended the Adventist service with three hundred people present on Saturday, and a Church of God service on Sunday.

As with many vacations, I paid for that one with lots of work when we returned. One patient was an old man who needed special attention for an infected foot. Another was a woman sick for two weeks with phlebitis in both legs. She arrived with her legs swollen hard, and we also took in her four-week-old baby because he was losing weight in the care of his 13-year-old sister who said she prepared his milk *by guess* and that he bothered her at night when she wanted to sleep.

The second week of May was busy—a picnic, five babies, a wedding, and the usual clinic work. The picnic for my Sunday School class was up the mountain side at the dam with swimming and lots of food. I took the cook along to help with the food—a pot of rice, another of beans, Dorothy's famous potato rolls, cheese, bananas, chocolate cake, and iced mint tea.

Four of the five babies arrived at night and the wedding was my former cook María's. All the missionaries and workers were invited to the cabildo to witness the brief ceremony. It was originally set for 9:00 a.m. then changed to 10:00 and finally started at 10:20 when the mayor and his secretary arrived. He asked them if they take each other as man and wife, and when they said they did, he pronounced them man and wife in the name of the law. His secretary then read the law so fast that I couldn't understand it, and that ended the civil ceremony.

María and Mr. Zapata led the way down to Cristales with all the guests following. She carried a bouquet of white paper roses and real ferns, and was wearing a tiny white hat and a street-length white taffeta dress with lace yoke and a full skirt overlaid with net. Her new home, which she did not see until her bridegroom led her there with all the guests, was a two-room mud house with an outside kitchen.

The missionaries were given seats of honor with the bride and groom while other guests, invited and uninvited, filled the room. Before long plates with fried beans, bread, and a cup of coffee were served to most guests, who ate and left. After that the cake was cut and served to the rest of us with soft drinks. I noticed no hard drinks were visible, not even María's little brother's dog named *Cerveza* or Beer!

The girl I hired to replace María had to be taught how to boil water, and since the missionaries drank only water that had been boiled, it was an important part of the job. After she brought me lukewarm water and said she had set the timer for five minutes after the water started to make noise, I realized I needed to explain and demonstrate again.

Many of the girls I hired to cook and care for the house came from homes with dirt floors where they swept very superficially so as not to raise dust. They also drank water as it came from streams and rivers where they washed their clothing and bathed. It was a total reeducation before they understood how to clean floors, dust furniture, hang clothes on a wash line with clothes pins, boil water, and even open doors with door knobs and turn on spigots to get water.

Among the patients at the clinic was a man brought in at 4:30 in the morning with a broken finger, and four dagger wounds—one a deep stab wound in the abdomen, which the doctor thought pierced the peritoneum. Fortunately a boat was leaving for La Ceiba in the afternoon, and after doing what we could, we sent him to the hospital for surgery. I think at least 30 people came to see him before he left, but I turned away all except his wife and another woman, whom I asked to care for him and watch the I.V. in his arm. The clinic, however, was like a place of entertainment for the women. Once while his wife was out of his room peeping around the curtain to watch what Ruth and I were doing to another patient, the man vomited. Since he was unable to help himself, we had quite a mess to clean up. Fortunately, the needle did not come out of the vein in his arm. The wife also kept insisting he eat cassava and coconut bread she had brought along, and in spite of the fact that I warned her he dared not eat, I think she fed him some.

A blessing that week was to hear one of the converts conduct his first children's meeting. He chose the creation story, and because it was still a new story to him, he read most of it. He later told me he wished Norman Hockman had time to hold classes to teach him and others so they could be of more help to the missionaries. One of the five babies born that week was that man's fourth daughter. He also had three sons but was hoping for another son and had planned to name him *Jesús Salvador* or Jesus Savior.

I was reminded of how good the Lord had been to me when a man with falciparum malaria was brought in from a village close to Tarros. Falciparum malaria was the rare and often-deadly kind which I had in 1952, only his affected the brain instead of the chest as mine had. He was in a coma most of the time he was with us, and after his common-law wife realized we could do nothing more for him, she took him home on a cot to die. My only other contact with the family was when the man had bought a New Testament from me several months earlier. His wife couldn't read, and I certainly pitied her with her three small children.

As I was trying to finish painting two chairs I had the carpenter make for our newly-enclosed porch, a woman who had been at the clinic for a prenatal examination a few days earlier came up to the screen and said *she came!* I asked if she wanted anything.

She replied, -*Me cayó el niño*,- "The baby fell."

I thought she was telling me she had miscarried, but when I got to the door I noticed she had a white package on her arm and I hurried her to the clinic and into the bed nearest to the door. The package was a fat, seven-pound boy wrapped in a white cloth. He seemed to have suffered no harm from being born somewhere along the beach or on the walk up the hill. Five days later we sent the two of them home in a car. Eight babies were delivered that May, and in July three babies were born early one morning between midnight and six.

After I had admitted and taken care of the woman and baby who came to the porch, Dr. Abularach and I worked most of the afternoon cleaning and suturing a drunken man with machete slashes to the right shoulder, face, and neck. It was the second time in two weeks he had been injured in drunken fights. Perhaps his mother thought her son would be safe in our clinic for she kept insisting that we admit him for several days. The police said she had been to see them earlier about someone who wanted to kill him, so I was very thankful the doctor sent him home to recover. I certainly could provide no security against avenging, drunken men.

Another patient that week was Victoriano Gil Medina, an early convert in Santa Fe, whose wedding we had attended in 1957. Although unable to read, he loved to attend services, hear the Bible read, and sometimes during the night when he couldn't sleep, he played gospel records on Murph's Finger Fono, a record player operated with one finger. His faith in God was an inspiration to me. He told me that sometimes there was nothing in his house to eat; once when he had no money, he got in his cayuco and went out to fish. He asked the Lord to take care of his stomach and give him something for the children. At Punta Piedra he caught a three-foot long cod plus another fish which he sold to buy the things he needed for the family.

Victoriano had tuberculosis and had been hospitalized in La Ceiba several times. We all knew he was gradually getting worse and nearing the end, but he was cheerful while he was with us and said he was praying that God would allow him to worship just once in the church they were building in Santa Fe. He said he wanted to pray in it twice: once in his own language (Garifuna) and once in the language of the country (Spanish). Toward the end he no longer prayed that prayer, but instead asked the Lord to come for him.

The church in Santa Fe was a big undertaking for the congregation in that small village. The people had started a building fund soon after there were several converts, and James began holding services in a home whenever he could get down on Sundays. Mother had sent a small donation after Father's death, and, in spite of their meager means, their monetary goal was reached in 1960.

After years of anticipation, disagreements, joys, and discouragements, they had located a suitable property and for a year had been making adobe bricks which were stored in a vacant house during the rainy season. Lumber was sawed in the mountains, carried to the sea on the shoulders of men, and taken to Santa Fe in dugout canoes.

When all the supplies were on hand, a carpenter was hired and the construction of the building began in March. Each member of the congregation donated two days' work each week; James went down frequently, sometimes taking some of the men from Trujillo. Even though the thirty-horsepower Johnson motor gave him occasional problems, he still thanked the Lord and was extremely grateful for the people who had donated the almost-maintenance-free fiberglass boat because it cut the trip from one hour of paddling to fifteen minutes under motor power.

By May the walls of the church had gone up on a street facing the sea, in the shade of two giant mango trees. The rafters were being roofed when I took a quick trip with James, who had to deliver some supplies. A small room was built on the one side so James would have a place to stay when the sea was too rough to return or for some other reason he would stay over night.

It was at that time Victoriano Gil told me he was waiting to go to *pasear* with the Lord. That word is hard to translate but means something like take a walk or go on vacation and enjoy oneself.

Near the end of June he made that victorious trip.

His wife said that just before he died, he had asked the Lord to come and take him. "And he did come," she exclaimed, "because Victoriano cried out, -*¡Que bueno el pasage, que buen cayuco!*- "How good the passage is, what a good dugout canoe!" Then he smiled and pointed upward and tried to speak again, but instead went to be with his Lord.

A few days earlier he had a dream in which beings with white faces like *Gringos*, Americans, wearing white clothes and carrying urns came and told him to go with them. He went as far as a river, and there he saw a *cayuco* but did not cross the river with them. When he died, his words indicated he had taken the good *cayuco* across. What a happy, victorious death!

Norman and Grace, James and Beaty, and I went down in the boat for the funeral. The sea was quite rough and I found myself reliving those frightening moments when I was in the water under the boat when Father lost his life. Almost simultaneously, the Lord took away all fear and I knew if the boat upset the next moment, I was still in His care.

A short service was held in the home of Victoriano's mother. She was sitting in a hammock facing us; the widow sat on a low chair in a dirty green dress, probably the only one she owned. Victoriano, Jr. stood in front of her wearing the outfit he wore every day—an alligator tooth on a string around his neck.

The body, in an unpainted mahogany casket, was carried to the new Santa Fe church for its very first service. The adobe mud bricks were plastered only halfway up the walls; the clay floor was not yet in, but the new backless benches were all filled. The service was joyous, with no tears, no wailing, and no candles. Most of the believers were there and several led out in prayer.

Victoriano had done what little he could to help build the church, and we couldn't be sad that he didn't see it totally finished because we knew he was seeing sights far more lovely where he had gone.

The church was completed and a dedication service was held in July. I donated a pulpit Bible in honor of my parents.

James tried to rent a boat to take people from the church in Trujillo to Santa Fe for the service, but Mr. Tatum, the British consul, offered him free use of the *Suyapa*. We had Sunday School in Trujillo and then went down to the wharf. Many more people than the boat could hold wanted to take a free trip, so the mate allowed the people from our church on free and charged the others a small fee. That cut the number somewhat, but even so the boat was crowded. James took our motor boat with about 15 people and at Santa Fe, where there was no wharf, had the job of ferrying passengers from the *Suyapa* to shore.

The plastering of the inside walls was completed and the clay floor as smooth and hard as concrete.

A bell from a Lancaster County school or farmhouse was in the rather large tower. Dicky Hess told me a bell was sleeping in that

Santa Fe church.

little house. Since the people had no clocks, the bell would announce services.

♛

Norman, Antonio, and Mr. July made an evangelistic trip to La Colonia and Chapagua, and five people accepted the Lord when Mr. July gave his testimony. Several weeks later I went along when they and several others made another trip. We left at 8:30 and traveled the 15 miles to La Colonia in about two hours. At the lagoon we put the car on a raft and Mr. July walked across the bridge pulling the rope attached to the raft while Antonio poled and Norman helped guide it so it wouldn't hit the piers of the bridge. I walked across the bridge on the way back and discovered it was higher than I thought with wide gaps to step over.

In La Colonia the men fanned out distributing pamphlets while I sat in the car playing gospel records over the loud speaker and telling Bible stories to the nearly 40 children and a dozen grown-ups who gathered. The men located three of the converts and were told the other two were working in the fields.

About noon we started walking through the woods to the next village, Chapagua, carrying the record player, loud speaker, pamphlets, water jugs, and our lunch. The 35-minute walk along the trail was pleasant and interesting, but muddy at spots and with the temperature at 97 or 98°. We saw lots of birds and huge trees but no monkeys or snakes. When we ate our lunch along the trail, the others sat down on a big rock and on the trunks of fallen trees. I knew the red bugs were just waiting to attack, however, so I ate standing up and moving around.

About 60 children, 20 women, and eight men from the 48 mud houses gathered for a service after we handed out the pamphlets and invitations. Most of the men were working in the fields. The people were typical of others in the country—poor, uneducated, courteous, and appealing.

♛

At 4:00 one morning the captain of the *Coronel Cruz* awakened me to ask if I would take in a mother who had delivered a baby on his boat. She was feeling perfectly well when she got on board in La Ceiba, but a short time later things began to happen and about two hours before they got to Trujillo, with the help of a Carib woman, she had delivered a fine boy. I called James and he went over to Millers and got the mission truck while I gathered some supplies. We drove to the wharf and brought our patients to the clinic. The new baby was named Cruz after the boat on which he was born. Cruz means cross.

Virgen María, one of the cutest babies I ever delivered, was born early one Sunday morning. Her mother had a hemoglobin count of 40 when she had registered a month earlier and I hadn't been able to build her up much. Neither of us thought she was due to deliver her seventh child, but the baby weighed six pounds and seemed perfectly formed and healthy. The father, Tango Negro, walked with a bad limp and made his living selling fresco and flavored shaved ice. He once used all dimes to pay a bill at the clinic.

After Holy Week with its celebrations that ended on Easter, the people looked forward to John the Baptist's birthday June 24. A five-section shelter built of poles and walled and roofed with palm branches was erected in the park that year about 15 yards from our porch. One part was for gambling, and in the other parts people sold things to benefit the Catholic church building fund and a relief fund for the needy.

Loud speakers announced every event and broadcast the singing, accordion playing by a blind man, and of course the Carib and marimba bands. My ears were apparently not attuned to the music because the songs sounded very much alike to me. I went to sleep every night with the noise going full blast, so I don't know how late or early it lasted.

All-night dances were held in surrounding villages with a final big one in the hotel across the street from our house.

At six one morning, the *saint* was brought from Rio Negro with an accompanying Carib band for the main celebration. The statue was erected on a concrete, palm-decorated platform in the park.

One day a queen was crowned and, as was to be expected, all week long firecrackers punctuated the other noise, starting as early as 3:45 a.m. By the time the week was over, I was sure most of the people in the town were very much in need of sleep.

The George and Grace Miller family, except for J. Mark, returned from furlough with everyone looking well and rested. Ruth was almost as tall as Grace, Miriam and Rachel had grown a lot also, and Daniel and Philip made things lively around the place.

Hesses moved over with me until it was time for them to leave on furlough. Hockmans moved into Hesses' house and Norman started preaching in Santa Fe. When the weather kept him home, the members there conducted their own service. One, a school teacher, gave the children an education in more than Bible stories. The ones that came without shirts were told they would not be admitted the following Sunday unless they wore shirts, and those who came without pants

The Miller family.

Back row: J. Mark and Ruth.

Front row: Grace holding Philip, Rachel, Miriam, and George holding Daniel.

The Hess family.
Dicky, James, Danny, Beatrice, and Gerald.

were sent home.

In September I made my first trip to Belize City, British Honduras, the capital of the country later called Belize. Since there were two doctors in Trujillo at that time, I closed the clinic and gave Tilda and Ruth their vacations while I was gone.

The Hockman family.

Norman and Grace with Larry, Dicky, Susie, and Joe.

Dorothy and I flew to Belize after a night's stopover in the Roosevelt Hotel in San Pedro Sula. The people were celebrating a special holiday, and we got to see Belize in all its finery. There were speeches in the park, and a parade with interesting floats, several bands, and thousands of school children in uniform. The people were every shade from deep black to almost white, with a few Chinese noticeable here and there. To the local people, our white skin was also most noticeable, I am sure.

Sunday we attended a small Baptist church in the morning and a much larger and livelier Church of the Nazarene in the evening.

Monday we changed our money to the local currency at the bank and got visas.

Tuesday Irene Snavely joined us, and Ada Smoker, an MCC nurse working in Orange Walk, came to show us the area. We went to Spanish Lookout, one of the three colonies of Mennonites that had originally settled in Mexico from Canada and then moved to British Honduras. Blue Creek and Shipyard Colonies were Old Mennonites and had been in Mexico over twenty years. I understood that only Peter Wiebe from those colonies spoke English. The Spanish Lookout people were Kleine Gemeinde and had left Canada only ten years earlier and could speak English although they used Plattdeutsch. They had left Mexico because they didn't want to contribute to social security, which financed things they didn't approve of such as pensions and theaters.

Many people who heard we were Mennonites thought we were affiliated with the colonists, but I felt far removed from them. Only a few of the leaders associated with the local people. The colonists were shy and appeared unsociable to outsiders because of not speaking the language and because of their desire to live lives free from worldly influences. If I was informed correctly, smoking and strong drink were not allowed in Spanish Lookout, but were not frowned on in the other settlements.

During one of the stops on the 67-mile bus ride over a one-lane, bumpy road, we purchased a lunch of *empanados* (fried cornmeal mush turnovers filled with beans), soft drinks, and banana cake. To pass oncoming traffic, each vehicle had to drive with one wheel off the road. After getting off the bus we walked another two or three miles in the burning sun over rough stones to a river where Cornie Reimer, a very sunburned, blond boy took us almost across on a hand-cranked ferry. We had to wade the last couple of yards to shore.

At Spanish Lookout we met the rest of the Reimer family and received a warm welcome at Isaak L. Dyck's home. Isaak was planning a trip to Belize City the following day and invited us to stay in the colony overnight and travel with him. He also drove us around the ten-mile colony, which included 18,000 acres with 71 families of around 600 persons. Their four schools had 25 to 30 pupils each, where they used a German reader with Bible lessons. The church was a palm-roofed shelter with no side walls.

Dorothy and Irene stayed with the John Friesen family for the night and Ada and I with the Dycks. Isaak showed us his dentist and doctor office. He was self-taught, had up-to-date medical and dental books, and must have been quite skilled because he said he had pulled thousands of teeth and even made dentures. The colony had midwives but called Isaak if there were complications, and he had delivered around 100 babies.

We spent part of the evening singing; first from an English hymnal and later from German hymnals and the *Ausbund* with the words under the music, which was written with numbers one to seven instead of notes.

It rained during the night and the black soil turned to mud, which I discovered collected like gum on my shoes. Dorothy and Irene arrived early in the morning on a tractor, and we started back to Belize City sitting on truck tires covered with a blanket in the back of a truck. The tractor went along to pull the truck up the hill and out of the mud when it got stuck.

When we reached the river, the tractor drove around in the water to wash the gummy mud out of the tire treads and wheels before returning to the colony. A caterpillar had scraped the mud from the road on the other side of the river, but the truck still had to be pushed by three men to get it up the hill. If Isaak hadn't been going to Belize City, I don't know how long we would have been stranded in the colony. The only way we could possibly have walked out was on bare feet because the mud was too deep for shoes or even boots.

Back in Belize City we waited for a truck to take us to Orange Walk, where Dorothy, Irene, and I spent the night with Ada. That truck had a wooden roof, and behind the cab were the seats, which were eight-inch-wide boards set in grooves like bed slats. A fence separated us from the freight they were hauling. Ada had not yet set up her clinic because her shipment of things had not cleared customs. She had been seeing patients, however, that came to her from Orange Walk and the Blue Creek and Shipyard colonies.

In the morning another truck with eight-inch planks for seats stopped to pick us up for an excursion trip to Chetumal, Mexico. Accommodations there were in a rooming house; Irene, Dorothy, and I shared a room with two single beds, slightly used sheets, no towels, and no running water. The cost was the equivalent of 70 U. S. cents for each of us. We toured the town, ate tamales, fried beans, tacos, and ice cream made out of canned yellow corn.

One U. S. dollar changed into 12.50 pesos so we felt as though we had a lot of money; however, one plate of ice cream cost two pesos so our money went fast. By that time we were carrying U. S. dollars, Honduras lempiras, British Honduras dollars, and Mexican pesos. The whole trip cost me $4.80.

The ride back to Belize City was faster than the trip out. The floor planks rattled, the curtains flapped, and the water splashed when we got into a rain storm, and I arrived back at the hotel aware of several muscles and vertebrae I hadn't noticed before.

Dorothy and Irene went on to Guatemala to the Central American Mission Bible Institute. I rested a day while waiting my flights back to La Ceiba and on to Trujillo.

Within hours of my arrival in Trujillo I was called to a home to care for a woman having a gall bladder attack. Next day it was a boy with a fractured arm that required attention until we could send him to the hospital in La Ceiba. While we were caring for him, a man was brought in with a big lump of something on his head. He had been struck with a bottle during a fight and both the bottle and his head broke. The lump on his head was from most of a box of baking soda his friends had put on to stop the bleeding. The doctor and I had to soak it all off and clean the wound before putting in seven sutures.

The *Comandante* decided the town would have a special celebration on the national holiday, *Dia del Soldado*, or Soldier's Day. He made up a list with the names of specially invited guests and sent it around to the homes. This special invitation was extended to the mission staff because we were neighbors. We felt it was important to attend as a sign of our support of community life.

The big doings began with a flag-raising ceremony at six in the morning at the *Cuartel*, or soldiers' barracks next door, which I watched from my window. That was followed by a Catholic mass at the same place and at nine o'clock the program started. All the children, in their school uniforms, marched in with their teachers and sat under a palm-leaf canopy. Several of the children gave highly emotional patriotic speeches which were spoken directly into microphones placed right in front of the mouth of each speaker, with the result being a loud noise thoroughly blurred. The school children were dismissed after being served soft drinks and then there were songs and music, including a nationally-known Carib guest singer with a beautiful voice.

About 11 o'clock the marimba, drums, and saxophones arrived and from then on the music was continuous. One Carib sat by a drum and slapped out a continuous rhythm with the palms of his hands while out in the blazing sun soldiers danced with girls dressed in their finest clothes. During most of that time I was with a maternity patient in the clinic.

Dinner was set up in the palm-leaf shelter in the *Cuartel* patio. The tables were loaded with big platters of rice, chicken, pork, spaghetti, potato salad, and bread, followed by soft drinks and ice cream. Those people certainly knew how to celebrate.

The missionary children also had their celebrations. As I stepped out on the patio to check the rain gauge one day, I heard Larry and Dicky Hockman celebrating mass under the coconut tree. A doll, representing the Virgin Mary, was sitting inside a little wooden frame; Larry, as priest, was instructing Dicky. "We are going to have the Catholic program now," he said. "Every time I kneel down, you ring the bell."

The bell rang and I heard Larry's voice, *-Santa María, dame tortilla, arroz amarilla, caliente y frio, abajo la silla, para mi tia.-* In Spanish it rhymes and means, "Holy Mary, give me tortilla, yellow rice, hot and cold, under the chair, for my aunt."

The children did a good imitation of a priest's tone and rhythm as he chants in mass, and when they noticed I was interested in their play, they invited me to another service in the house.

There was no laughing or giggling as they solemnly went through the ritual. The doll once again held a prominent place as Dicky, behind a pulpit made with a pile of cushions, read Latin out of a Bible. Every now and then he would pick up a cup from a nearby stand, turn his back to the audience, face the doll, and drink. At one point he chanted -*Santa María*- at least six times very rapidly.

Larry closed the service by once again singing the rhyme to the doll. They said they had learned how to do it from schoolmates in Siguatepeque, although Dicky's mother said he frequently stole across the street into the Catholic church in Trujillo to observe the mass.

Both Dicky and I had birthdays in October, and for my birthday Dicky made me a little red bench or stool. He had made one for himself and I admired his work so much I asked him to make me one, but I didn't expect him to give it to me as a gift. In 1999 I still use that little red bench in my apartment.

We held communion every three months in our church, and in October, 24 persons participated. George Zimmerman and Elam Stauffer, Pax men from Tocoa, were visiting, and six church members from Santa Fe also joined us for the service.

A blast of a cannon or some equally loud sound jerked me from a good sleep at four o'clock one morning in mid-November. At about five the church bells started ringing and rang most of the day. Boys were in the belfry pulling on the bell ropes. Shots were fired and firecrackers exploded. A little boy said he thought it was the President's birthday, but later I was told the international court had granted a decision in favor of the Hondurans in the boundary dispute between Nicaragua and Honduras.

The school children in uniform paraded the streets followed by the soldiers, a judge, the mayor, and the priest. Following that the town folks gathered for lots of impassioned speeches which they punctuated with shouts of *Viva Honduras*.

I was busy in the maternity ward, but with the loud speakers I didn't miss much. An all-night dance in the hotel across the street concluded the celebration.

The next exciting event was that the monkey became an Evangelical. He started out as a Catholic, but the priest gave him to Norman so the children decided he had changed religions. He was black with a white face, head, and shoulders, and stood about 12 inches high and was 16 inches long. His home was a barrel under the mango tree, but he spent most of his time up in the tree. Whenever Norman came near, Pancho rushed to jump into his arms to be held like a child.

I had a wonderful reason to be thankful on Thanksgiving Day. Norma, my new house girl, a half Indian 15 years old from Rio Negro, asked me how one goes about becoming a Christian. A sister was Catholic, the Jehovah Witnesses visited her home regularly, but she attended our Sunday School classes and was soon doing a Bible correspondence course with my help.

1961

The holidays and New Year were so busy that when I finally sat down to write my mother a letter on January 4, I couldn't remember all that was already accomplished in 1961. I did remember we had several emergencies in the clinic including a patient who had been beaten with a whip. Seventy persons had attended the Watch Night service at our house, and I had gone down to Santa Fe for Sunday morning worship and then hurried home for the service in our own church. I had also delivered two babies.

I worked hard to complete the end-of-month and end-of-year reports for 1960 before I needed to pack my suitcase, typewriter, and all the Christmas cards and letters that needed answers and fly to Gualaco for two weeks of Bible School. Besides patient records and orders for medicines and medical supplies, I kept the financial reports for the clinic and sales room and also recorded the rainfall for our area—134.75 inches for 1960 with most of it falling from January to March, and in December.

Before I started for Gualaco, however, I had one more patient. A young man was brought in with three long, ugly, ragged, and deep cuts on his head. Cutting his hair so the doctor could stitch him up was like chopping my way through the jungle. I told myself that maybe I should use a machete.

The man was a clerk at a store in Chapagua and had been robbed as he was counting the money at the end of the day. His 17-year-old assailant had given him three whacks over the head with a piece of wood and then dropped the wood to attack with a knife. My patient said that if he had had his machete, he would have killed his attacker. As it was, he had picked up the wood and struck the knife out of the boy's hand.

When he returned to the clinic to have the wounds dressed, he told me what he intended to do when he found his attacker. "Yes," I said, "the human thing is to want revenge, but that is not what God says we should do." I read him some verses from the Bible, and he was dumbfounded to discover that God said he should love his enemy and do him good.

I was amazed when he said he could do that only if God gave him a *gift*. I hurried on to tell him that was exactly what God wanted to do. As I explained the gift of salvation, he took it all in and accepted the Lord with a faith that was wonderful to see. He said this was the second time he had almost been killed, and God must have been keeping him so he could hear the gospel. He was blind in one eye from the first attack.

A week later the sister of his assailant told me that she had met him on the street, and they had sat on the curb and talked about the problem. Her brother was still in hiding and she was very concerned about him because it was raining daily.

Months later the brother was brought to the clinic on a cot in a hysterical condition. He and an older brother had been fighting, one with a machete, the other with a pistol. I found him a very likable person when he was not allowing Satan to control his life.

To get to Gualaco I first flew to La Ceiba and from there the plane followed the coast east before turning south over the mountains. For awhile we skimmed along between the mountains and the clouds and then climbed above the clouds.

We stopped at Catacamas, and the pilot did some fancy spiraling as we descended through the cloud cover. Our next stop was at Las Limas where we landed in a large pasture to load some *guayacan*, a very hard wood. The logs were four feet long and twelve to eighteen inches across. The weight was painted on the ends of each log, and I noticed one that weighed 446 pounds. After they were put into the plane, they were lashed to folded-down seats across the aisle from the passengers.

In Gualaco I visited with the missionaries, had nine students in my Bible School class, picked coffee beans one afternoon, and made house calls with Becky Herr. One patient, in the middle of the night, was a boy with dysentery and vomiting. He was in a state of shock with a pulse rate of 176. The priest had already been there with a monk who had given him injections of liver and B-12. We gave him more of the same plus something for shock and stayed with him all night. When we left, his pulse was down to 160; when we checked him later in the forenoon, it was 140. I thought he might recover, but he died before noon.

Most mornings the mist rolled up the sides of the scenic mountains that surrounded us, but the day Lorraine Roth and her parents flew in, it didn't roll away. A group of us waited on the field right in a cloud of mist as the plane circled overhead until a tiny break allowed the pilot to see the landing field.

Upon my return to Trujillo, the nurses told me that the clinic had taken care of three macheted victims. One had a slash wound on his shoulder about a foot long. The other two men had been fighting and had to be kept in separate rooms with two soldiers guarding them at all times. One eventually lost all the fingers of his left hand, but the doctor had spent seven hours suturing because he thought he might be able to save them. The other man had a horribly slashed arm and part of his skull almost sliced off.

By the end of January I was rejoicing that I had the foresight to buy a set of old-fashioned sadirons when I was home on furlough. Most of the people ironed with charcoal or gasoline irons, but I didn't like the smell of them or the safety hazard. My electric iron was useless when the electricity went off, and we were told it would be nine days before repairs were made. Before long they said it would be 30 days; then it was extended to 60 days.

Attendance at our evening church services dropped because of dark streets and buildings. I used a flashlight to see the words in the hymnal until we installed hooks in the church ceiling and hung several gasoline lamps Millers and the Pax men brought along for evening services.

The next inconvenience occurred when the burro that hauled the garbage went lame. No garbage was picked up, and in the warm climate it quickly became a constant reminder of the lack of service. I wondered why another burro wasn't used, but the owner apparently didn't share my idea of a solution to the problem. The next report was that the burro had died, and the smell grew even stronger before garbage collection was resumed.

A tall, humorous old fellow who was a friend to all the children and answered to the name "Rice and Beans" died in our clinic the beginning of February. He was brought in unconscious and died six days later without regaining consciousness. He was an English-speaking Negro, had no family, and lived alone. A stroke several years earlier had left him crippled and slightly mentally impaired, but it was quite apparent he had had a good education and was intelligent. His burial was a community affair—a merchant in the town donated lumber, a man from our church made the coffin, prisoners were sent to dig a grave, and George Miller held a short service.

A month-old baby girl was brought to the clinic looking like a wrinkled old woman. The mother said the baby was nice and fat when born but kept losing weight even though she gave her formula. On questioning I learned she hadn't bothered to measure the formula and the baby girl was so dehydrated and malnourished she hadn't the strength to even move her arms and legs. Five days after being admitted, the little girl had gained seven ounces and was moving her hands.

The Hockman family transferred to Tocoa in February when George Zimmerman and David Bange, a new Pax worker, moved to Trujillo to help George Miller with the work. The next new faces were those of LaMar and Catherine Stauffer, who came to Trujillo until a house was ready for them in La Ceiba. They all stayed in Hesses' part of the house, and the weekend Pax men Elam Stauffer and Sam Lapp came over to visit, the house rang with laughter and good will.

I thought I would have a mini vacation Easter weekend and gave the two nurses time off. Then the patients started to arrive and I had to call both women back to work one night each. One patient was so horribly chopped up by a machete that the doctor and I only cleaned the wounds, gave him medication and intravenous fluid, and sent him to La Ceiba on the *Suyapa*. Fortunately the doctor was going too, so he had medical care, if needed.

Grace Miller came over with an infected finger that needed to be opened, a boy arrived with a fish hook I had to get out of his finger, and a number of other people came with one thing or another. I got to the Easter Sunrise Service but missed Sunday School. The following Sunday I was called out of church to attend to a man bleeding from his mouth and ears. He had been cutting down a tree and when the tree fell it knocked him down and crushed his head between a rock and the tree trunk.

The next serious case was the young man who had joined our church in spite of his family's opposition. He was working on his farm, and as he cut a big stem of bananas, his machete slipped and cut his knee. He walked the six miles home but had lost so much blood he fainted on arrival. The family notified the doctor, who asked for the mission truck to pick him up. He said he thought he had lost at least a quart of blood.

After the doctor was finished, I invited the patient to eat with me. As we ate, he asked me why I thought this had happened. I said I thought it was just an accident, perhaps he had been careless and perhaps not. I suspected his family had taunted him with suggestions that it had happened because he had become a Christian.

When he returned for a clean dressing, he told me he agreed with me that it was just an accident and confirmed my suspicions about his family. I then mentioned that most of the macheted victims were not church members which seemed to help relieve his fears that he was being punished.

A mother of several children had a stillborn son early one morning. The father accepted the death casually with the words, "For my part, I give him over to the Lord with pleasure because we already have a lot of boys and they are stubborn."

April seemed to be baby month. I delivered six, and another six I was supposed to deliver were born before the mothers got to the clinic, but the beds were full anyway. One woman with amebic dysentery was brought from quite a distance, traveling first by hammock, then by cayuco, and finally in the mission truck from the dock. Although she was carried into the clinic, she was able to walk out several days later.

A man who attempted suicide was quite upset that we saved his life. He declared if he got well, he would simply try again—but with a better gun. He had tried to shoot himself in the chest while drunk, but the bullet only plowed a five-inch jagged tear along the chest wall. He bled a lot and since the doctor was away sewing up a man with a machete cut on his leg, I had to stitch the chest wound. As I worked, he told me he no longer believed in God. I knew he had a wife and child, and wondered if anything or anyone but Satan could deceive that normally intelligent, good-looking young man into attempting to end his own life.

May was a month of wind with only a few calm hours at night. The grass dried up and the ball field next to our house became a sea of dust. In waves the dust blew into the house at every crack and cranny and settled on floors and furniture to the extent that even Pax man George Zimmerman asked for a dust cloth when getting ready for the Youth Meeting. On the streets the dust stung our legs and blew into our eyes and nose and even between our teeth.

I wasn't sure what to expect from the training school I registered to attend in Siguatepeque, but it was more profitable than I could have imagined. Jean Garber, Rebecca Herr, and I were from Mennonite missions. Ruth Bregenzer was from the Moravian Mission; Diemut Heller, Magda Kroehler, and Ruth Strauss were students from Evangelical and Reformed Mission stations; and Eleanore Entz, Kathleen Gute, Betty Leach, Jean Pulkin, Janyce Smith, Jenta Strombeck, Phyllis Taylor, and Verna Van Wingerden were from Central American Missions. Our instructors were Doctors McKinney and Marx.

The 15 of us attended lectures on the philosophy of medical mission work, as well as on diseases, diagnosis and treatments, and how to recognize cases we could not treat that needed to be sent to hospitals. The doctors spoke on dentistry, dermatology, medicine, gynecology, urology, ophthalmology, obstetrics, and pediatrics. We had demonstrations on nose packs, pressure bandaging, splints and casts, starting I.V.'s, physical exams of children and adults, as well as ear, nose, and throat exams.

Between and after classes we shopped, toured the town, and had fun. Dr. McKinney and his wife invited us all to dinner the last evening. For entertainment, we nurses got a skit together where we diagnosed the medical conditions of the doctors and Mrs. McKinney. Jean had the honor of being Dr. McQuack. I remember we told Dr. McKinney he had a decomposition of the heart and it would be fatal—and next time he shouldn't wait so long for medical treatment. Dr. Marx was told he had a pain in the neck. The treatments we recommended were equally outrageous.

While in Siguatepeque I attended a piano recital at the school the missionary children attended. Ruthie Miller, Alice Hamilton, Miriam Miller and Larry Hockman all played pieces.

Shortly after I got back to Trujillo, Irvin Weaver and Henry Shenk stopped in on their way to Tocoa for conference meetings. They had just delivered a plane load of 15 pigs and eight heifers to Paraguay.

A 12-day celebration was held that year for John the Baptist's birthday—the longest I could remember. Lots of all-night dances and four coronations were held—a queen in Cristales, another queen in Rio Negro, and a *Rey Feo* or ugly king in Trujillo and Cristales. The gown for the queen in Cristales was said to have cost 200 lempiras for 30 yards of material embroidered with silver. The printed program indicated drinks would be available for those who paid, and I could only wonder how many patients I would have to care for as a result of drunken fights.

Visitors arrived from as far away as Tegucigalpa and with the pole and thatch shelter for gambling and other entertainment only feet from our house, willing or not, we couldn't avoid the noise of the festivities. I didn't see, but I certainly heard, the shouts and applause when a small contestant, equipped with sand, was able to climb a 30-foot greased pole and bring down a flag mounted on the top.

In contrast to that method of honoring a long-dead saint, two men walked from La Conce, a 12-hour walk, to attend our church service and hear a stirring message about not putting off the day of salvation. The next Sunday J. Mark Miller returned for the summer. He led the singing in the English service and because he was home, we had a Youth Meeting. Seven young people attended in spite of the festivities in the town. J. Mark also had a children's meeting and I told him he spoke Spanish just like the locals. I remember he and Francisco walked to Santa Fe and bought 100 mangoes for one lempira. They were tired young men by the time they carried home what they didn't eat!

Although my mother was in Pennsylvania, I had a party in honor of her birthday in Trujillo. I invited two couples who attended our church and planned a special menu. I wasn't sure if my guests would come since the people were not accustomed to being invited out for meals, but they came. After the meal as we were preparing to read some verses from the Bible, a man rushed in and said the doctor wanted a bed prepared for a patient. As I worked in the clinic I heard my guests reading and singing and was able to rejoin them before they went home.

The patient, shot through the foot, arrived with a lot of friends and relatives—all smelling of liquor. His drunken friends continued to visit after his wound was dressed, and I warned him he would have to leave if he drank in the clinic. He was a young, successful businessman, but lived a very sinful life. Even though he had a wife and some children, one of his many girlfriends had been admitted to the clinic just the week before after a miscarriage. That girl had never seen a Bible before and was interested enough in what she heard that she bought a New Testament before leaving.

My mother was a woman of prayer; therefore, when I wrote home I would tell her about these people and request prayer.

♔

Monday morning I got up at 5:15 to go to the *matanza* (the killing) for meat. Every week or so a cow was killed at a roofed concrete slab beside a stream. The carcass was then brought into town in the garbage cart. It was hung up in a room and sold as fast as pieces could be cut off. Forming a line and waiting for your turn was never introduced in Trujillo so I was surrounded by a pushing, yelling, demanding bunch of people.

July 22 I saw an eight-month-old Carib baby that weighed nine pounds. His fever was 105° and his chest congested. I gave him a shot of Distrepdipen and told the mother to bring him again the next day, but Sunday was a day like I never had before. Hurricane Anna arrived with rain off and on the evening before; in the morning, just as we came out of church, the wind began to blow. Through heavy rain and strong winds I went to the home of the businessman to dress the wound on his foot. On my way home I heard screams coming from a house; then the front door opened and someone called for me to come and help. A woman had slipped and fallen on the wet stones outside her kitchen. The son and husband had just laid her on her bed and it was obvious to me that her hip was broken. I sent for George and we splinted the leg and hoped the weather would allow a MAF plane to come in the next day to take her to the hospital.

I decided to spend the night with the woman, but just as I was about to go to the clinic for a few things I heard a terrible crash. The tin roof of the school near the clinic had blown off. As I hurried home, I stayed as close as possible to buildings to keep out of direct blasts of the wind and to avoid being hit by wind-blown objects. At the clinic a quick glance showed the grapefruit and banana trees were blown over, tree limbs were strewn around the patio, the concrete block chimney on Hesses' part of the house had blown down, and the radio aerial and pieces of roof tin were loose and flapping. It took my whole body weight to push the double patio doors shut against the wind which was coming from the north. After two hours in the calm eye of the storm, the wind shifted and came from the south with the same strength and I had an equal struggle to open a door against it.

On my way back to spend the night with the broken-hip patient, I met an *army* of people carrying the postmaster on a cot. A flying piece of tin roofing had struck him in the back of a leg and I embroidered the cut shut with 13 stitches. All of this occurred the day after the MAF plane had taken the doctor to the hospital in Tegucigalpa with an apparent kidney stone.

Thirty-seven houses were blown down in Trujillo, Rio Negro, and Cristales, and hardly a house escaped some damage. The building that held the telegraph office and was the home of several people lost its roof and all records and personal possessions got wet. The telegraph lines were down, and just days later we lost our radio contact when a tube burned out in the set and we had no replacement. Half the church roof had to be replaced and Hesses' roof, chimney, and the radio aerial needed repairs. Lots of the fruit trees were blown down and many *milpas*, *bananales* and *plantanales* (corn, banana, and plantain plantations) were destroyed. As a result, food was scarce for a long time. In Castilla, across the bay, Mr. Brooks, the Methodist preacher lost his life trying to save his boat, which was being swept out to sea.

Everyone was busy Monday and the sound of hammering resounded throughout the town. Because we had been in the eye of the storm, damage had hit from every direction and trees had fallen haphazardly and were mixed with debris of all kinds. Practically all my little mango trees were blown over, but I replanted them and hoped the roots would take hold again. The poinsettias were shredded and the patio strewn with limbs and leaves and chimney blocks. The Miller house had very little damage beyond a few pieces of loose roofing and a fence blown down, and I was grateful when George, J. Mark, Mr. Luby, and Francisco came to clean up at our place.

The young Carib mother brought her tiny baby back to the clinic, and I was amazed to find his temperature was normal. I had expected to be told he had died over the weekend. The MAF plane was able to land and take the woman with the broken hip to the hospital in San Pedro Sula, and our clinic made the front page of the newspaper when the postmaster whose leg I had sutured wrote an article about the storm and of being cared for at the Mennonite Clinic.

The Hess family was due to return from furlough and we announced at church that we needed to clean their apartment. There was some water damage from the storm as well as plenty of dust that had accumulated after the Pax men had moved out. People came to help on cleaning day and by evening the house smelled and looked fresh and clean. Friends sent flowers and everything looked nice and welcoming the day the Hesses arrived.

Once again I was entertained by the Hess children. Gerald said a little deer was down the bank and Dicky asked, “Is it a rain deer or a snow deer?”

Another time I heard the mournful whistle of a train and found Dicky supplying sound effects while pushing little plastic train cars along the walk. I said, “That sounds just like a train.”

Dicky replied emphatically, “It is a train!”

“How old are you?” Dicky asked one day.

“Fifty,” I replied.

“That’s older than my mother,” he said.

“Yes, older than your mother, your daddy, and Uncle George,” I agreed.

“You’re gonna die before us, I believe,” he said, then after a moment added, “I hope they can fix you up alive when you’re half dead!”

I still love Dicky for those words because it showed he loved me.

At that time Dicky wanted to become a missionary doctor. Danny wasn't quite sure but thought he might be a pilot. Gerald wanted to be a popsicle man.

James Hess resumed Sunday visits to Santa Fe with 80 children in Sunday School and 30 adults for the worship service. He also held a week of evangelistic meetings in Trujillo using the parable of the prodigal son as the theme. Six persons accepted the Lord. The afternoon James and a number of us met with the new believers for the first time was also the day my nephew, Donald Taylor, was married to Erma Horst in Ohio. When I read my mother's account of the wedding a week later, I felt a twinge of regret that I had missed yet another family event. But immediately I realized I was not really sorry, because the joy of the salvation of six new souls more than compensated for missed personal pleasures.

September brought many blessings. Three Pax (overseas Voluntary Service—VS) men arrived one Friday on the *Suyapa,* and before they left Monday by plane for their assignment in Savá, they blessed us in our Sunday morning service. Mardene Sensenig from New Holland, Pennsylvania, led the singing in the English service; Menno Coblentz from Indiana gave his testimony; and Ray Horst from Iowa delivered a fine message.

Another blessing was the arrival of Hesses' shipment which included packages for me—music books, my sewing basket, cake and pudding mixes, dried fruit and corn, and as noted in a letter, peanut butter that *certainly won't go to waste.* Someone had sent me white stockings, but since I didn't wear stockings except for church or when I went on vacation, I used a tea bag to dye them.

The Honduran Independence Day brought a lot of work to the clinic. The celebrations on the plaza across from the clinic got louder and louder, and at one point the women selling food in the booth ran into the clinic for safety. Political discussions turned into arguments and finally into fights. We saw a group of men run out of the booth and across to the hotel where more men joined in; then all disappeared up the street in an uproar of shouts followed by gun shots. I rather innocently asked, "Why don't the authorities do something about this?" A little later I discovered some men who should have been breaking up the riot were actually part of it. One even waved a gun at and threatened Grace Miller and a few other women who were outside as the pack ran past.

It wasn't long before I had a man on the examining table with gunshot wounds to the wrist, thigh, and abdomen. We cleaned him up and started fluids and turned to the next victim, his brother. That patient was unconscious and had lost a lot of blood. He was shot in the chest and abdomen and died about 30 minutes later. When his drunken friends came to take him away, they ignored my suggestion to carry him on a sheet and simply picked him up by arms and legs and carted him off. One of my nurses said he left at least three *wives* and a half dozen small children and several grown ones. The other patient died early in the evening. By then we had another shooting victim with several wounds above the ankle that had broken both leg bones. Like the others, he was drunk when brought in.

Satan and his evil work was all around us, but the Creator was more powerful than the created fallen angel and protected us during spiritual warfare. A concealed letter was discovered in the VS unit house in Savá, which translated read, *"Oh powerful ghost, companion of Lucifer, Oh devil, devil, king of treasures, on my knees I ask thee that this family may flee from here, that they may have neither peace nor unity until they are far from here. If thou doest for me this that I ask thee, I will be thy servant. Amen."*

We were told that such a curse on a family that didn't have the protection of the Spirit of the Living God could cause the people in that house to see ghosts and hear screams and that they were even molested so that they couldn't sleep at night. People were frightened nearly to death and usually moved out of houses that had been cursed. The Christians in the VS unit house were unaffected by the curse.

The beginning of October two ladies, Wycliffe Bible translators, arrived in Trujillo to work on the Moreno language Bible. They stayed with me for two weeks, but we had little time to talk because they spent most of their time visiting Moreno Christians in several towns to have their translations of Luke and I John checked and corrected.

The end of October the Missionary Aviation Fellowship did a trial run of a new project—a dental clinic. Dr. Kenneth Cole from Bell, California, and his wife flew in with a portable dental chair and drill which was run by battery. I wasn't sure if the people had paid any attention to the notices I had posted, but there were more patients than could be treated Monday afternoon. A lot more people came the second day, which had to be shortened so the dentist could pack up and fly out before night fell. Fourteen teeth were filled and 45 pulled. The team then went to Tocoa and Gualaco.

Irene Snavely

In November I took a short vacation. Grace went along as far as La Ceiba where she planned to have dental work done, and I continued on to Tegucigalpa where I met Irene Snavely, my vacation companion. Irene and I stayed at the Central American Mission that night and next day applied for visas at the Mexican, Salvadoran, and Guatemalan consulates.

Our luggage was searched by customs officials at the border into El Salvador, and again a short time later by soldiers probably looking for communist literature. When a soldier opened Irene's bag on top of the bus, I overheard him say something about evangelicals being good people and figured he had seen some of the tracts she was taking along. I told him he wouldn't have to open my bags and he promptly dropped my keys down to me. San Salvador was a beautiful city and the missionaries we met showed us most gracious hospitality.

We traveled on the paved Pan American Highway through El Salvador, but it became a gravel road in Guatemala until we drew close to Guatemala City, where it was again paved. A 45-minute flight (it would have been 12 hours by road) took us to Huehuetenango to visit friends and see Indian ruins at nearby Zacaleu. At the CAM (Central America Mission) school I got new instructions on how to make good peanut butter. I had apparently always dried the peanuts too much in my prior attempts and on my first try after learning this important step, I didn't dry them enough. Even so, the results pleased me.

The next year I sent to La Ceiba for five pounds of raw peanuts and tried again with excellent results. That time I apparently roasted them just right because I needed almost no oil to get the right spreading consistency, and I discovered I didn't even need to remove the red skin from the kernels. The four and a half big jars of peanut butter cost only $1.25 for the peanuts, a little cooking oil, and some time grinding and preparing them while anticipating the delicious results.

Irene and I continued by bus to the Mexico border and after wading through mud several inches deep, we passed through the immigration office (hut) and caught another bus to Oaxaca, Mexico. We visited some marvelously fascinating ruins and saw a tule tree that was 38 meters around, 40 meters high, and 2,000 years old, as well as ruins at Mitla and Monte Alban.

After spending a night in a small hotel in Tlaxiaco at a cost of 80 cents per person, we took a small local bus to the tiny Indian village where Claude and Alice Good worked with the Trique Indians. The Goods and their two little girls lived in a three-room house built with hewn lumber—not sawed—where Wycliffe translators had lived while translating Mark and John into the Trique dialect.

When we arrived, at an elevation of approximately 8,000 feet, we felt we were at the top of the world. We could look down on other mountains blanketed with clouds, and although the air was quite chilly, the fellowship was warm. The Goods said they had only seen two sunsets during their time there because mist moved in early every forenoon and lasted until a wind blew it away—usually in the evening.

During a few hours of clear weather Claude took us up a high hill behind their house to a place where we could see the opposite 8,000-foot mountain that had a 4,000-foot drop into the Putla Valley. On our way back down to the house, I found a broken arrowhead, and we saw an Indian steam bath. The bath consisted of a little hut built of sticks and leaves just large enough for an adult to crawl into. At one end was a stone fireplace where water was poured over heated rocks to create the steam.

During a trip to Puebla and Mexico City, we saw snow by the side of the road and passed a few volcanoes.

In Mexico City Mennonite missionaries Esther Detweiler from Cuba, Rosanna Roth from Oregon, and Cora Yoder from Ohio took us sight-seeing before we went to a YMCA camp near Cuernavaca to attend several sessions of a Christian Businessmen's Spiritual Life Conference. It was quite encouraging to hear the speakers and meet with a group of dedicated church and mission workers.

A stop at the Wycliffe Bible Translators' headquarters also made us aware of many other areas where Christians were out in God's service.

♔

Suddenly, 1961 was almost over. Thanksgiving was a meal of beans, rice, spaghetti, fruit salad, and pumpkin pie for all the people from the church. We then swung into Bible School with an average attendance of over 100 and finished out the year with more patients in the clinic, including the suturing case of a man bitten by a pig, a cast put on the broken arm of a little boy, and three babies—one a tiny two-pound seven-ounce girl. That baby, whose mother came in comatose with eclampsia, actually lived. We kept her until she weighed about six pounds and we all became quite attached to her.

Goldilocks didn't ask for my help when she delivered six kittens. Goldilocks belonged to the Hess family and I think she must have had more than 100 kittens in her lifetime. I had kept one of the ten kittens she had during Hesses' furlough, a pure yellow one. I thought she looked like a little lion and named her Leona. When SHE turned out to be a HE, the name was shortened to Lee. After James Hess returned, he suggested we should neuter Lee. I was unfamiliar with animal surgery, so I administered a bit of anesthesia while James did the operation.

1962

By the middle of January the tiny baby, Dulce María (Sweet Mary), born the month before weighed almost four pounds, and the doctor said it was a *triumph* how she was developing. The mother had gone home and when she or the father visited, they were amazed at how well their daughter was doing. This was another case of an unwed mother living, at least part time, with a man who had a wife and family. I hardly knew how to talk with people like that because their viewpoint of sin was so compromised that they felt they could live as they wished and that God would understand their circumstances and not condemn them.

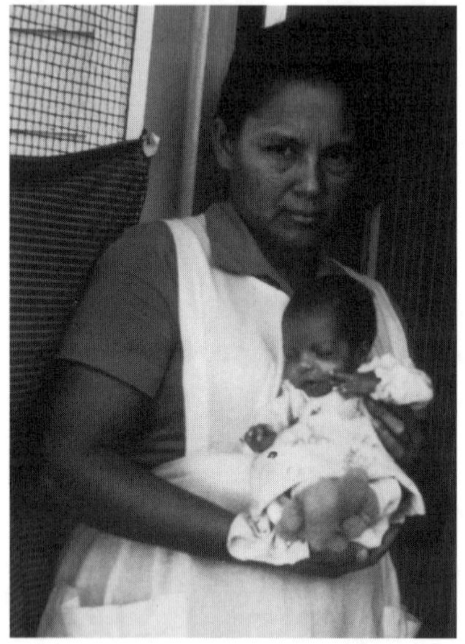

Tilda and Dulce María.

Before long we noticed Dulce María had discovered that we picked her up if she cried and we knew she was developing as a normal, healthy child. I also discovered she had quite a temper if not picked up quickly, and it wasn't long before she would stiffen her little body and practically stand on her feet when I did pick her up after any delay. I tried to wean her from expecting constant attention; as she grew stronger, we sometimes allowed her to cry herself to sleep. I knew she would soon go home and her mother, who had begun teaching school in Santa Fe, could not be at her constant beck and call. In fact, I met her father the day after she went home and he said she had cried most of the night.

We saw Dulce María again at 15 months when her mother brought her in with diarrhea. She weighted 14 pounds and had a four-month-old brother who weighed almost the same.

Chester Denlinger from Belize and Virgil Hostetler of Beltsville, Maryland, visited our mission in January. George Miller showed them around, but their much-anticipated trip to Santa Fe was aborted because of problems with the motor on the boat.

The weather also cut down attendance at the ten-day Bible Institute held in Tocoa the beginning of February. Several men from our church and a few from Santa Fe attended, but 15 inches of rain raised rivers and flooded paths and kept others from getting there. Two of the Savá VS men and two local men walked nine hours to get to Tocoa. Later in the year I walked part of that road and learned firsthand just how deep the mud could get.

Norman Hockman, James Hess, and Lorraine Roth were the teachers with about 20 persons in the daytime classes. Evening classes had slightly higher attendance. The Tocoa church provided the food: one man gave a pig; others gave rice, beans, plantains, and even corn for tortillas. Everyone agreed the meetings were a great blessing even though most of the men had to sleep on hard church benches at night.

♛

February also brought about the beginning of the end of the mission clinic in Trujillo when the government began building a hospital. Earlier when Trujillo officials had discussed plans for a hospital, they had requested that we Mennonites run the institution. This hospital, however, was being built by the Honduran government, and it was unlikely we would be a part of its administration. Knowing how often the governing party had been overthrown, and how frequently projects were begun and not completed, such as a dam to supply round-the-clock electricity, it was far too early for us to make any decisions about our continued medical work in Trujillo. We asked for the Lord's direction and went on with our usual tasks.

In April I had my first tour of the new hospital. The bricks were only up about three feet, but the engineer showed me the layout. The wards would be for six beds each—men's surgical and medical, women's surgical and medical, pediatrics, and maternity, and an out-patient department. Dr. Hernándz thought it might be in operation by the new year. When he told me that, I wondered where I would go and what I would be doing in 1963. My conclusion was, "As He leads."

♛

The dam above the town had been started with enthusiasm and promises but was still incomplete, and neither of the two old fuel-powered electric plants was in working order. Mr. July's son finally received the parts to repair the one plant and I was so glad for the bright lights because the house was dark and dreary with only candles and lamps during the rainy season.

The two plants ran on different cycles, and the one he repaired provided bright lights but could not be used for any appliances with motors. The other one operated motors without damage, but produced weak lighting and barely heated the electric iron.

♔

Patients in February included a 19-year-old from the prison who had a guard with him every day, and a young woman whose mind was affected by cerebral malaria. At times she lived in total torment from delusions brought on by high fever.

Later the 12-year-old houseboy of the president of a lumbering company was brought in with an almost circular cut on his back. He had fallen down some steps while sleep walking and landed on an opened tin can. The doctor sutured him and we kept him in the clinic for several days.

♔

Mr. July planned another speaking trip to La Colonia and Chapagua and James, Beaty, and I took him as far as we could go in the Jeep. In the jungle where the road was swampy, two- to four-inch poles had been laid side by side with ground packed over them. Several kilometers didn't have ground on the corduroy bed and the going was rough and bumpy! It took three tries to get up the banks of one stream we forded because of loose soil. In the second stream we wobbled and jiggled crazily over rocks the size of my head. Although James was sure we could ford the third stream, he doubted the Jeep could climb the steep bank to get out, so we prayed with Mr. July and said good-bye.

When Mr. July returned a week later, his face beamed with joy at being allowed to witness for his Lord. From the place where we had left him, it had taken him four hours to walk to La Colonia because for one kilometer he walked through mud and water up to his knees. At each village he had handed out tracts and held a meeting. At one village he said there was *bastante interés* (plenty of interest). He said they needed a lot of teaching in another village where few people could read, and he was ready to take another trip the following week.

Almost every time Mr. July returned from his evangelistic trips he reported people had accepted the Lord because of his witness and testimony. A young man who spent several days in the clinic as the result of a fight was an example of the far-reaching witness of Mr. July. Our patient was so drunk when he had the fight that he didn't even remember who he had fought with or why. I asked him where he lived, and he said he ate in a Moreno home in Rio Negro and slept in a cayuco on the beach at night.

When I talked to him about the Lord, he mentioned that he knew Mr. July and how he had changed when he started believing in God. He apparently hadn't listened to Mr. July, however, because he was totally ignorant of even the basic facts of Christianity. When I asked him if he knew who God's son was, he suggested *San Pedro* (Saint Peter). A short time after explaining the reason and results of Christ's death, I returned to talk with him again and asked if he remembered who it was that had died for his sins. His hesitant reply was, "The devil?"

The day we dropped Mr. July off at the stream was clear with beautiful blue sky, and Beaty and I thoroughly enjoyed the little outing. On our way home we stopped at the brick factory where workers were making the bricks to build the hospital. It was interesting to watch the process from pit to kiln. One man was digging clay. An old man was patting the mud into a five-brick form, then dumping out the bricks. Younger men were hauling the bricks in a wheelbarrow to the furnace where once a week they were burned for 48 hours. One of the men showed us the factory kitchen. The stove was a piece of tin just a foot off the ground with a wood fire underneath. He joked that they had a mad dog to wash the dishes!

One day I saw a woman walking down the street with a pan on her head. Extending over the front about two feet was the head of a kingfish and over the back an equal distance was its tail. She brought it to the clinic and I purchased it for two lempiras or one dollar. It weighed about 16 pounds and I got 24 nice-sized slices from it. Jean was visiting me that week, and I invited the Hesses to join us for a fish dinner which included boiled yucca, tomato sauce, *patastillos* (squash-like vegetable that grows on vines) fried with onions, and dessert of pudding and cookies. The Miller family missed out on the fish but didn't mind because they were in Siguatepeque with their daughters celebrating Danny's fifth birthday.

Holy Week was wet! Over eight inches of rain fell, and although the priests could collect the Holy Water that was given out each Good Friday, none of the processions with the statues of Mary and Christ, and with the little girls dressed as angels could be held on Good Friday. Our Thursday and Friday evening services were attended by several persons who normally didn't attend, but rain kept many away from the Friday morning service.

The skies cleared and our Easter sunrise service began at 5:30 at the *mirador.* (Mirar means to look—the mirador was a place behind the town hall with a couple of benches where one could sit and enjoy the beautiful view of the bay and the Bay Islands in the distance.) Sunday School and the English worship service were held in the forenoon, and a wedding in the evening service was followed by a reception in my living room. Grace, Beaty, and I each made a gallon of punch and baked a cake for the reception, and about 55 people were there. The happy couple even had a few gifts to take home.

We missionaries viewed this wedding as a highlight because of the Christian witness the wedding conveyed. James used it as an example in his evening sermon, saying that others who say they believe but don't keep God's commandments are deceiving themselves.

♔

Just before sunset on Easter Monday I went to the *mirador*. I could see a rain shower between the islands of Cayos Cochinos and the mainland and another on Cayos. Big clouds were piled up all over the bay and as the sun dropped it painted the clouds and water in amazing and changing colors. Through breaks in the heavy clouds, I could see the pink of more distant clouds.

A cayuco, with two adults and a child in it, raced through a calm sea towards the pier. On the beach three young men hurried to beat the storms. Their frequent rests indicated the big brown package they carried was both heavy and awkward. As they drew closer, I saw it was a marimba.

As I watched, rain started falling in the bay from two separate storm clouds. I could see another storm out at sea—three storms within sight all at the same time. The water in the bay and under the storm clouds was a dark gray. Just beyond was a shiny strip of colorless water which later turned pink. The more distant storms faded away, but the closer black clouds seemed to increase in size and I realized they were drawing closer.

Two men came and sat on the next bench and asked if I was *contemplando el paisage* (contemplating the landscape). My cat also came out and after stalking back and forth on the bench several times finally settled down for some petting.

The cayuco was nearly at Cristales, the marimba and the young men had disappeared, and the storm clouds drew closer. First I felt mist in the air, but when big drops started falling I went home. Two hours later a lively shower was still falling, bringing an additional two inches of rain to our already wet Holy Week.

Rain, however, didn't stop the noisy soccer players on the lot next to our house. They slipped, slid, and fell until they resembled dogs or pigs as they raced around butting the muddy ball with their heads.

Soldiers were standing around the playing field, so I assumed the teams were made up of prisoners. Crime in the country had risen dramatically, especially murder. People talked about it on the streets and more than once I heard, "Getting ready for elections next year."

♔

Bible School at Santa Fe was held in May. Lorraine Roth came on the MAF plane from Tocoa to help; she, James, and I went down to Santa Fe every day before lunch. We held classes from 4:30 to 6:00 and from 6:40 until 7:30, thereby getting in our two-week material in one week of classes. Before the classes began, I spent some time studying my lessons in the little belfry room halfway up to the bell tower. When one of the VS men and a friend found James taking a *siesta* one afternoon in a cayuco, he had a rude awakening—he got dumped out.

The weather was good and we got wet only one day, from the spray blowing on us. Of course, I always used my umbrella as a shield which gave some protection. It made a trip special when one or more porpoises joined us.

James drove us to and from the beach in the mission truck, and it took us almost as long to get home from the beach as it did to come from Santa Fe in the boat. The truck needed a carburetor, and one evening as he got in, James dropped the keys—right through a hole in the floor onto the sand below. Time and salt air had rusted the floor.

The church at Santa Fe had been growing slowly, but over 100 children regularly attended the Sunday School, so they knew many of the songs we sang during Bible School. I wish I could have recorded them as they sang with enthusiasm and their own embellishments to the tunes. They certainly made a joyful noise unto the Lord. I really enjoyed teaching God's Word to the fourth, fifth, and sixth graders.

Attendance was good even though one school teacher threatened punishment for the children coming to our meetings. I had 18 pupils with perfect attendance. One girl missed a day because she had been bitten by some animal in the sea. We had to limit enrollment because of available space in the church, but those that did attend certainly heard more than when we held classes in a house or under a tree. I remember the year I helped Esteban teach in a house—after we closed the door to begin the lesson, children climbed in and out of the windows so fast I doubted we ever did get an accurate enrollment.

Conference for our mission workers came next. Grace, Beaty, and I planned menus and sleeping arrangements. LaMar Stauffers came from La Ceiba, James Sauders from Gualaco, and seven of the eight VS workers gathered in from their various locations. One VS man stayed in Tocoa so he could go every day to give injections to a dying cancer patient in a neighboring village.

I put eight pounds of red beans to soak before leaving for church on Sunday. They were my contribution to lunch that day along with mango sauce.

We had hoped to use the clinic for sleeping space for four of the VS fellows, but then a patient arrived. He was drunk when brought in and had been fighting over a woman. The doctor was amazed to discover that none of the seven bullets had struck a vital organ or broken a bone. Two had entered and exited the abdomen, two went through his thigh, one left a four-inch graze wound on the other thigh, one went through his right arm, and another grazed the left arm. Including the entry and exit sites, the doctor had 12 wounds to dress; he then ordered intravenous fluids and bed rest for four days.

At first that patient seemed to improve, but then a fever struck that didn't respond to any medicine. The doctor thought he might have advanced TB, and after 16 days in our clinic he was sent to a hospital. Another patient brought in with malaria and anemia was also sent to the hospital, but an American from Mississippi with a finger almost cut off was treated, sutured, and released by the doctor.

A 60-year-old man with high blood pressure and heart problems was in our men's ward for two weeks. His family brought his meals and he was able to take care of himself, so except for medication and keeping him under observation, he created no work for us. He went across the street to the Catholic church twice on Sundays and attended our church in the evening. It was the first time he had been in an Evangelical service. When I discussed the need of accepting the sacrifice of Christ for our sins, he admitted that everyone sinned, but added that he had never done any great sins.

The dental clinic that May was successful. In four and a half days Dr. Ken Cole from California and working with MAF pulled 171 teeth and filled 37. There would have been more work for him, but he usually didn't stay even that long in one place. Ruth Cole was a nurse and worked as his assistant and I acted as receptionist—and patient. I asked him to pull a tooth that had been giving me pain in my jaw. After he started, he informed me the root of the tooth next to it was infected and should also come out. I gave him the go-ahead and I experienced almost no pain. Tilda took out the stitches a few days later.

Jean mentioned in a letter that Dr. Cole pulled 113 teeth and did 17 fillings during the three days he and his wife spent in Tocoa and there were more he could have done if he had been able to stay longer.

♔

Firecrackers tied to the iron fence around the park announced the beginning of John the Baptist's birthday celebration one evening in June at 10 o'clock. My comment was, "At least they didn't set them off at two in the morning like last year!"

John's statue was carried through the streets and spent one night in Cristales and one night in Rio Negro before returning to Trujillo. I'm not sure if he attended the dances in those towns, but in Trujillo he was standing in the park while the dances went on in the cabildo next to our clinic one night and in the hotel the following night. The music was quite wild, and when the dances ended at five in the morning, I couldn't miss the yelling and whistling that accompanied the departure of the participants.

The last day of the holidays was much quieter and I guess gave the people a chance to catch up on sleep and get sober before returning to their work on Monday. I knew none of the celebrations was pleasing or honoring to John the Baptist.

♔

My holiday was a vacation week on Cayos Cochinos in the Griffiths' house. It was delightful but began with a strong land breeze which stirred up the sea as Sam Lapp; James, Beaty, and Gerald Hess; and I left Trujillo at noon on Sunday on the *Suyapa*. It took almost an hour to get to Santa Fe. There two men in a cayuco came out with a tub of mangoes, a rice mill carved out of wood, and various pieces of luggage. They bobbed around quite a bit but came up expertly alongside the boat. After unloading, they returned for two women.

We watched rather breathlessly as they battled the mounting waves and didn't seem to get anywhere. Sometimes they disappeared behind waves, but just as we thought they would have to give up and return to land, they made one more effort and reached the boat. The women were drenched, and getting up the ladder dangling over the side of the *Suyapa* wasn't easy. The first was a little old woman who slipped and fell as she got on board and then almost slid off the deck before being pulled to safety.

The waves were six to ten feet high, but later when I talked to Captain Cooper, he said they were up to 15 feet at times. For the first time in her life, Beaty Hess got seasick, and we all were glad for the warm welcome Hanno and Hessie Griffith gave us to Cayos Cochinos. Hessie served a good meal and requested we have a service for them in their living room.

By Tuesday the sea was calm and the sky so clear that the mountains ten miles away seemed much closer. The five of us vacationers took long walks and drank in the beauty of the island, sky, and sea. Some of the hikes turned into rather rough going; once Beaty lost her footing on a steep hillside made unstable with loose shale. It took both James and Sam to get her back on the path on both feet. The vegetation on another hillside had been chopped, and I felt quite worn out after negotiating its deep carpet of dried branches and tree trunks. A shower, meal, and rest were all that was necessary to make me ready to strike out again in another direction. Right in front of the house was a wide white beach where by day we swam and by full moon saw a picture-perfect view of coconut palms leaning out over the shimmering seascape.

James and Sam had brought our boat along, so we enjoyed rides around our island and a smaller island to look at caves and water-carved rock formations that played musical sounds when the wind blew. On the north side of our island the sea dashed against huge stone cliffs where even in a calm sea the water was thrown up in curls of spray.

A ride to one of the keys gave the men an opportunity to swim in the bright blue-green water and Bobby and me an opportunity to walk on the white sandy beach and collect miniature shells whose beauty made it difficult not to go home overloaded. Bobby was Griffiths' son and although not quite eight years old, he knew the sea and told James where to go to avoid reefs, rocks, or shallow places.

Hessie was concerned about the salvation of the other residents of the island and invited them to attend the services she requested we hold each evening in her home. The island's population was 31, and each evening, after the first, I gave a flannelgraph-illustrated Bible story for the children, which was equally enjoyed by the adults.

The meals were wonderful. Breakfast was at six and was a full meal of tomato juice, fried ham and eggs, fried beans, oatmeal, platanos, toast, marmalade, coffee, and milk or tea. We had meat three times a day. Lobster was mentioned one day and soon a boy was sent out in a dory. He returned with a big lobster which appeared on the table in a delicious lobster salad. Hessie had a cook and a maid but did a lot of the work herself.

Hanno was building a new boat which was to be 76 feet long, four feet longer than the *Suyapa*. Each rib had a slightly different curve and the siding was being put on. One thousand pounds of five-inch spikes were being used to put the boat together. Seven spikes weighed a pound. Holes were bored, and after the spikes were driven in, they were painted over. Wooden stoppers were dipped in paint and driven in over the recessed spike ends. The protruding ends of the stoppers were then sawed off and sanded smooth.

Hanno said he couldn't be happy without boats. He designed, built, and sold them. This particular one would probably be sold in the Bahamas. He said it cost about $20,000 to build and would sell for around $30,000.

Three days after arriving we said good-bye and rode off in our boat. We crossed diagonally to the mainland and stopped at Farallones, where Doña Chon, or Concepción, lived. (She was the woman mentioned earlier who had walked to Trujillo for instruction and baptism.) Rocky cliffs dropped sharply to the water's edge and we had a stiff climb to her house. Because of rocks we had to leave our boat out from shore a short distance and had thrillingly tippy rides in and back out, but thankfully were not dumped into the sea. As Sam lifted Gerald into our boat from the cayuco, he said, "Well, we got here all right."

Gerald replied, "Yes, but I didn't love it!"

It was my first visit to the home of Doña Chon. We stayed less than a half hour, but we all enjoyed it.

Dr. McKinney came out from Siguatepeque to hold clinics. Becky and Jean had him examine their obstetric patients in Tocoa, and I lined up all my obstetric patients too. Sixteen came and the instructions and pointers Dr. McKinney gave were very helpful. He also saw a number of the mission personnel and went over my drug supply.

During his visit he toured the new hospital being built in Trujillo and expressed concern about the missionaries' working for the government. Everyone seemed to be in agreement that when the hospital opened, my work would be over. The hospital walls, however, were only up to the windows so there was still time to adjust to the idea and too early to make any definite plans for the future.

Jean and Lorraine flew into Trujillo in early July. They were leaving for furlough, and when they flew to La Ceiba I went along. Two days later the alarm clock woke us at 4:30, and by six we were on the early Fruit Company train to Olanchito. The train had nine cars which looked like small wooden sheds with windows. The windows were also wooden, so I was glad it wasn't raining because the car would have been dark if they were closed. Trees with lavender blooms and bird-of-paradise flowers appeared framed in the windows for a few seconds and then disappeared as we rattled by.

Before we had traveled far, I decided the designer of the seats must have won the prize for *most uncomfortable design*. The seats were slats of wood about ten inches wide, dipped out in the center so that the front edge cut into the back of my knees. When the conductor came through to punch our tickets, he was followed by a man dressed in khaki wearing a gun and a belt full of cartridges. I was unsure of his job and toyed idly with the idea that he would threaten to shoot anyone without a ticket. Whatever his role, the gun and cartridges made him an impressive figure.

For awhile we traveled between the sea and the mountains with stops every few kilometers at Moreno villages. The popular pastime was eating. At each stop men, women, and children came on board with buckets of mangoes, dishpans of tortillas, fried beans, cheese, yucca with cracklings, coconut buns, etc., and threaded their way back and forth calling out their wares. The vendor that shouted *-El cafe,-* had a pot of coffee in one hand and a can of water in the other. In the water were two or three cups—automatic dishwasher?

Even though we had a good breakfast before leaving Betty Brown's home in La Ceiba, I couldn't resist buying a tortilla filled with fried beans. As we got further inland there were fewer villages and less stops, and the vendors sold only *frescos*. In spite of the convenient open-window garbage disposal, by 9:30 the floor of our car was littered with fish bones, mango seeds, and bottle caps.

The train crossed several high trestle bridges, went through one small tunnel, and had to slow down frequently for curves as we climbed the mountain.

We arrived in Olanchito sometime after two and were met by Jaime Clark, a young missionary who took us to his home, the Baptist Mission house. He and his wife had met in language school in Costa Rica.

The next morning we went to the Bible Institute and sat in on some of the classes with the twelve young men and women in various stages of the three-year course. In the evening we attended a prayer meeting; the following morning we took a little bus to meet a local train going as far as Elixir. Our destination was Savá, but the train didn't go there, so we got out and started walking in the hot noon sun.

Don Pancho Flores met us at the train to guide us to Savá. In the beginning of our five-mile walk, we followed the railroad and then turned off through banana fields. Once we found a bunch of bananas discarded on the ground and ate all we wanted.

Around two in the afternoon the sky clouded over. Just as the rain began to pour, we came to an empty *champa*, mud and thatch building. It was only a porch with palm leaf roof and one room with ground floor.

Before long a man walked into our shelter and then a man and woman came down the hill in an oxcart. They left the cart at the roadside and came in with their umbrella over their heads. The umbrella was a big banana leaf with the front end impaled on the man's machete and the other end held up by his wife. Next, two men, overseers in the banana fields, rode up on horses and joined us.

When the rain was over, we were invited to ride in the oxcart to the river crossing. I pulled on the boots I had with me, and Jean, Lorraine, and I were soon in the cart bumping and sliding down the rocky slippery hill. At the crossing we thanked the couple for the ride and got on the raft that, for a dime, took us across by the power of the current and guided by an overhead wire. The next creek we crossed in bare feet; then it was only a steep muddy hill to climb to get to Savá.

Elam Stauffer and David Livengood were living in an ordinary mud house with three rooms and a smokeless mud stove they had made. David said Elam had studied the cookbook for almost two days so he could prepare tasty meals for us, and the food was good. A pudding was especially delicious.

The two days we were there Don Pancho and his oldest son slept in the VS house; his wife and two boys shared one of the beds and I used the other in their house. Lorraine and Jean slept in the same room on bunk beds the VS men had made using cowhide strips for springs. The native bed I used was a wooden frame crisscrossed with rope and topped with matting for a mattress. The one the mother and boys used had metal strips for a spring. The fourth boy used a cot brought over from the VS house. All the beds had sheets. The only light in the house was a tiny kerosene lamp, but we all went to bed at 7:30 so lighting wasn't a problem.

The house was really two houses built together. The kitchen was about 24 x 30 feet with a thatched roof and pole ceiling where the corn was stored. Drums provided storage in two corners of the kitchen; one was filled with beans. A small table held the *tinaja* or clay pot of water, the tortilla maker, a bucket, and a couple tins cups. On one wall was a wooden box painted green holding a half dozen soup plates, some cups, and a glass or two. The corn sheller and the round stone corn grinder were on a box. The table was in the center of the room.

The other room had a tin roof which made it hot during the day and cold at night. It was divided into two parts with a cardboard wall covered with newspapers. The doorway to the bedroom was a panel of yellow cloth.

Lorraine had 33 in a children's Sunday School class Sunday morning. Don Pancho had 21 adults in his class which included the eight that came from Tocoa to take me there to catch the plane back to Trujillo.

The fellowship and hospitality left me with a feeling of grateful thanksgiving as I climbed into the four-wheel drive with the Tocoa group plus several additional passengers for what became an adventurous trip home. Lorraine and Jean headed back to La Ceiba where they had left their luggage, and then on to the States and Canada for their furlough.

Grace Hockman and Don Pancho's wife and youngest son were in the front seat with Menno Coblentz driving. I shared the benches in the back with five women, five children, Becky Herr, and Becky's dog, Prince, who had stayed with the VS men while Becky was on furlough.

The 20 miles to Tocoa were on the old unused railroad bed road, but Norman was at La Conce and we planned to stop there for the evening service. La Conce was off the main road, and we went along fine except where there used to be bridges that had since washed away or deteriorated and were unsafe for travel. One stream we forded had a steep hill up from the banks and all of us passengers had to get out and walk up the hill. Menno, only after several tries, backed once more and then came flying up after us.

Another stream almost conquered us. It had a lot of stones in it and a slippery hill on the way out. Menno had a terrible time backing straight and on every new try he backed into the bank. Men and boys from the area came with all kinds of advice while we gathered stones and cut bushes to throw in the path and shoveled mud. Finally, after an hour of work and with lots of pushing, Menno got the vehicle to the top. Everyone was wet and muddy by that time but eager to get to La Conce.

The little thatch-roofed, whitewashed mud chapel at La Conce was almost full for the meeting. It had a concrete floor, a bell, and six benches on each side of a center aisle. Before the service we ate the lunch Grace had brought along and immediately after the meeting left for Tocoa with Norman driving. Menno joined the 12 of us in the back.

It was a beautiful night with moonlight revealing the tall trees and tangles of thick vines. Ten minutes after starting, we got into deep mud and the wheels under us turned slower and slower and finally stopped. Norman knew the four-wheel drive was out and there was no way he could get out of that mud or through the several other even worse places ahead—so we all climbed out in the mud to walk the eight kilometers to Tocoa! I was the only one with boots, but at the two wide rivers we crossed the water came up to our knees. The other women, except Grace and Becky, walked barefoot on soles toughened by daily use. Becky had shoes she could tie tight, but Grace had flat, low, loose shoes that stuck in the mud at every step. It wasn't long before the shoes were full of mud and her feet had blisters. The local women thought nothing of the walk, and I wrote in my journal that I hadn't had so much fun in a long time. Until after her blisters healed, Grace would have preferred it had never happened.

Looking back, I realized how once again the Lord had taken care of us. Without the brilliant moonlight, it would have been pitch black under the tall trees; with only a few flashlights, the walk would have been dangerous, especially with all the small children to keep track of in the mud and rivers we crossed.

When I flew back to Trujillo the next day, I discovered three babies I hadn't expected had been born in the clinic and the two I had told the nurses to expect had not arrived.

As soon as I was home I had a job getting all my belongings cleaned up from the trip through the mud, and then it was back to babies, book work, and entertaining guests. Menno and Irene Coblentz came with two teachers from Tocoa; two women Jean and Lorraine had met in the San Pedro Sula airport also visited for several days. One was from the U.S.A. and the other a Honduran. They were working with SCIDE, an organization for the betterment of schools in Honduras.

The road between Tocoa and Trujillo had been improved with rafts at the lagoon and the Aguan River, and 13 new bridges on the three miles the other side of the river, but with four inches of rain that week, everyone wondered how the return trip would be. Menno had fixed the four-wheel drive, but didn't trust it completely.

Friends sent me a bag of fruit including two big Hayden mangoes.

They were almost two pounds each and had small seeds. I shared one with J. Mark and Ruthie Miller who were back from the states for summer vacation, and had enough left to send slices home for George and Grace. I think they were the most delicious mangoes I had ever tasted, and I certainly hoped the Hayden-grafted tree James had planted would bear the same quality of fruit.

I kept busy in August. First I had Captain Cooper and his wife invited for a meal when his boat had a layover at Trujillo. Then Dave Sharp and LaMar Stauffer spent several days in Santa Fe. They came to Trujillo first and Mardene Sensenig and Marlin Ebersole came up from Santa Fe to take them down in a cayuco. Cathy Stauffer stayed with me, but before they left I had them and the George Miller family to dinner. J. Mark and Ruthie Miller were almost ready to leave for school in the states, and Miriam and Rachel had just come home from school in Siguatepeque.

Before J. Mark left for his first year at Eastern Mennonite College, he took Mr. July out as far as the car could go to start him on his way for another visit to La Colonia and other villages. Mr. July had not been there for some time, mostly because the roads were so bad.

A little girl with a crochet hook in her hand was brought to the clinic. It wasn't hard to get out, but she needed a tetanus shot and bandaging. A 20-year-old school teacher was admitted with gastroenteritis, and a small baby was left with us for 18 days while his mother was away. He was quite skinny when he arrived, but he was a good baby, and by the time his mother returned, he had gained over a pound and was sleeping all night.

Among the usual parade of expectant mothers coming to deliver we had several abnormal deliveries including a set of twins. Earlier I had mothers who had delivered one twin arrive in distress over the second birth, but these were both delivered in the clinic. The mother arrived to ask me when she would have her baby and said, "I'm tired." I examined her and advised her not to leave, but she had no money to pay for a stay at the clinic. We made arrangements to cover that problem, and when I took her medical history I asked the name of the father.

She said, "I don't live with the father of my two boys, and this one doesn't have a father."

Upon further questioning she said, "Oh, in Puerto Cortes."

Because of her condition I decided to induce labor using Watson's method. Several hours later she delivered a girl breech and three minutes later a boy in the normal position. Each weighed over six pounds.

One woman came in for her sixth delivery, but her baby was stillborn and badly deformed.

Four teenage *primiparas* (first-timers) delivered at the clinic in August. One had had rheumatic fever earlier which concerned me, but she delivered with little trouble.

August also brought Dr. Gustafson from Omaha, Nebraska, on a MAF dental clinic program. He was with us two and a half days and pulled 143 teeth and filled 26. His name was familiar because of his being with Bob Pearce of World Vision on his crusade in Tokyo.

My grace is sufficient for thee sang itself over and over again in my mind the day one of my workers left early with a threat never to return and another arrived in a bad mood and said she was quitting the end of the month. When a third worker asked what we would ever do without the two, I could reply with confidence, "The Lord will help me. He has never forsaken me yet."

The special evangelistic services we had the end of the month uplifted my spirits, refreshed my soul, and sustained me for the next three months which were far busier than the previous eight months. During the meetings one worker recommitted her life to Christ which resulted in a wonderful change in attitude and made our work together harmonious.

Don Enrique Peñalva of Tegucigalpa was guest speaker for our five days of meetings. James Hess again placed benches on the clinic porch and set up the loudspeaker system so those wandering around in the park could hear the messages even if they were not inclined to attend the meetings. He broadcast music for a half hour and by the time the message began the porch was full. Don Enrique's messages were Biblical, practical, and interestingly presented. His illustrations were most fitting, and I greatly admired his skillful use of the Spanish language.

I had felt a great burden to pray for those meetings and invited several women to join me in prayer the previous two Wednesday evenings. Don Enrique fasted and prayed each afternoon, and I decided to skip my evening meal and also spend the time in prayer.

Our prayers were answered, and at least 34 persons indicated they wanted to accept Christ. From past experience we knew only a portion would move forward toward baptism and church membership, but several were children of current church members, and we were confident they would return regularly.

One woman who attended the women's meeting the following

week prayed a beautiful prayer of repentance for going back on her prior commitment. As she prayed asking the Lord to help her, I tasted again the pure, high joy that comes only in service of the Lord, a joy of soul that makes anything worthwhile—years of work, suffering, and denying oneself.

Independence Day, 1962, did not bring the tragedies of 1961. I dreaded the holiday which had resulted in the deaths of two men in the clinic the year before and wondered what to expect. Instead of victims of too much celebration, I had two babies born that day. In fact, by the seventeenth of the month, there were eight.

The music professor asked if he could bring the school children to my house to practice the national anthem and several other songs on my piano. He moved it to the porch for their practices and then to the park for the performance.

The following week I felt I was celebrating when a friend sent me a piece of beef. Meat from the cattle butchered locally was then being shipped to San Pedro Sula or other large towns or cities because a higher price could be charged than in Trujillo, so I seldom had fresh meat.

Two months later another friend gave me some beef bones to make soup, and a piece of liver—something I hadn't had for a long time.

Harvey Kauffman, his wife and ten-month-old daughter, Lydia Mae, VS leaders in a program in El Salvador, along with John Glick from Lancaster, Pennsylvania, and Ben Stoltzfus came to visit the three VS units in Honduras: Tocoa, Savá, and Santa Fe. The Kauffmans were an Amish couple from Ohio. Mrs. Kauffman was disappointed there would be no accommodations for her in Santa Fe, but I think she enjoyed her stay with me. I know I enjoyed having her company.

For a few days during Mrs. Kauffman's stay, the beds in the clinic were empty. Then one afternoon I heard a loud crash that I soon learned had come from the new hospital construction site where work was going on day and night to complete it on schedule. Before long two men were carried in. One had a gash in the head and was in shock. The other man had a bruised foot and I suspected broken bones.

The doctor also arrived; as he worked on the men, he joked that they should have waited to have an accident until the hospital was completed. As it was, the one with the foot injuries had to be sent to a hospital in La Ceiba for x-rays.

Philip Ray Sauder was born in Tegucigalpa on September 16 to

Rhoda and James Sauder, and a week later LaMar and Catherine Stauffer had a boy, Dean LaMar, in La Ceiba. I was also busy with babies. Twenty-seven were born in the clinic the last three months of 1962 bringing the total for the year to over 50.

I was hurrying to get a letter finished the afternoon of October 16, when I heard a laugh from Hesses' apartment that sounded like Paul Kraybill. I dropped everything, forgot the mailing deadline, and rushed over to greet him and Aaron Shank, who had arrived on the MAF plane for a mission conference. Norman Hockman, James Sauder, and LaMar Stauffer arrived the following day, and we had several days of reporting on past developments and making future plans for the mission work in our various areas.

I thought that conference would result in definite plans for the remainder of my mission term. After discussion, however, the best plan we could make was to have our clinic close when I left on furlough or when the new hospital opened, whichever came first. I couldn't help wondering if my days in Honduras were numbered.

Another decision was to name George Miller as bishop overseer to the churches in Colón and to have him and Grace go to Costa Rica to complete their interrupted training in the language school. Upon their return the following May, they packed their household belongings and moved to Tocoa to replace the Hockmans who took their furlough after attending the funeral of Grace's father in the States.

It was a good conference in spite of the inconvenience of having no electricity. The plant had once again broken down in September, and the part needed to repair it had to be ordered from England. It was back to kerosene lamps and the old-fashioned irons. Of course, the lamps were always ready anyway because we never knew what time of evening the lights might go off. Power was finally restored the end of November.

A sailor from British Guyana was brought to our clinic about 24 hours after being burned by boiling soup when his ship lurched during a storm at sea. By then he was near death from second and third degree burns, but with care he gradually recovered. For some time he ran a high fever and suffered a great deal of pain, especially when we changed the dressings.

He was a black man, and as new skin gradually grew in around the edges of the burn area on his chest and abdomen, the skin was pink with tiny dots of black here and there. As healing progressed, the black dots grew and took over until the skin had his normal color.

The sailor was a Methodist by infant baptism, knew some of the Psalms by heart, but didn't seem to grasp the message of the gospel. His company had arranged for his meals to be prepared and brought in, and I was certainly glad because he complained constantly that nothing tasted good and everything made him feel sick. He was with us for more than a month—two weeks, in fact, after we had discharged him because his company didn't reply to our telegram immediately and he didn't know where to go. Finally, word arrived that he should rejoin his ship when it docked at Cortés and he left on the *Suyapa* the middle of December.

A second burn patient was brought in before the sailor left. She was a young Carib girl who worked for a family in Trujillo. Kerosene flames had burned her forehead, ear, and upper arms. She was wild with fear and pain when brought in and remained a problem throughout her stay. I remarked that she drew people like flies to molasses as she sat by the window of her room in the clinic. Friends and relatives flocked to visit as she held court daily, enjoying the prestige her experience gave her.

The next major case was a woman brought in in a coma with eclampsia. She went into convulsions, and we had to send for the doctor in the middle of the night and twice the following day. Two days later she opened her eyes and asked where she was. When I placed her baby in her arms, she asked, "Whose is this?" I told her it was her baby and she had no memory of the birth.

It took some time for the woman to recover, but gradually the headaches diminished and her blurred vision cleared. After being released she soon returned with high fever and an abscess. The baby, although 18 days old, weighed the same as at birth so both were patients.

Another baby was born Thanksgiving Day, when the whole church family was invited to our big dining room for a fellowship dinner. The mother, a believer, arrived in the forenoon for an examination and I told her she had better stay. "But if I stay," she said, "I can't come to the dinner." The outcome was that at 12:15 I took the newborn to the dining room and introduced him to everyone.

Tears came to my eyes when that mother and child played the parts of another mother and child in the Christmas Eve program at the church. Baby Ayax Tedy lay in his *cuna* (cradle) of straw waving tiny fists in the air as, in the glow of the footlights, his mother gazed down at him with love written on her face. His father, acting as Joseph, looked on.

The Osorto family
1962
Pedro Pablo and Argentina Osorto and their first three children:
Xiomara Delycia - 27 months
Denys Henry - 14 months
Ayax Tedy - 1 month

The Osorto family
1981
Pedro Pablo, pastor of the Mennonite church in Progreso, with his wife, Argentina, and part of their family.

James and Beaty Hess sang some songs, several poems were read, and Miriam Miller was a beautiful angel. Even the town lights cooperated and didn't go off until twenty minutes after the meeting closed. The whole Christmas program was the most pleasant and least stressful I had ever planned and conducted—even though Dicky and one other wise man appeared in bare feet!

A group of us went caroling and ended the evening at the Miller home. A young man who had been away for some time was back in Trujillo and went with us. At his mother's house he insisted we go inside and after we sang, he read the Christmas story from Luke 2 and continued with a short description of what it means to accept Christ. His enthusiasm was wonderful to see because although I knew he had heard the Word, he had left Trujillo without ever making a decision to accept Christ himself.

I looked around the room as we had refreshments and felt there could be no greater joy in life than to have friends whose lives had been so dramatically changed by Christ.

I thought I was too busy to help in our end-of-November Bible School, but there was no way out. Mrs. July brought the children for my class over from the church after the opening program each day, and we had our classes on the porch. That arrangement made it possible for me not to be away from the clinic during a time when one of my workers was ill and the one on duty did not give injections or handle medications.

The doctor sutured two men cut with machetes. The one had been fighting while drunk and had several bad cuts. The other man was cut in an accident. That man was not admitted but slept at the clinic because he had no place to live except in a house in Cristales which was too damp for him during the rainy season.

"It seems strange to have no babies here," I typed at the beginning of a letter to my mother near the end of December. I ended the same letter with a handwritten note, "Well, we have a baby now—born half an hour ago. He's yelling!"

We rarely had no inpatients, but occasionally the ones we had took little care, which gave me time to catch up on record keeping. At other times I felt stretched to the limit and longed for a vacation. The babies were always a pleasure, but the personalities and problems of some patients sometimes sent me to my knees seeking forgiveness for harsh thoughts. I was grieved over my selfish desires for a life of easy answers and people who would accept my instructions without question. God was always gracious when He needed to remind me that sometimes I was hard and demanding when I could have been more generous and thoughtful, but He was faithful in forgiveness when I saw myself as He must have seen me, and asked His forgiveness.

1963

Jesu, Joy of Man's Desiring—the phrase repeated itself over and over in my mind the day after attending a piano concert by Ricardo Foulkes in Tegucigalpa during my vacation in January. Foulkes' selections included pieces from Scarlatti, Weber, Liszt, Chopin, Bach, Debussy, and Rachmaninoff. As he was playing the last selection on the program, I thought to myself, *"Jesu, Joy of Man's Desiring" would be the piece I would choose as an encore*, and when he announced it and began to play, I was flooded with joy and really worshipped Jesus, who had died for me and was my joy.

All rooms at the Central American Mission were filled for a mission conference. My accommodations were with the La Ceiba delegation to the Youth Convention—a bench in a Sunday School room. I hadn't packed any bedding, so when I telephoned greetings to Arab friends in Tegucigalpa, I gladly accepted the hospitality they offered—a bedroom all to myself. Their cousin, the oculist who had tested my eyes the year before, invited me to a delicious Arab meal that ended with their traditional tiny cups of thick, sweet coffee.

The attitude among all the Arabs I knew in Central America was to make me feel I was granting them a great favor whenever I accepted gifts or their offers to share home and meals.

After the conference was over, I enjoyed their quiet spacious home. When I sealed my fifty-eighth letter, I felt I had accomplished the almost impossible. Set free from that backlog of correspondence, I could go out and snap some pictures of the older streets of the city, take a few side tours, read two Christmas-gift books, do some errands for folks back in Trujillo, and attend services at the church of Don Enrique, who had conducted the revival meetings in Trujillo. I was also able to help two families by house-sitting a few nights while they were out of town. The one was the Irish family of a SAHSA pilot who attended the same church as my Arab friends.

Irma Moody, a World Gospel Mission missionary from California who had been in Honduras for 34 years, invited me to visit her at El Hatillo, the Bible Institute, five miles outside Tegucigalpa and 1,500 feet higher up the mountain. She showed me around the school as well as San Felipe, the charity hospital, and the sanitarium.

My trip back to Trujillo began at 3:30 one morning. A real bus, not a truck like the one I traveled in ten years earlier on the same road, stopped to pick me up and then traveled around the city for 28 more passengers. We stopped in San Antonio del Valle for a breakfast of fried egg, fried beans, tortillas, fried pork, fried *plátano*, and coffee, and were back on the road by 6 o'clock.

The morning light revealed we were traveling on a two-lane road that wound up and around on turns tighter than hairpin curves—more like bobby-pin curves. At times it seemed we were trying to find our way out of a maze. The middle of the road seemed to be the choice of travelers going either direction, but when we met oncoming trucks, buses, or jeeps, everyone yielded to the right. On curves, all traffic announced its approach by very adequate blasts of the horn. Our driver didn't take undue chances, but we didn't suffer from the dust of other vehicles because he always got ahead of anything traveling in the same direction. Motion sickness seemed to be expected because the driver's helper had a supply of bags and kept an eye out for an emergency. Eight hours after starting I was dropped off at the Roosevelt Hotel in San Pedro Sula.

The next morning I boarded the train for Tela at 7 o'clock. For that trip I got a first-class ticket which instead of plank seats around the edges of a car provided a straw-upholstered seat. Every stop turned the train into a smorgasbord and an open market, and every imaginable local food was offered for sale and eaten with obvious enjoyment. A man in the seat behind mine bought a live chicken and a four-foot iguana. As he left the train in Tela he commented, "I have my dinner and my supper."

At noon I changed trains and was in La Ceiba at 6:30 after watching a repetition of the selling, eating, and drinking that again occurred at almost every stop. I decided people rode the trains to eat.

♔

A plane ride completed my journey home. The nurses had delivered four babies while I was gone, and one of the nurses had gone to the hospital in La Ceiba with appendicitis.

James and Beaty reported the Bible Institute they had held had been a success. Church members contributed food, and women from the church had used my stove and refrigerator to help Beaty prepare meals for the 25 to 30 attendees. They served the meals on my porch, and I wished I had been there for the meetings and to help with the cooking, but it probably was better for the women to have the experience and responsibility.

One result of the meetings was an increase in church attendance. Also two couples decided they should marry rather than just live together. The one man even came to tell me he had been to the government offices to start the paper work.

His wedding occurred during a morning church service in August. The bride and groom were the parents of three girls and five boys and a baby was due within a month. Beaty and I made cakes and *fresco* for the reception at my place that afternoon with 35 relatives and church friends. I thought it would be nice to sing a few of the church songs, but after we got started no one wanted to stop. After most of the guests had left, the bride's mother accepted Christ, and then to top off a wonderful day, the newlyweds and four other new believers were baptized during the evening service at our church.

Sam Luby

Sam Luby, the 83-year-old man who was a member of the church and lived in a little one-room house outside town was having health problems and could no longer be trusted with cooking fires. We had been sending his meals to him but realized he needed even closer supervision and decided to move my maid into another room and give him the maid's room. Although I considered him feeble, he still walked all over town and liked to help wherever he could. When Hesses were away, he took care of their chickens.

In February when the nurse I could most rely on began working additional days, I was free to do more visitation in homes. Some of the women promised to come to church and Sunday School, and I looked forward to seeing them grow in the faith that had taken root during the revival meetings.

One obstacle to regular attendance was that the meals they cooked frequently required several hours of preparation, and since cooking was done on wood-burning mud stoves, they could not leave them unattended. Evening services were also difficult, especially for a mother with three or four children used to going to bed at sundown.

One woman told me she wanted to attend, but sickness or

something always got in the way. She was the mother of ten children, the youngest a one-year-old, and a grandmother of four.

Another woman never failed to send her little girls to Sunday School but was unable to attend herself because she sold lottery tickets to earn money for her family. Sunday was the day the awards were announced and was, therefore, her busiest day. She said she wanted to get another job so she could attend church, and before Easter she did quit. She then salted fish and took them to Cortés to sell. I later hired her to work in the clinic when another worker left, and I felt fortunate to have a Christian woman as my helper. Being able to attend church and receive religious teaching, it wasn't long before she was teaching a Sunday School class.

The husband in one family didn't attend regularly, and when I visited the home I learned he was deeply involved in politics and felt uncomfortable in church. His wife was ready to be baptized, but he wanted her to wait until he had another job; then he would join the church with her. He planned to get out of politics, but before that happened he landed in jail along with many others ousted by a political coup.

♔

The ninth baby for the year was born March 2, to one of my former maids. She had run away from home with a young man who after a short time lost interest in her and moved on to another woman. She had written me a letter and said she was *mil veces arrepentida* or repented a thousand times, but when she returned to Trujillo she was quiet and sad. Apparently her repentance only meant she regretted running away and ending up with shattered dreams.

She had no money to come to the clinic, but when she started having difficulties she was afraid she would die and sent a sister to ask if I would see her. Of course I told her to come and found her with dangerously high blood pressure and other complications. By her delivery date, we had managed to get her blood pressure down and she had a normal delivery.

I feared the baby would see very little love. The whole family had hoped the child would be a girl. When the sister came to see the little baby boy, she said, "This is God's punishment." She herself was an unmarried mother of four children whose father had children to several other women.

The new mother assured me her mother would take care of the baby so she could get a job and earn enough to pay her bill at the clinic. The father, however, came one day and acknowledged the baby was his child and paid the bill.

While she and her baby were still with us, a man was brought in with a terrible machete cut in the head. The doctor said, "The people from the country have a marvelous resistance. Anybody else would have died from this type of wound."

I agreed with him. I had seen some of them who thought nothing of a machete wound, and never even winced while being sewed up. Yet I had also seen some of those same people shrink back in fear from an injection.

The man experienced some paralysis but got well and went home. I witnessed to him, but he wasn't willing to accept Christ although I was sure he understood and even seemed to enjoy listening. In September he was brought back almost comatose and with severe head pains. The doctor recommended they take him to La Ceiba, but they took him home instead where he soon died. When he was brought into the clinic, I said, "What a pity he had not accepted the Lord."

"Oh, but he did," his mother said. He had asked for Don Edgardo Hernández to come to visit and had accepted the Lord at his invitation. The mother said she had accepted first, then her son, our former patient accepted, but they were still waiting for a sister to yield herself. These were simple, barefoot, illiterate people, but the change that came into their lives when they accepted Christ was so good to see. Don Edgardo, himself, died a short time later after being bitten by a snake. He left a wife and nine children.

A woman, also with a head wound, was brought in by her mother and brother. The bone was cut through and splintered, but the skull was not depressed like the man's had been. The doctor came and sutured her head and then started to suture a cut on her arm only to discover both bones were either cut through or broken, so she needed to go to the hospital in La Ceiba. The brother said, "I don't know why her husband had to use his machete—he could have beaten her with a belt!"

The next seriously injured patient was a man who worked for the Plywood Company. A tree had fallen on his head, and he was brought in in a coma. He too was sent on to La Ceiba for surgery.

I had nine deliveries registered for April, and before the end of March had two deliveries I hadn't expected. The day those two mothers and their babies left, a Carib man was brought into the clinic. He had been chopping wood and cut his foot with the ax. He had already lost a lot of blood when he arrived, and just after the doctor had finished suturing and dressing the wound, blood gushed out again.

We started intravenous saline and were relieved when the flow stopped. The doctor was afraid to touch the dressing again because he was sure the man wouldn't survive another hemorrhage.

Almost a week later he hemorrhaged again. I quickly elevated his leg, put on a tourniquet, and told the nurse to summon the doctor. She dashed out the door, but even though it was an emergency, she rushed back in to get a rag to cover her head because it was raining. As with many of the people, she was afraid some harm would come to her if she went out in the rain after dark with her head uncovered.

The bleeding was under control by the time the doctor came, so he redressed the wound and gave the man an injection. He also told him he should go to the hospital, but the family came and took him home. The doctor said one of their superstitions was that dead people draw blood out of living people and since people had died in the clinic, the family possibly thought it best to get him away.

The Ides of March brought in the strong winds that started blowing around noon each day and grew stronger and stronger the rest of the day and into the night. The house had more windows than before the renovations, but the louvers above some of the old windows and the screen in the bathroom window gave easy access to dirt and grit. Everything turned red with dust, and the floor of one room would yield as much as two tablespoons of dirt at one sweeping!

What a relief when the rains came a week later. The wind had sucked the moisture out of the soil and plants, and although Mr. Luby watered my papaya trees daily, I feared they wouldn't survive. As soon as the rains came, however, they revived and practically jumped in height. The grass turned green and the dust settled during the eight inches of rain we got in four days. We swept, dusted, and washed curtains and clothes, and gradually the house started to feel clean again.

It was during those dusty, windy days that LaMar and Cathy Stauffer came to visit with their not quite six-month-old son Dean, and LaMar's father on his honeymoon with his new bride, Ruth Miller, a former missionary in Tanganyika. The wind made the sea too rough for the boat, but that didn't stop LaMar from immediately going to Santa Fe to visit the VS fellows—he walked. He took the rest of the family later in the week in the boat.

The rains also changed our plans about the Christian Life Conference in Tocoa. We had planned to take a truck load of passengers from our church and the church in Santa Fe, but bridges were out and the raft on the river could carry only small cars. Also, all the mission trucks were just about falling apart. We wondered what we should do. Finally, James voiced the words everyone was thinking, “I guess we’ll just have to give it up.”

As James said those words, something said inside of me, “The Lord would just delight in working it all out to get us there.” Somehow I had an assurance we would get to the meetings. A day or two later I was reading how God took the Israelites across the Jordan and kept them dry and I thought, “If He could take those thousands across like that, He can surely take the few of us across these rivers.”

That night as I was going to sleep, I suddenly remembered a sizable check I had received with no indication of how the donor wished it to be used. Although it was made out in my name, I considered the amount too large to be a personal gift. In my letter of thanks I had asked to be advised about what area of our work he wanted the money applied, but no answer had come.

My mind raced with an idea. Could we use the money to subsidize plane tickets for those wishing to attend the conference? Had the Lord sent His answer before we even knew we would need money? I could hardly wait for morning to share my thoughts with James.

I knew James had already inquired about airfare for the seven-minute flight, and when I proposed the solution to the *muddy-road problem*, he quickly went back to SAHSA. If 15 persons bought tickets, the cost would be about eight U.S. dollars per person. We decided that each person should pay $2.50 and the check I had received would cover the balance. The fee did cut the number able to go, but 21 eager persons left from Trujillo—more than enough to get the 15% discount. Included in our group were several from Santa Fe, and Doña Chon and Pablo from Farrallones, the woman and her son who had walked to Trujillo one Saturday in 1960 to be baptized the following morning.

James Sauder and four men came to Tocoa by mule from Gualaco. The ride took three days, eight hours to San Antonio the first day. The second day they were on the trail 11 hours—six of those hours over mountain trails so steep the men sometimes had to dismount and urge the mules to jump. Curves were so close together James said the mules were sometimes still getting around one curve when they had to twist into the next. At times the trail was so narrow there was barely room for the mules’ feet. At other places rain storms had eroded the path into deep canyons so narrow the men had to lift their legs up in front of them on the mules. Where coffee had been transported through such areas, the sides of the gorges were scraped wider by the saddle bags hanging on the sides of mules.

Arriving in Tocoa.

James was so thankful for a safe arrival, but I knew the ride back would be even harder because Gualaco was several thousand feet higher in elevation than Tocoa.

Between 60 and 70 persons attended the daytime conference sessions. Evening services were held in the grassy area between the church and the school which the cows, horses and donkeys kept trimmed. There was plenty of help to string up lights each evening, and carry out the pulpit, church benches, and school chairs. The work was well worth the effort because about 250 people filled the seats and stood around the fringes listening.

Various church members led a 5:30 prayer meeting each morning. Bro. José Antonio Santiago from Puerto Rico was guest speaker. James Hess, Norman Hockman, Mr. July, James Sauder, and others also brought stirring messages on the Discipline of the Christian Life, Stewardship, and Consecration. Special music was scheduled into the program each evening.

Mr. July was one of the first to speak during testimony time, and the woman who had left her job selling lottery tickets and was working for me was another who stepped forward to tell what Jesus meant in her life. It was wonderful to see the Lord working and to watch people responding to His call. I wrote in my journal that I didn't think the intense joy I felt could be surpassed this side of heaven.

The meals were prepared by the women on the smokeless mud stove in the school kitchen and on two cut-down drum stoves outside. Wash tubs were used as kettles. Tocoa church members donated the food. One man butchered a pig and others brought ducks and chickens.

Mealtime at Tocoa conference

Corn for tortillas, rice, beans, and cheese were also donated, but as good as everything tasted, the spiritual food was even better.

Sleeping accommodations, using *petates* or small pieces of matting for sheets or mattresses, were provided in the church and the school buildings. The older men used the church as their dormitory, the younger men used the classroom of the newer school building, and the ladies used the large room of the old school building. A lot of chatter filled the air, and the young girls had an especially hard time settling down at night. As some of the older men were returning the benches to the church one evening, I heard one ask another for help in carrying *his bed*.

Just before the meetings ended, Grace Hockman received word of the death of her father and within two hours the family had left for the United States.

After the last meeting, Irene, Alma, Dot, Becky, and I invited the VS fellows to an ice cream party. Ray Horst and Ernest Hostetler were there from Savá, Mardene Sensenig and Marlin Ebersole from Santa Fe, and Paul Hess and Menno Coblentz from the Tocoa unit.

The Ides of March, March 15, had brought the rain, but the Ides

CONFERENCIA DE LA VIDA CRISTIANA
Semana Santa=IO al I4 de Abril de I963
Iglesia Evangélica Menonita
Tocoa, Colón, Honduras

PROGRAMA DIARIO

Miércoles, IO de Abril
Llegada de los hermanos de las otras congregaciones
5:00 Cena
7:00 Servicio Evangelístico. . . José Antonio Santiago
Palo Hincado, Barranquitas, Puerto Rico

Jueves, II de Abril
5:30-6:I5 Culto de Oración . . . . Francisco Flores
Sabá
6:30 Desayuno
8:00 La Mayordomía en la Vida Cristiana . Norman Hockman
Tocoa
9:30-IO:00 Recreo
IO:00 Clases divididas-Jóvenes=Como Dios nos Guía . Santiago
Casados=El Concepto Cristiano del Sexo . .Jaime Hess
Trujillo
II:30 Almuerzo
I:30 Disciplina en la Vida Cristiana . . . Hess
3:00-3:30 Recreo
3:30 Clases Divididas-Jóvenes=Como Atraer la Juventud a Cristo . Santiago
Casados=Deberes de los Maridos
Jaime Sauder
Gualaco
5:00 Cena
7:00 Servicio Evangelístico. . . . . . . Santiago

Viernes, I2 de Abril
5:30 Culto de Oración . . . . Pedro Paz
6:30 Desayuno La Conce
8:00 La Mayordomía en la Vida Cristiana . . Hockman
9:30-IO:00 Recreo
IO:00 Clases divididas-Jóvenes=La Organización y Reuniones de la Juventud . Santiago
Obreros en la Iglesia
Profa. Dora Membreño
II:30 Almuerzo
I:30 Disciplina en la Vida Cristiana . . . . Hess
3:00-3:30 Recreo
3:30 Clases divididas-Jóvenes=El Noviazgo Cristiano.Santiago
5:00 Cena
7:00 Servicio Evangelístico . . . . . . Santiago

Sábado, I3 de Abril
5:30 Culto de Oración . . . . .Arturo July
6:30 Desayuno Trujillo
8:00 Manteniendo una Visión Misionera . . . Santiago
9:30-IO:00 Recreo
IO:00 Manteniendo una Vital Vida Devocional . . . Sauder
II:30 Almuerzo
I:30 Servicio de Consagración . . . . Sauder
3:00-3:30 Recreo
3:30 Preguntas y Respuestas, a cargo de los conferencistas
5:00 Cena
7:00 Servicio Evangelístico . . . . . . Santiago

Domingo, I4 de Abril
5:30 Culto de Resurrección . Escuela Evangélica Menonita
6:30 Desayuno Tocoa
9:00 Escuela Dominical
IO:00 Predicación y Comunión . . . . Hess
II:30 Almuerzo
2:00 Testimonios y Mensaje de Consagración
"Presentando Nuestros Cuerpos Vivos al Señor. Santiago
5:00 Cena
7:00 Servicio Evangelístico. . . . . . . Santiago

Copy of the conference program.

of April, April 13, brought to me a new peace and a sense of being able and willing to relinquish my work in Honduras.

My furlough was to begin January 2, 1964, but the mission board had advanced it to December 15 so I could be home with my family for Christmas. Grateful as I was for their thoughtfulness, I couldn't help wishing I could stay for one more Christmas program in the church, one more Honduras *juventud* or youth (AJEH) meeting in La Ceiba, one more Bible Institute, one more Bible School. . . .

I knew in my mind that **AS HE LEADS Is Joy**, but my heart was bound up in Honduras. During the meetings something seemed to grow inside of me as I fellowshipped and listened to the stirring messages and testimonies, until sometime in the hours before dawn the night of April 13, my heart was finally ready to bid farewell to Honduras because I knew the Lord leads unerringly, and in His will is my joy, no matter what the cost.

As I lay awake, I reviewed the wonderful events of the conference. Then I recognized it was self-pity for not being able to be a part of the next conference that was holding me back from making definite plans to leave the country. I acknowledged to the Lord that I was hanging back when He was leading me out of Honduras, and I acknowledged that *to do His will* was far more important than *wanting to do it.* Suddenly, and I can't say how it happened, I realized I would go home on December 15, without any questions or reserves. Immediately the Lord Himself became so real, so precious, and so near that I just loved Him.

It was eight months before I would leave for home, but it was not too soon to start making plans. The piano was soon sold to the high school. Even though I might return to the mission field later, it wasn't practical to ship the sewing machine home. Besides, it had had termites in the wood earlier, so I promised one of the new converts first option to purchase it. But what about the dishes, pressure cooker, canner, pots, pans, rugs, books, and the many things that accumulate over a twelve-year period? Some of my clothes were too worn to bother taking home, but every item demanded a decision.

Patients had a different concern. "What are we going to do when you leave?" The hospital didn't seem to be as near completion as the schedule had predicted, but the mission board had made a firm decision to close the clinic when my term was over.

Meantime, babies were born, and other cases arrived as before. I was always grateful when I could discharge someone who had found new life in Christ. When feasible, I challenged patients to begin Bible correspondence courses for I knew the Holy Spirit could teach them direct from His word long after I was gone.

A young man was brought in one day whose leg was cut almost the whole length with a hatchet. It was the biggest wound we had had for a long time; it took the doctor an hour and a half to suture it. That young man couldn't read, so one of my nurses played gospel records for him, and before he left, he accepted Christ. Even after the doctor discharged him, he stayed with us because he needed dressings changed regularly and had no place to live in Trujillo. I sent for an Alfalit primer, a Spanish literacy method, and tried to teach him to read. He seemed to be an intelligent person, but had very little training of any kind and didn't seem able to remember things.

While he was with us, I became a patient also—but not in the clinic. I spent several days in bed with malaria. I hadn't had malaria for a long time and then just before our conference in Tocoa I had had a light case that responded to Aralen. After getting home, I had it a second time.

Don José Santiago, the evangelist for the Tocoa conference, returned to Trujillo with us for several meetings in our church. One evening the men took the loud speaker to Cristales and held an outdoor meeting where several persons responded to the invitation to accept Christ.

A street meeting was held in Rio Negro another evening, and when Don José went to Gualaco, James Sauder met him at San Esteban, and they had a meeting before going on to Gualaco and several other villages by horseback.

The day Don José left, Irma Moody, the World Gospel Mission worker, arrived to visit. Several mornings later the *Betty B*, a boat owned by Bruce Borden and named for his daughter, pulled into the dock. A few minutes later Irma, with shining eyes and eager face, proposed that she and I go to Guanaja, the island farthest east of the Bay Islands, for a few days.

I had a week's vacation coming, no seriously ill patients in the clinic, and although just recovered from the second attack of malaria, I made a quick decision to do it. An hour later we were off. The boat stopped at Santa Fe and Mardene and Marlin, the VS fellows, come aboard. They were on their way to Limón to show educational films.

Irma and I reached Guanaja about 2:30 Monday afternoon and immediately went to the home of a woman I had met when Grace

Hockman, Dorothy Showalter, and I had visited the key several years earlier. Mrs. Phillips had invited me to return any time, and this visit suited her just right. Her husband worked in the United States and he was leaving Guanaja that very evening to return to work. She said our fellowship would, "Help me get over the miss of him." Not five minutes before we arrived he had asked her if she had heard from me recently—and there I was!

Their house was built out in the sea over the water like many of the houses on the key. Streets were narrow boardwalks and bridges. There were no vehicles and no electric lights. Swimming was just back of the house and Irma and I went out with a neighbor girl.

Phillipses' house built on stilts over the sea.

The Phillipses were Christians and it was a delight to hear Mrs. Phillips singing around the house and to pray with her. We attended her church, visited neighbors, and when it was time for Irma and me to leave on Wednesday, Mrs. Phillips went along to see us off.

It was an hour's trip in a motor dory from the key to the main island. One man stood in front holding up a piece of canvas to protect us from the spray. A second man steered through the rough sea. We landed at Savanna Bight and walked about an hour to get to the north side of the island to a little flat space where a small Cessna with room for three passengers could land.

The plane stopped at Roatan, the next island, for the third passenger, and when we landed at La Ceiba, I bid farewell to Irma and took another plane to Trujillo.

I had brought the Hesses a parrot from Guanaja and it became a great pet. She was tame and spent as much time outside her cage as in it. The mango tree, the wash line post, and a swing were favorite recreation areas, but an offer to ride on someone's arm was seldom turned down. Old Mr. Luby spent a lot of time talking to her, and I noticed the noise of the washing machine or splashing rain turned her into a chatter box.

James found a lizard one day and put it on a board where the parrot was sitting. The two animals looked each other over carefully and neither seemed afraid of the other. They were just about the same bright green color.

One evening when the young people were meeting in my big living room, the three Hess boys burst in shouting, "Daddy, Daddy, something's happening to Raisin."

We all ran out to the patio and there was a big dead toad. The dog had bitten the toad and was having convulsions from the poison in it. Ten minutes later Raisin was dead—the dog and the toad had killed each other. The next day James buried them both in the same grave.

About that time I began noticing the symptoms of malaria for the third time within a month. The doctor came and did a slide, and put me on a series of Plaquinol which was to hit the parasites in the organs. My spleen was sore and the doctor said my liver was enlarged.

It was also in April that James Hess turned over to me the Luz Y Verdad Bible correspondence lessons which he had been correcting since Millers left for Costa Rica. Every mail seemed to bring more lessons and I found the work very interesting and enjoyable. Whenever possible, I corrected them the day they arrived and sent them back in the next mail. But when the count ran as high as 325 in June, I felt I was never caught up.

About 30 people in Santa Fe began taking the lessons and news spread like wildfire with friends recommending friends. In October I had 600 lessons mostly from Santa Fe. Many were from young people 12 to 16 years of age. How I prayed that the lessons were more than interesting stories. By Christian standards, the lives those young people lived were terrible. As soon as they were matured physically, they paired off and they changed partners whenever the whim struck them.

If a few became saved, they could be living witnesses of a different way of life.

When I left Honduras, Isaac Frederick took over the correspondence lesson work.

♔

June 3 found all of us missionaries flying to the island of Utila for conference. Our first stop was a night in La Ceiba. We spread around the city—Millers in a hotel; Dot, Becky, and I at Camerons; the VS fellows at the VS Unit house; and Alma and Irene at the home of Rev. Heavilus, a Methodist preacher, who was going along to our conference and would give devotional messages.

The other missionaries arrived before we left the next morning on the *Mary L.*, a 45-foot-long boat. Utila is 17 miles from La Ceiba and is about nine miles long and two or three miles wide. The population was around 1,500, mostly people of English origin with names like Morgan, Eden, Borden, etc. The island had four churches; Methodist, Baptist, Adventist, and Church of God.

We stayed in private homes and had our meals in the hall where we had our meetings. Wednesday evening we attended services in the Methodist church. They liked our four-part singing and enjoyed a song by our quartet. The last evening of our conference the Baptist church offered us the use of their building.

Our afternoons were relaxing—more so than at conferences on a mission station because no one had to plan and prepare meals or arrange accommodations for guests.

Back in La Ceiba, on our way home, we met Orie Miller, Ira Buckwalter, and Adam Martin to discuss mission plans, and we learned that Mennonite Central Committee was turning over their work in Belize to the Eastern Mennonite Board of Missions.

♔

My journal on June 16 records the following: *George (Miller) preached his last sermon as a Trujillo resident tonight. They leave Wednesday for Tocoa. And in six months from today is my date to leave. "I'd rather walk in the dark with Him than walk alone in the light." Walking with Him is joy and it is peace.*

The joy I felt when I saw fresh growth in new believers was indescribable. Pancho and Miguel sang a song at church that evening, and when they had come to practice it that afternoon, Miguel talked about using the Bible *when he goes out to preach.*

After an announcement was made in church that a night of fun and games was planned for the youth group, word filtered back to me that some of the boys would prefer that instead of all games, I would tell stories with figures. It took a little time for me to grasp that they meant flannelgraph-illustrated Bible lessons. A few of them had been asked to conduct children's meetings in church Sunday evenings, and they felt it would teach them how to use the flannelgraph board and figures. I was delighted to comply and a group of 25 young people gathered.

I invited a few of the new adult believers to come also. We sang a lot and I showed them my files of flannelgraph figures, gave some pointers about telling stories, and then illustrated by telling the story of David and Goliath. Everyone enjoyed the evening, including the root beer and cookies, and a baby in the clinic waited to make his appearance until after everyone had left.

John the Baptist's birthday celebrations were the cause of one patient for the clinic: a drunken man with a four-inch-long machete cut through the skull, and another cut that severed two tendons on one arm. He was a Panamanian, a seaman from a boat in port. While the doctor stitched from 2:30 to 4:00 in the morning, the dance music which had started at 10:00 the evening before played on.

That patient was put into a room with a man who had been gored in the side and leg by a bull. A boy, brought in later in the day, who had accidentally shot himself in the leg was sent home after being sutured.

A 16-year-old boy, run over by the wheel of a trailer, was brought in and then sent to La Ceiba for x-rays of a possible fractured pelvis. His father was a prisoner in the jail, but was given furlough to take the boy to the hospital.

A piece of firewood was the weapon used to club a man who had once expressed interest in joining the church. His head was cut open but the skull not cracked. I gave him a Gospel of John booklet to read and prayed much when I noticed him reading it hour after hour.

A woman who thought herself very sick asked to be admitted. She had been going from doctor to doctor, but never waited for them to complete tests or read x-rays. She also left our clinic undiagnosed because she simply couldn't wait for her x-rays to be forwarded from La Ceiba.

There was no doubt about the diagnosis of the old woman who was brought in later that month. She had had a stroke and her blood pressure was higher than my instrument could register—260 over 160. The doctor drew out 200 cc of blood and how I wished we were able to type it to see if it could be given to another woman who had been hemorrhaging and registered no blood pressure.

There was nothing further we could do for the old woman, and her family took her home to die. Two weeks later I saw people coming out of the Catholic church after celebrating her funeral mass.

Trujillo, Honduras, C.A.
June 20, 1963

Dear Friends,

For some of you it has been a long, long time since I sent a letter your way. When I came back to Honduras for this term I brought a hektograph to use for form letters, but I never could get the liquid to work; it just made gummy strings when I melted it. But now we have a duplicator on the station and I'm going to be the first to use it.

What can I write that will be of interest to people living in very differing circumstances in about 16 different countries? If I would write you what is in my heart it would be joy-joy-joy. This is an isolated and obscure (but beautiful) little spot in the world and my work is insignificant. Every month I attend a few mothers who come here to the clinic for their deliveries--but the babies would be born anyway. The people here are unimportant to anyone but themselves. Then why this abounding satisfaction with life and exulting happiness of each day?

It is the Lord, walking with Him and speaking with Him, and hearing His voice--living with Him. It is seeing His working in other lives and sharing their joy. Like a young man who has known Him for about three months. He was telling me Sunday that a neighbor offered to sell him a Catholic Bible. He has his own Bible, but said, "I have to go out and preach the Gospel and it will be useful to me for that, so I want to buy it." And the High School student praying earnestly that the special song in which he was to have part might mean the salvation of some soul. And a young mother looking forward eagerly to giving her first children's meeting because she loves to teach children, then bringing three neighbor children to church the next day.

Tomorrow my good helper in the household tasks, María Luisa, will be 16 years old. It is also my yellow cat, Leona's, second birthday. And tomorrow marks twelve years that I arrived in Trujillo. So we are going to celebrate with fresco and cake. It looks as though my days here are fast coming to an end. The government is building a hospital near us and when it opens our clinic will no longer be needed and it will be closed, either then or when my furlough begins in December. I don't know where I will be after that but the Lord will lead as He has done in the past, that is enough to know.

Your prayers mean much. Please continue to be faithful. May He bless each of you daily. "The blessing of the Lord, it maketh rich, and he addeth no sorrow with it." Proverbs 10:22.

Yours sincerely,
Dora
Dora Taylor

Home Address: ELVERSON, R. # 2, Pennsylvania, USA

Letter I sent to friends and prayer partners.

In July 250 pastors, missionaries, and lay workers attended a Honduras Evangelism in Depth seminar in San Pedro Sula. Thousands of souls had been saved in Guatemala the year before in this program, and the San Pedro Sula meeting was to familiarize workers with the plans for the Honduras campaign. Don Enrique Peñalva was the chief director; George Miller was regional director for Colón, our area, as well as Gracias a Dios and La Mosquitia.

Home cell groups were formed to get believers together to pray weekly prior to and during the campaign. We had seven cells in our area. I was part of one in the Osorto home in Rio Negro. Lay people were trained for personal visitation and literature distribution, and the goal was to reach every home in Honduras by May 1964.

The first official meeting in our church was held in September to coincide with the national independence day celebrations. The church was almost full that evening and the meeting lasted until almost midnight.

The need for changed lives was brought home to our little group of mission stations when the first member of the Gualaco mission was killed. For some time Daniel had been absent from church services, and then we heard he had gone back to his former life-style. We were informed he had gone to collect a $3.50 debt and his debtor attacked him with a machete. He was struck in the head, neck, and arm and died immediately. I suspected one or both of the men had been drinking.

Immediately after the killing there was fighting between the two families. Grace Miller wrote me a note from Tocoa saying nine men had been killed in less than two weeks. She had seen one headless corpse carried past their house.

When one of the murderers was being brought to the jail in Trujillo, some of the victim's friends ambushed the guards and drove them away from their prisoner. The prisoner was helpless because his arms were tied but the attackers showed no mercy—they cut him to pieces. A week later one of those men was in our jail. There seemed no end to the evil, anger, and hatred.

Two brothers who had attended our Sunday School at one time were fighting one day; the one got so angry he got his machete to kill his brother. He was stopped, however, before he accomplished the deed. I went to visit them and we had a long talk. I reminded them of things they had learned in Sunday School and asked them if they didn't want to accept the Savior. The 14-year-old, who had wielded the machete, laughed and said no he had no interest in such things.

The 15-year-old discussed his problems thoughtfully and thanked me for coming. He said he was afraid he would become so angry that he would kill someone some day, but he wasn't ready to accept Christ. My heart ached as I left and I could only think, "What will it take?"

Many of my patients, except for the midwifery cases, would now be considered emergency or trauma unit cases. That was certainly true of the two brothers brought in after a vicious fight with machetes. The first brother was carried in on a board. The fight had been two days before and he was in critical condition. With every breath fluid bubbled up from the wide and deep chest wound.

We had to wait almost an hour for the doctor to arrive. When he began to work, he thought the wounds were already filled with pus, but the father said, no, they had poured hot cooking oil into the wounds and also put in tobacco. Coffee grounds were all over the man's back, and in my opinion he needed a bath as much as he needed medical attention. The doctor did temporary repairs and ordered him taken to La Ceiba.

Before we were finished with him, the second brother arrived. He was afraid of his brother and asked if he was still armed. That man had a long cut in his skull and two cuts several inches long through one cheek causing the face to hang down. These cuts had also been treated with the yellow cooking oil.

I had opportunity to discuss the gospel with that brother. He said he had heard Don Jaime (James Hess) when we had the outdoor meetings.

In September we had three more macheted victims. As soon as they were able to leave the clinic, they were taken to the jail and then brought back daily to have their dressings changed.

The day after Danny and Dicky Hess returned from school in Siguatepeque, I took them and the three Hanna children for a Sunday afternoon *paseo* or walk. We first went to inspect the school being built on the hill back of the town. The two buildings, one for boys and the other for girls, had 11 rooms each built in a straight row. The walls were of kiln-dried bricks and cement. The setting was beautiful, so much nicer than the old school wedged between the jail and the old ruins.

We hiked on up to the reservoir and had a good time clambering over the big rocks that the boys in their long pants turned into huge sliding boards. The children and I had a lot of fun as we laughed, talked, and thoroughly enjoyed our outing, but the day was hot and the pitcher of cold punch waiting in the refrigerator finally drew us back home.

Isaac and Mary Frederick and their children, Sharon (12), Marilyn (10), Duane (8), and Debra (almost 4), arrived in Trujillo the last day of August and got a warm reception. The weather was hot and mucky. Towels and wash cloths used in the evening were still wet the next morning. Dresses washed in the morning weren't dry enough to iron by evening. My handkerchiefs were quickly soaked with perspiration, and I decided the prisoner brought in by a guard for treatment at the clinic each day was pretty smart to come with a towel draped around his neck.

The Frederick family. Marilyn, Isaac, Mary, Debra, Duane, and Sharon.

The Fredericks moved into the empty Miller house, but when Isaac and Mary went with James Hess to look for a permanent location, I kept the three girls at my house. They fit themselves right into the household helping with the cooking, doing the dishes, baking cookies while I was busy in the clinic, and one day gathered up all their dirty laundry and washed it so their mother wouldn't have that work when she returned.

While the parents were gone, little Debbie's throat became quite sore and I had the doctor check her when he came to the clinic to see other patients. She braved the injection without a whimper and before long her dolls were all in a *hospital* having their temperatures taken and getting shots. She then *read* them a story about how Joseph went to Bethlehem and called, "Samuel, Samuel!"

A property was rented for the Fredericks in Tegucigalpa with plans to open a school for missionary children in 1964. Rachel Mohler was to be the teacher when it opened.

We celebrated Dicky Hess's ninth birthday while the Fredericks were in Trujillo. I asked Beaty if Dicky had requested the flavor of his cake and ice cream. "Yes," she said. "He wanted chocolate cake with chocolate icing and chocolate ice cream with chocolate sauce."

About that time the Hess children lost another pet. I'm not sure what kind of animal it was, but the children called it a kitten. Locally it was called a *tigre*. The VS fellows brought it from Santa Fe and the children fed it with a bottle and nipple I supplied from the clinic. The first time I heard it howl I thought it sounded like a night hawk. The poor little animal had a hard life—it was always getting trampled and never seemed to learn to move when anyone came near. It even got run over with a bicycle. Another time it fell off the truck onto the concrete and that was the end of its life. Danny dug a grave with a machete and shovel under one of my trees. He invited me to view the grave site and said, "We buried Tigger in a cereal box. I think it was a Special K® box." Dicky fashioned a cross out of two sticks and printed Tigger on it and the boys circled the cross and grave with stones.

♔

My next house guests were Elam and Sharon (French) Peachey from the Belleville, Pennsylvania, area. They were directors of the VS unit in Costa Rica, visiting the VS units in Honduras. George and Lois Zimmerman from La Ceiba were with them and spent the night with the Fredericks. Once again our boat motor refused to start and changed plans for our guests. The Santa Fe VS fellows came up in their cayuco the next day and took the ladies down while the men walked.

While they were visiting, my work in the clinic went on as usual, including two births, a man brought in after an epileptic seizure, and an old man from La Colonia with pneumonia who eventually spent three weeks with us.

The old man was a believer and when his son came to take him home, I asked if he was the son who had accepted Christ. He said his brother was the one, so I went through the plan of salvation to be sure he understood and then asked if he was ready to accept. He hesitated only a moment and then with a gleam in his eyes he said, -*¡Si, yo acepto*!- "Yes, I accept!"

He then told me he had a dream of being in a church and that he had stood up and said, -*Yo acepto á Cristo por mi Salvador,*- or "I accept Christ as my Savior." How grateful I am that I did not ignore the opportunity to speak, for it appeared the Lord had prepared his heart. He was the eighth person to accept the Lord in the clinic that year.

One of the new converts from church told me she was talking to her neighbors about the happiness she felt since accepting Christ. She also had a dream—about me standing at the door to a big ark inviting her inside. When she entered, everything was bright and shiny. Then she started to pray, and apparently she prayed aloud in her sleep because her husband woke her up and asked what was going on.

♛

Shots interrupted my dreams around 4:30 the morning of October 3. They sounded from the direction of Rio Negro, and once awake I got up and dressed in anticipation of victims.

Instead, I saw soldiers running in formation out of the *Cuartel* with their guns held the way they did during drill. They surrounded the hotel and soon brought out a man and took him to the *Cuartel*. After that they spread out in groups and before long other prisoners were ushered to the *Cuartel* at gun point. By 7:00 they had most of the men they wanted—the mayor, governor, school principal, head of the post office, the man running for representative in congress, and other men active in the Red (Liberal) Party. Among them was Pedro Pablo Osorto, the man who had earlier asked his wife to wait to be baptized in our church until he could get out of politics and be baptized with her. Pedro was right-hand man to one of the Red candidates running for an office.

Stores and schools were closed the first day and many people were afraid to be out of their homes. The only thing we sold in the clinic was nerve pills. The wife of one of the arrested men came to my door and said she needed help. I expected her to be in financial need, but all she requested was prayer. She said the three shots I heard were fired through the door of their house when the soldiers came to arrest her husband. She and the children were still suffering reaction from being awakened in such a frightening manner.

All day and for several days thereafter women were constantly up and down the street taking provisions to the prisoners—sleeping mats and pillows, and food in *portaviandas*, the little kettles that set one on top of the other and fit inside a rack.

Pedro's wife stopped to see me on one of her trips. She said she had to leave her little children alone when she took Pedro his food three times a day, and when she got home one time, they were all out in the rain and later got sick. She asked James if he would try to get Pedro released, but because of Pedro's political connections James' visit didn't appear to accomplish anything.

Mr. July took a book to Pedro from me and Pedro's wife said he had asked her to bring his Bible. James and Beaty visited him, and several days later when I went to offer to send in some of his meals, his wife said he was home. She said she was sure he was released because of our prayers. I immediately asked if we could have a prayer meeting in their home, but she said he was prohibited from having meetings in their house. I sent a letter asking for special permission to have a religious meeting and my request was granted.

As soon as I got to the house that afternoon (the night curfew was still in effect), Pedro's wife went to invite a few of the other believers. Pedro told us of his fear when they threatened to shoot him and that Jesus became very real to him. He believed God had allowed his arrest for his own good.

I told him that even before this had happened I had requested prayer for him from my family and church back in the United States. Also, in a prayer meeting the week before in Trujillo we had prayed for him and discussed how prayer was the key that opened the prison doors for *Pedro* or Peter in the Bible.

Pedro then confessed that he had gone a long way from the Lord, but had returned and wanted to serve Him with all his heart and tell his friends about Jesus. As we went to prayer, he was the first to pray. He admitted his failure to do what he knew was right, that he had listened to the deceiver, and he asked God to help him live for Him. His wife's prayer was full of joy and praise.

What a joyous time we had in that meeting. My heart thrilled to have been a witness to answered prayers. Those were among the happiest hours of my life.

A month later the family left Trujillo. Pedro was being harassed by soldiers who beat on the house door at night and shouted threats. He feared he would be killed or thrown into jail again. One night, at dusk, the family left their meager belongings in their house and quietly boarded the *Mary John* for Cortés.

Time magazine reported that was Honduras' 136th revolution in 142 years of independence from Spain, and that only two constitutionally elected chiefs of state had ever completed their terms of office. They also said Hondurans called their country the land of the 70's—70% illiterate, 70% rural, 70% illegitimate, and they probably should add 70% politically unstable.

The coup ousted President Ramón Villeda Morales only ten days shy of completing his term of office. Elections for October 13 were canceled and Colonel Osvaldo López, who masterminded the revolt, took over as one-man ruler of the country. The ex-President and the ex-presidential candidate were sent to exile in Costa Rica. Once more there seemed no end to the bloodshed. Street fighting broke out, and university students in Tegucigalpa even shot at soldiers patrolling the streets. Over 100 lives were lost. The new government was the fifth holding office since my arrival in Honduras in 1951.

Babies about to be born didn't obey the strictly enforced night curfew from 6 to 6, and the soldiers allowed two women to come in during the nights that followed the uprising. Whoever accompanied the women, however, had to wait until morning to leave the clinic.

The street in front of our house was again busy when the prisoners were released. They went home carrying their bed mats and pillows, and I saw one man walking through heavy rain carrying a cot.

♛

The first 13 days of October we had 15 inches of rain. When I was out one afternoon, my shoes got filled with water, not because the water was deep, but because the rain was coming down at an angle and was driven right into the tops of my shoes.

The storms apparently blew migrating birds off their normal routes because I awoke one night to the sound of hundreds of chirping bird calls. The Hess boys found numerous dead birds and a few injured ones. One was a young male redstart.

"Aunt Dora, Aunt Dora," I heard coming from the patio, but it wasn't the Hess boys calling. It was their parrot. She had learned to talk and she sang phrases of a few songs so well that sometimes I thought it was one of the boys.

♛

My time in Honduras was coming to an end and there were still several things I wanted to do before I left. One event I hadn't planned. I ended the life of a snake in my living room with a fly swatter. It was a young one; very thin but over a foot long.

One of the things I did plan was a trip to Tocoa and a trip from there to Salamá. It rained so much I wasn't sure the plane could land in Tocoa. After we did land, Danny Miller told us that another plane had slipped around in the mud so much it barely got up enough speed to lift off. I observed that there were more pigs in Tocoa than people, and the pigs certainly enjoyed the mud more than the people did.

The trip to Salamá in a four-wheel drive Chevy was equally

slippery but the fellowship there was blessed. The Sunday morning service was handled entirely by local believers. I thought of Proverbs 11:25, *". . . he that watereth shall be watered also himself."*

Group who attended the service at Salamá in front of Pastor Pedro Paz's new house.

The pace of my sorting and packing picked up. The clinic was to close December 1, and for months I had been trying to lower my inventory and yet not run short of essential items. My sewing machine had left town with Pedro Pablo and his wife, but there were so many things that I needed until almost the last minute.

A boat carrying 40 passengers capsized near Castilla, spilling all passengers and cargo into the sea. One family which consisted of a father, mother, two daughters, and three grandchildren was sent to Trujillo because the father had a dislocated or broken arm. The family had been moving and all their possessions had been lost as well as the lives of a third daughter, her two children and one son of the older daughter.

The whole family was Christian and attended our church services Sunday morning and evening. James, Beaty, and I went to visit them in the afternoon at a little house on the beach where they were staying until the father was discharged from the clinic. Beaty took food and children's clothing. As I thought of their loss, my possessions became a vast supply, and I gladly gave a quilt I had made when I was eight years old, a dress and underwear for each of the women, and the plastic dishes and silverware we had been using for the clinic. The women wore the dresses to church for the evening service.

The testimonies in the Thanksgiving evening service were treasures to take home in my heart. All rang true and faces beamed with joy as believers spoke of repentance, the faithfulness of God, and the blessings and peace He gave.

Dicky Hess gave me one more memory to take home. Sometime after we received the news of President Kennedy's assassination, Dicky came over to the clinic with more news. "They found the man that killed Kennedy," he said. "They found him sitting in a field like a cow, just moving around worried. Kennedy couldn't get well even with 12 doctors. Twelve doctors is a lot, but still they couldn't fix him."

The last two patients left the clinic November 30, and I could finally end my chart-keeping and close the books.

Hesses had moved to the Millers' empty house and I used their rooms to store the items I would take home. Mr. July hunted out my drums and then it was rush, rush. Marlin and Jay came up from Santa Fe to help me close the drums and to get them and my trunk to the dock. Mr. Griffith's boat, the *Caribbean*, was to take them to La Ceiba where I would meet the *Orpheus*, a Standard Fruit Company ship, which would sail December 16. At the last minute, however, the *Caribbean* was not able to come because of the weather, so the things were sent to La Ceiba by plane.

When the VS fellows returned to Santa Fe, I went with them for one final visit. We left early in the morning and people coming towards us said the one river was chest high. Fortunately when we got there, a man with a cayuco was willing to ferry us to the opposite side. On the way we met some girls taking bread to Trujillo in boxes about the size and shape of chicken crates. They carried them on their heads.

In Santa Fe I first stopped to visit a friend who treated me to cookies and coffee. Jay, meantime, had gone to the VS house and prepared breakfast.

The rain that fell did not take away any of the pleasure I felt as I walked the sandy streets and greeted and was greeted by old friends. I spent almost an hour with one woman who accepted a Gospel of Luke and immediately started reading out loud to me. The story of the Good Samaritan caught her interest. As she read about the priest passing by on the other side, she paused to say, *-Esto da lástima-* or

"That makes you feel bad."

I visited the twins I had delivered in the clinic and got to see Don Emilio's new house. It had a cement floor and pictures on the walls—quite different from his old house where I had stayed while conducting Bible School years earlier. And then a perfect ending to a wonderful day was the evening service in the church. Almost 100 people gathered to hear James Hess's teaching on the Christmas story. He and his three boys had come down to hold the service and take me home in a motor cayuco.

Friday, December 6, I had sale day for the things left in the clinic. Two of my workers helped me and I was certainly grateful.

My last Sunday in Trujillo, an evening wedding was held in our church followed by a joint reception for them and farewell for me.

Monday and Tuesday I disposed of the last medicines in the clinic, packed the records, balanced the books, welcomed a constant stream of visitors, and packed my suitcase.

Wednesday morning three of my former workers came to help clean the house and I was glad to share with them some of the things I didn't want to take home. More and more people arrived and it was nice to have the house filled with friends. I was wearing a dress I made from a beautiful piece of material given to me by a friend especially for my going-home dress. Just before James brought the truck to take me to the airport we joined hands and prayed. As I rode in the cab with James and one of the older women, I asked a young man standing on the running board how many people had piled onto the back of the truck and he counted 19.

The peace and calm I had found in Tocoa about my departure from Honduras sustained me as the plane lifted off toward La Ceiba. As I watched my friends disappear from sight, my eyes felt hot and misty for a moment, but my grief was at saying farewell to people who had become most dear, not from a desire to linger after my work was finished.

The new hospital—1963.

There were also friends to see me off when I boarded the *Orpheus* in La Ceiba. One was a young man who had just joined the VS unit, Ira Kurtz, Jr. He was from the Conestoga Mennonite Church in Morgantown, Pennsylvania, the local church Mother attended after Father's death and which became our home church upon my return although we still had ties to the church at Frazer.

Sunday, December 16, 1963, as the ship left dock, I thought of the many changes I had seen in Honduras—even the way bananas were shipped. When I first arrived in Honduras, bananas were shipped on the stem, but the *Orpheus* had a cargo of 45,000 pounds of bananas, all packed in 40-pound boxes. Cost of transportation had changed also, but my complete trip from Trujillo to New York cost me only $170.50 including shipment of three drums and a footlocker.

I had said good-bye many times in my life and would say it again many more times. The sadness of farewell, however, was always tempered with anticipation. Where would God send me next? Where would He lead me? I knew that **AS HE LEADS Is Joy** that would far outweigh any broken earthly ties.

P. S. If I had known where He would lead, it wouldn't have been so hard to leave Trujillo. But that is another story, **More Joy AS HE LEADS**.

Epilogue

As I wrote this book, I had a growing conviction that it was destined to lead someone to Christ, would strengthen someone's faith, or encourage someone to be faithful to a calling from God, and that that person would cause great joy in heaven.

The reasons I feel this will happen is because Satan has tried in many ways to keep this book from being written:

- In 1952 he tried to take Dora's life through sickness. God, in answer to her prayers and the prayers of her fellow missionaries, saved her life.
- In 1972 Dora's journals were stolen. They held the little details of daily life in Honduras that were needed to write this story. They were also a record of her heart-felt desire to serve Christ and praises for His leading and keeping power. Once again Dora's prayer was answered when someone hiking on a mountain near her home found the water-stained notebooks and returned them to her.
- As I was writing the 1952 chapter, the year she almost died from malaria and which includes many Bible verses, I started having difficulty concentrating on the work, and my computer screen distorted so that I was unable to read my entries. I called Dora and asked her to pray for me; I also asked my pastor to pray for me and my computer. The problem never occurred again.
- During the typesetting of the final draft of the book, I upgraded my computer equipment. After transferring the book into the new computer, the dedication page was totally changed from written words into the symbols often used to indicate swear words. That page also increased in size so that it took up more computer space than the entire book when completed. Next, certain paragraphs on one page in the 1952 chapter compressed and refused to obey any of the commands of the program and the computer *crashed* repeatedly. After several hours of work by the computer technician, who reinstalled the entire operating system of the computer and the layout application, he had to leave for his next appointment with my problem unsolved—the text

on page 46 was still compressed. I reinstalled clean copies from a back-up disk, but page 46 continued to distort as soon as I did any work on that chapter. When I tried to shut down the computer, it crashed again. I spent some time in prayer and praising God for being greater than any power working against the completion of this book, and when I reopened the 1952 chapter, it no longer had the compressed text, and I was able to continue typesetting.

Because of the strong conviction that Satan did not want this book published, I again asked my pastor for prayer. He and an elder from my church and a group of intercessors have prayed for God's protection over this book as it is taken through the final steps of completion and is sent to the printer. I know that greater is He that wants this book published, than he that has sought to prevent and destroy it.

Dora did not want this book written to glorify her or the work she accomplished, but rather as a challenge to you to be obedient to God's calling. She has freely admitted shortcomings and her need to ask forgiveness, and she hopes you are encouraged to make your life count for Christ.

After Dora's work was completed in Honduras, the Lord led her to Belize for three years. He then opened doors for her to make numerous annual trips with Christian Medical Society medical teams.

She now lives in the Virginia Mennonite Retirement Community in Harrisonburg, Virginia, and would have no greater joy than to know that you have been blessed by this book.

Marie E. Cutman